Revelation: Dawn of All Hope

Chapters 1 to 11 of John's Apocalypse

Leo De Siqueira

Unveiled Publishing
Calgary, Canada
Revelation: Dawn of All Hope – Chapters 1 to 11 of John's Apocalypse
Leo De Siqueira
Copyright © 2021 by Leo De Siqueira
All rights reserved.
ISBN-13: 978-1-9995060-6-3

Printed in the United States of America and Canada

For permission, please contact the author through www.leodesiqueira.com.

DEDICATION

To the descendants of Abraham. To the nation of Israel. To the Jewish people of the past, present, and future. Romans 9 to 11 will come to pass.

CONTENTS

FOREWORD

Revelation is one of the most fascinating, inspiring, and misunderstood books of the Bible. It's the whole culmination of the Bible, the final chapter, but it isn't a narrative (like the Gospels) or a body of doctrinal teaching (like the Epistles), it's an apocalypse – a big-picture look at the sweep of God's redemptive plan, in the language of symbols. In some ways it is like an art gallery, with different paintings showing different, yet interconnected stories; in other ways it is like a theatrical performance outlining the big parts of God's work in human history. It is usually regarded as a book of endings – it is the last book of the Bible and it ends with a new creation, yet in other ways it is a book of beginnings, a new Genesis – it shows the new Covenant, the new Age, the new Kingdom that is emerging and transforming creation.

I think the reason that Revelation has caused so much confusion and controversy is because we tend to separate it from the rest of the Bible and try to interpret it on its own, with a Western worldview and a set of Western categories that we can extrapolate into a list of 'coming events.' That is true both when Christians read the book, and also when Hollywood uses it for their latest apocalyptic movie. None of that is the purpose of the book and that is not how the original readers would have understood it.

Leo has started at the beginning, with the Aramaic language and Hebraic culture that permeated both the Jewish people's understanding of the world, and also that of most of their geographical neighbours (Syrians, Parthians, and those in Asia Minor to whom the book was written). Aramaic was the base–language of most Semitic groups, and it brought a particular worldview or psychology with it—it tends to view things as 'whole' whereas Greek tended to talk about things as 'parts' (for example, an Aramaic person might describe an elephant as large, mighty, magnificent; whereas a Greek person would describe its parts; its trunk, legs, ears, etc.). Aramaic is 'big-picture-thinking' and Revelation, as Leo points out, is painting a big picture:

> The Old Covenant is fulfilled, and the New has come.
> God's Kingdom is here and will continue to expand.
> Everything from the Old Covenant—blessings and curses,
> priesthood and sacrifice, law and kingship—is all fulfilled by Jesus.
> And a whole New Age, Covenant, and Kingdom are here.

All prophecy is now fulfilled in Jesus, and what has been accomplished spiritually by Christ's death, resurrection, ascension, and outpouring of the Spirit, will be seen in the physical time-space world as His prophecy (Olivet Discourse) is fulfilled and the entire old system, Temple, priesthood, and sacrifice are finally and fully done away with, as every prophetic word is fulfilled to the letter, in the destruction of Jerusalem in AD 66–70.

Leo is painting a big picture in this book, one that involved painting with the colours of Deuteronomy, Daniel and Ezekiel, as well as the words of Jesus and the apostles. If you know scripture well, but don't see how all the pieces of the jigsaw puzzle fit together, Leo will show you the picture on the jigsaw puzzle box, the picture Revelation reveals, and how everything God has done, is doing, and will do, find their place—in a full unveiling of Jesus Christ. Let your faith soar and your mind be enlightened with truth, as you read this book.

Dr. Martin Trench
Apostolic Leader, Author, Lead Pastor
Martintrench.com

PREFACE

I f I were to draw a contemporary analogy to illustrate the structure of this book series, I would liken it to The Matrix trilogy. The first installment of the movie could be considered a standalone work in that it encompasses the main story as well as a sufficient glimpse of future installments. The same can be said of my first book, Dawn of This Age. The second and third installments of the movie were actually two parts of a single story. Again, the same may be said of this book you are about to read and the book that will follow: they are in fact one book, but to keep the content digestible, they are divided into two bite-sized parts.

As for theological basis, this book stands on my well-supported belief that Revelation serves primarily to maintain Israel's centrality in God's grand narrative of restoring all creation. Limiting Revelation's context to 1st century Rome or 21st century America, as many scholars have, violates the covenant of the Cross of Jesus and neglects to address the evils of other empires like the Mongol, the Ottoman, and the Third Reich (Nazi Germany). Many empires have committed evils much worse than the Romans. Why would God punish one civilization but not another? Is it possible that Revelation is not focused on judging empires at all?

That withstanding, this book seeks to explore the prophetic summons placed upon John as an explanation of the horrendous events that befell Jerusalem and the Holy Land, just as God did through Isaiah, Jeremiah and Ezekiel. It is my hope you will discover, as I have, that the visions of John not only fit within the context of an Old Covenant judicial framework, but it also explains why we see such a grand reckoning this side of the Cross.

FLOW VERSUS FRAMEWORK

I am aware of the long-standing tradition of listing all previous Revelation frameworks and giving equal praise and attention to each before presenting one's own framework. This sort of process never crossed my mind. My focus is not to prove, disprove, defend, or destroy another's doctrinal framework. My aim is to elucidate the grand love story of God written in the journals and documents of the Holy Bible.

When it comes to understanding God's overarching testimony, I believe there are two main parts:

First, He is a loving Father actively involved in the lives of those He made in His image. His grace is revealed through healing and prophecy, dreams and visions, and appearing as the "Man in White" to liberate the captives of demonically dark and oppressed nations. Regardless of what we believe or know, God is always working for the good of those who love Him and serve His purpose (Romans 8:28), and no amount of books could possibly contain all He has done, is doing, and will continue to do (John 21:25).

Second, the Bible is a collection of books that include experiential stories that take place at specific points in history. Most importantly, it includes vivid snapshots of what God has done and plans to do through people's intimate encounters and interactions with Him. These personal diaries have been preserved through oral and written tradition, and they afford us the privilege of witnessing God's grace and the power of faith in action.

The testimonies of the Bible are written in a rich, beautiful, and often enigmatic manner. On a side note, there are few publishers who appreciate this fact more than Robert Alter, who has devoted his life to conveying the literary genius of the Hebrew writ into English (*The Hebrew Bible*, Alter, 2018) while preserving tone, word-play, humour, and nuances. The Hebrew-style literary flow also happens to permeate the Book of Revelation. It is rife with deep meaning, powerful images, and constantly drawing on the Hebrew mind to recall their rich heritage in Yahweh.

Like the prophets of old, John's encounter with God became a powerful testimony. Revelation is the final word of God's masterpiece woven through the Jewish people and thus must be approached the same way a student of the Hebrew Scriptures approaches Isaiah, Jeremiah or Ezekiel. My overarching goal as I unpack Revelation from the language of Jesus is to stay true to both God's Biblical testimony and to the Hebrew-style narrative flow. Consequently, my translation and interpretation will not stay true to any one doctrine. And that should be quite liberating I hope!

PESHITTA (ARAMAIC) PRIMACY

"We all fell to the ground, and I heard a voice saying to me in <u>Aramaic</u>, 'Saul, Saul, why do you persecute me? It is hard for you to kick against the goads.'" Acts 26:14 (NIV)

Mel Gibson got it right when he used Aramaic as the spoken language of his movie, *The Passion of the Christ*. Aramaic is the older sister language of Hebrew—a Semitic language of the Middle East—and is very similar in construction, alphabet, and vocabulary. Aramaic is related to Hebrew much like Portuguese is related to Spanish. For centuries it was the language of the surrounding Mesopotamian empires (Persia, Assyria, Babylon, etc.), much like the countries that surround Brazil speak Spanish, while in Brazil Portuguese is spoken.[1]

> "I had always imagined the original New Testament might be discovered in a manuscript from the first century, unearthed from a cave, as were the Dead Sea Scrolls. As it turns out, the original was buried, not under the earth or in a cave, but under centuries of ignorance, obscurity, and misinformation—perhaps deliberate misinformation…
>
> Many may concede an Aramaic original for the Gospel of Matthew and perhaps Hebrews, as Eusebius and other early writers (Papias, Hesesippus) wrote of an original Aramaic Matthew and/or Aramaic Hebrews…
>
> [But] the entire Aramaic text was translated into Greek, under the auspices of the apostles themselves, for the Greek speaking Roman nations, as Greek had been the "Lingua Franca" (common language) of the Roman Empire since Alexander's conquests of 330 BC. (There were exceptions to this trend, however, in Israel and the Middle East (Asia Minor), Aramaic

---

[1] "The Jews stopped speaking Hebrew during their Babylonian captivity in the 6th century BC. Even earlier, the Assyrians imposed the Aramaic language on the Jews, and on the entire Middle East, which they conquered in the 9th century BC. Aramaic continued as the lingua franca (language of commerce) in different forms, from that time until the Muslim conquests replaced it largely with Arabic in the 7th century AD, over one thousand years later. The first Christians and churches were Jewish converts, to whom the Apostles proclaimed the risen Messiah Yeshua." Bauscher, David. *The Holy Peshitta Bible Translated*, Lulu.com. (Kindle Edition), p 7.

had been established since the Babylonian and following Persian Empires as the common tongue."[2]

So, what does "Peshitta" mean? It is a Syriac word meaning "simple," "straight," or "common." So the Peshitta Bible is the ancient Aramaic Bible, using the simple or common language of Jesus' day. The Old Testament Peshitta was, like the Talmud, an Aramaic copy of the original Hebrew Old Testament.

> "What is especially interesting and valuable about the Peshitta Old Testament is that it is represented in the oldest Semitic manuscript of the complete Old Testament extant, in the Codex Ambrosianus, commonly dated to the 6th or 7th century AD. The Peshitta Old Testament is commonly believed by scholars to be a 2nd century AD translation. I believe that it is older than that, based on its readings and also on many of the headings of the Psalms in Eastern Codex Ambrosianus of the 6th century, several of which actually date the original text in the 1st century A.D...

> "Christians wanted and needed the written books of scripture for their assemblies, to read and preach, and to carry to other places for evangelism and teaching, and of course, to train young pastors and evangelists. The New Testament was the volume of first importance. The Old Testament would be scarcely less desirable, especially for the Jewish converts and future Jewish audiences. The Hebrew Bible would no longer be read in the Christian assemblies, but the Aramaic Targums would be needed in writing, whereas formerly they were primarily oral only, being spoken in the synagogues. The Peshitta Old Testament most likely was translated in Israel by Christians who had converted in the 1st century and were familiar with the Semitic names of people and places in Israel at that time. They most likely had a strong command of the Hebrew language and Hebrew Bible, as well as the Aramaic

---

[2] Bauscher, David. *Divine Contact: Discovery of the Original New Testament,* Apple Books. https://books.apple.com/ca/book/divine-contact-discovery-of-the-original-new-testament/id508414851, p 29–30.

language which was the language of Israel, Syria, and the surrounding Fertile Crescent."[3]

The Aramaic New Testament is not a copy, it is original. Given that Aramaic was the Language of Jesus, such a statement would seem intuitive. Consider the following passages from the New Testament taken from one of the most common translations to date, the New International Version (NIV):

"Some time later, Jesus went up to Jerusalem for one of the Jewish festivals. Now there is in Jerusalem near the Sheep Gate a pool, which in Aramaic is called Bethesda and which is surrounded by five covered colonnades." John 5:1-2 (NIV)

"When Pilate heard this, he brought Jesus out and sat down on the judge's seat at a place known as the Stone Pavement (which in Aramaic is Gabbatha)." John 19:13 (NIV)

"Carrying his own cross, he went out to the place of the Skull (which in Aramaic is called Golgotha). Many of the Jews read this sign, for the place where Jesus was crucified was near the city, and the sign was written in Aramaic, Latin, and Greek." John 19:17, 20 (NIV)

"When they heard him [Paul] speak to them in Aramaic, they became very quiet." Acts 22:2 (NIV)

"We all fell to the ground, and I heard a voice saying to me in Aramaic, 'Saul, Saul, why do you persecute me? It is hard for you to kick against the goads.'" Acts 26:14 (NIV)

For those still hesitant toward the notion that the Aramaic preceded the Greek, here are some further points for consideration:

- The Assyrian, Babylonian, and Medo-Persian Empires (the nations surrounding Israel) all spoke Aramaic. When the Ten Tribes of Israel were assimilated by the Assyrians, the Aramaic

---

[3] Bauscher, David. *The Holy Peshitta Bible Translated,* Lulu.com. Kindle Edition, p 6-8.

language would have become their norm over time. And when Daniel was captive under the Babylonians, he spoke Aramaic, and his book was written in Aramaic too.

- Evidence suggests that from a cultural perspective, the Greek language was seen with disdain. Consider the following quote from the Babylonian Talmud: "At that time, it was declared… cursed be he who taught his sons Greek."[4]

- Consider the Talmud in Soferim 1:7–8, speaking of when the Torah was translated into Greek, "[It] was as difficult [a time] for the Jewish people as the day when the Golden Calf was made."

- Judeans were strongly opposed to Hellenization. This is perhaps best illustrated through the Maccabean Revolt.[5]

- The Septuagint (Greek translation of the first five books of the Old Testament) was created at the request of the Egyptian King Ptolemy II Philadelphus for the great library in Alexandria. It was not written for Judean use.[6]

- Josephus, a Jewish POW turned Roman historian, lamented in the introductory remarks of his great work, "Antiquities of the Jews," that it was painful for him to translate his great work from Aramaic into the Greek language.[7] He even went on to say:

"For those of my own nation freely acknowledge that I far exceed them in the learning belonging to Jews: I have also taken a great deal of pains to obtain the learning of the Greeks, and understand the elements of the Greek language, although I have so long accustomed myself to

---

[4] Babylonian Talmud, Tract Baba Kamma (The First Gate), Chapter 7, online: www.sefaria.org/Bava_Kamma
[5] This event is celebrated even to this day through Hanukkah. And it was also commemorated during Jesus' day. Back then it was known as "Dedication Day" (See John 10:22).
[6] Josephus, *Antiquities of the Jews,* 1:10; 12:12–40, online: www.penelope.uchicago.edu/josephus
[7] Ibid, 1:3–12. See also, Josephus, *Against Apion*, 1:3, 50.

speak our own tongue, that I cannot pronounce Greek with sufficient exactness… for our nation does not encourage those who learn the languages of many nations."[8]

- Consider the fact that the apostles were "unschooled" and "common men" (Acts 4:13). How then could they have written so eloquently in Greek while an educated man like Josephus had struggled with the language?

- In Josephus' most famous historical work, *The Wars of the Jews*, he wrote these words:

"I have proposed to myself, for the sake of [those who] live under the government of the Romans, to translate those books into the Greek tongue, <u>which I formerly composed in the language of our country</u>, and sent to the Upper Barbarians; Joseph, the son of Matthias, by birth a Hebrew, a priest also, and one who at first fought against the Romans myself and was forced to be present at what was done afterwards."[9]

- The Roman Empire had two official languages: Latin and Greek. Latin was more official, and state documents were most often written in Latin.

- Several works from Qumran, such as Enoch and Tobit, are preserved in both Aramaic and Hebrew versions.[10]

- Discrimination against Greeks was evident even in the first days of the Church. *"And in those days, when the number of the disciples was multiplied, there arose a murmuring of the Grecians [Jews] against the*

---

[8] Ibid, 20:26.
[9] Josephus, *Wars of the Jews,* Preface 1:1, online: www.penelope.uchicago.edu/josephus
[10] "Aramaic was the Near East 'lingua franca' of the Biblical period, and it is still used among several Christian communities today. Just like the Hebrew Scrolls, the majority of Aramaic manuscripts were written in standard 'square' (Jewish) script. Represented in the Dead Sea Scrolls are a variety of Aramaic dialects: Official Aramaic, Jewish Palestinian Aramaic, Nabatean, and Christian Palestinian Aramaic." The Leon Levy Dead Sea Scrolls Digital Library, 2019, online: www.deadseascrolls.org.il/learn-about-the-scrolls/languages-and-scripts

Hebrews, because their widows were neglected in the daily ministration."
Acts 6:1 (NKJV)

- An interesting reference is made in Acts 1:19 to the Aramaic language: "And it was known unto all the dwellers at Jerusalem; insomuch as that field is called in their proper tongue, Aceldama, that is to say, The field of blood." As Ewan MacLeod points out:

    "This phrase is made up from the Aramaic hakel, meaning field, and dama, meaning the blood. (The KJV is translated from Greek, and Greek has no letter h, so hakel becomes acel or akel when written in Greek). But, critically, Aceldama cannot be Hebrew. It can only be Aramaic. In Hebrew, the word for field is not hakel; it is sadeh. In Hebrew, the equivalent phrase would be sadeh haDam. Aceldama uniquely and precisely identifies "our own tongue," the phrase used by both Josephus and the New Testament, as Aramaic, rather than Hebrew."[11]

- Matthew 5:22 and 27:46, Mark 5:41 and 7:34, John 20:16, and 1 Corinthians 16:22 are examples of Aramaic, not Hebrew, words being quoted.

- In addition to Irenaeus, who I quoted above, Papias and Eusebius agreed that Matthew was not written in Greek but in his native tongue.

- Papias (c. 60–163), an early church father, disciple of John the Apostle, and contemporary of Polycarp, wrote:

    'So, then Matthew wrote the oracles in the Hebrew language, and everyone interpreted them as he was able.' And the same writer uses testimonies from the first Epistle of John and from that of Peter likewise. And he relates another story of a woman, who was accused of many sins before the Lord, contained in the Gospel according to the Hebrews. These things we have thought it necessary to observe in addition to

---

[11] Ewan MacLeod, *Discover Aramaic* (JesusSpokeAramaic.com, 2016) p 139, e-book.

what has been already stated."[12]

- Eusebius, a fourth-century church father and historian, made several references to the Aramaic dialect of the apostles and their writings. Below are some of those references:

"For Matthew, who had at first preached to the Hebrews, when he was about to go to other peoples, committed his Gospel to writing in his native tongue and thus compensated those whom he was obliged to leave for the loss of his presence." (Eusebius, *Ecclesiastical History*, Book III, 24:6)

"And in how many provinces Peter preached Christ and taught the doctrine of the new covenant to those of the circumcision is clear from his own words in his epistle already mentioned as undisputed, in which he writes to the Hebrews of the dispersion in Pontus, Galatia, Cappadocia, Asia, and Bithynia." (Eusebius, *Ecclesiastical History*, Book III, 4:2)

"For as Paul had written to the Hebrews in his native tongue, some say that the evangelist Luke [or Clement] translated the epistle." (Eusebius, *Ecclesiastical History*, Book III, 38:2)

"The whole church [of Jerusalem] consisted then of believing Hebrews who continued from the days of the apostles until the siege which took place at this time; in which siege the Jews, having again rebelled against the Romans, were conquered after severe battles." (Eusebius, *Ecclesiastical History*, Book III, 5:2)

"And he (Hegesippus) wrote of many other matters, which we have in part already mentioned, introducing the accounts in their appropriate places. And from the Syriac Gospel according to the Hebrews he quotes some passages in the Hebrew tongue, showing that he was a convert from the Hebrews, and he mentions other matters as taken from the unwritten tradition of the Jews." (Eusebius, *Ecclesiastical History*, Book IV, 22:7)

Since, in the beginning of this work, we promised to give, when needed, the words of the ancient presbyters and writers of the Church, in which they have declared those traditions which came

---

[12] Eusebius, *Ecclesiastical History,* Book 3, 39:16, online: www.earlychristianwritings.com/eusebius.html

down to them concerning the canonical books, and since Irenæus was one of them, we will now give his words and, first, what he says of the sacred Gospels: 'Matthew published his Gospel among the Hebrews in their own language, while Peter and Paul were preaching and founding the church in Rome. After their departure Mark, the disciple and interpreter of Peter, also transmitted to us in writing those things which Peter had preached; and Luke, the attendant of Paul, recorded in a book the Gospel which Paul had declared.'" (Eusebius, *Ecclesiastical History*, Book V, 8:1-3)

"Pantænus was one of these [Saints], and is said to have gone to India. It is reported that among persons there who knew of Christ, he found the Gospel according to Matthew, which had anticipated his own arrival. For Bartholomew, one of the apostles, had preached to them, and left with them the writing of Matthew in the Hebrew language, which they had preserved till that time." (Eusebius, *Ecclesiastical History*, Book V, 10:3)

"He (Clement of Alexandria) says that the Epistle to the Hebrews is the work of Paul, and that it was written to the Hebrews in the Hebrew language; but that Luke translated it carefully and published it for the Greeks, and hence the same style of expression is found in this epistle and in the Acts." (Eusebius, *Ecclesiastical History*, Book V, 14:2)

"Among the four Gospels, which are the only indisputable ones in the Church of God under heaven, I (Origen) have learned by tradition that the first was written by Matthew, who was once a publican, but afterwards an apostle of Jesus Christ, and it was prepared for the converts from Judaism, and published in the Hebrew language." (Eusebius, *Ecclesiastical History*, Book VI, 25:4)

Lastly, several Biblical scholars have explained in great detail the Semitic (Aramaic and Hebrew) grammar that is embedded in the Greek New Testament. Here are a few to consider for further research on this topic:

- *Aramaic English New Testament, 5th Edition*, by Andrew Gabriel Roth
- *Was the New Testament Really Written in Greek?*, by Raphael Lataster
- *An Aramaic Approach to the Gospels and Acts*, by Matthew Black
- *Documents of the Primitive Church*, and, *Our Translated Gospels*, by Charles Cutler Torrey

- *Semitisms of the Book of Acts*, by Max Wilcox
- *The Aramaic Origin of the Fourth Gospel*, by Charles Fox Burney
- *The Aramaic Origin of the Four Gospels*, by Frank Zimmerman
- *The Words of Jesus in the Original Aramaic*, by Steven Andrew Missick
- Various translations and commentaries by David Bauscher
- *Jesusspokearamaic.com*, by Ewan MacLeod
- *Dukhrana.org*, by Lars J. Lindgren

TRANSLATIONS FROM THE ARAMAIC

For the texts of Revelation itself, I provide my own translation from the Language of Jesus: Aramaic. So whenever you see a Scripture quote end with "Aramaic Text," that is my translation from the original language. To satiate the curiosity of the scholarly, I have used as a base the BFBS and UBS Peshitta[13], along with the Syriac and Hebrew Peshitta NT based on George A. Kiraz's SEDRA 3 database, and cross references with the Crawford Codex. The Khabouris Peshitta text does not have the book of Revelation in it. I also owe a great deal of thanks to Lars J. Lindgren and his site, www.dukhrana.com. It is jam-packed with every lexicon available, and was a critical key to my research. Please check it out and support his work.

---

[13] The British and Foreign Bible Society B.F.B.S. and United Bible Society U.B.S. Text of the 1905/1920 Aramaic New Testament is said to be a Critical Text of about 42 Aramaic Manuscripts.

THE DESTRUCTION OF JERUSALEM BY TITUS

1846
By Wilhelm von Kaulbach (1805–1874)
Oil on canvas,
Neue Pinakothek, Munich
Photographed on 11 April 2016
by Ad Meskens
(Creative Commons)
.

1 DIRE STRAITS

"Behold, I bring evil upon this place, [even] all the words that are written in the book that was read before the king of Judah; because they have forsaken me, and burnt incense to strange gods, that they might provoke me by all the works of their hands; and my wrath is kindled against this place, and it shall not be quenched."
— Huldah the prophetess, 2 Chronicles 34:24-25, LXX

King Josiah's spine must have tingled and goosebumps set his hairs on end as he heard the words quoted above. In those fateful days the golden age of the Davidic era were but a distant mirage in the Judean desert. After the death of Solomon, the united Hebrew kingdom had split into the northern kingdom of Israel and southern kingdom of Judah.

As Isaiah, Hosea, and Amos prophesied, around 722 BC the northern kingdom of Israel was conquered and its inhabitants displaced by the superpower of their day, the Assyrians. The ten tribes that were displaced became known as the "lost tribes of Israel." Because of their great apostasy, the terms of their legal contract were violated repeatedly, and opportunities for repentance were mostly ignored. This was a legal course of action.

The southern kingdom of Judah was spared for a brief time because of the prayers of the prophet Isaiah and King Hezekiah (2 Chron 32). But the atrocities of Manasseh, the king who succeeded him, and his son Amon steered the proverbial Titanic straight into the iceberg.

Some of Manasseh's abominable acts included building alters to foreign gods *inside* the Temple of Solomon and shedding "innocent blood until he had filled Jerusalem from one end to another" (2 Kings 21:16). But what solidified his dark place in history was his trip to Gehenna[14] (yes, the Gehenna you read of in the Gospels) where he submitted his children as burnt sacrifices to the god Molech. As he led the inhabitants in like manner, the stench of burnt flesh filled the air. This demonic fire would become the primary symbol by which the Prophets, and later Jesus, would denounce Israel.

Having repeatedly violated the contractual requirements of the Law of Moses, it wasn't long before the legal consequences of the Law were felt. The Northern Kingdom of Israel fell to the Assyrians, and the Southern Kingdom of Judah was sacked by the Babylonians. Solomon's Temple was destroyed, and Jerusalem was set ablaze. **It was the end of the world for Jews in those days. The Day of the Lord had come.**

Fast forward roughly 650 years. For both Jews and Christians of the known world in 68 AD, it must have felt as though life as the they knew it was about to end once more. Following the suicide of Caesar Nero, Rome, the greatest and most powerful empire of their day was plunged into chaos and civil war. The monolithic kingdom was shaken to the core when, over the course of a single year, a total of four emperors assumed and lost the throne of Rome. Each one was killed by the next, save for the fourth, Vespasian, who remained in power.

At home in the regions of Judea, Vespasian led a full-blown Roman assault upon the Holy Land with his son, Titus. The pair commanded several legions and began by laying waste to Galilee, the homeland of Jesus of Nazareth, as they moved southward town by town. By the year 70 AD,

---

[14] The Hinnom Valley (ge-hinnom in Hebrew) was a valley just south of Jerusalem, which you can still visit today. Gehenna in early Jewish and Christian culture represented fire of abomination. Jerusalem also has a valley to the east, the Kidron Valley, which is perhaps also the Valley of Jehoshaphat. This was the "valley of the shadow of death" referenced in Psalm 23.

Jerusalem and the Temple would be completely razed, and hundreds of thousands of people slaughtered. Judaism was fundamentally changed from that time forward.

Within the communities of believers in Israel and throughout the Empire, devastating events shook them as well. The vast majority of the city of Rome was either destroyed or diminished by the Great Fire of 64 AD. Christians were used as a scapegoat by Nero, and three and a half years of persecution ensued. Then in 67 AD, two pillars of the early church, Paul and Peter, were both put to death. By 68 AD, Andrew (brother of Peter and one of the Twelve), was crucified on an x-shaped cross. Luke (the Gospel writer) was crucified. Bartholomew was crucified in Armenia. Mark (the Gospel writer) was tortured to death in Egypt.

"For it is time for judgment to begin with the household of God; and if it begins with us first, what will be the outcome for those who do not obey the gospel of God?" 1 Peter 4:17 (NASB) [15]

With pressure mounting on every side, the people of God no doubt felt tremendous tension in every aspect of their lives. In Judea, which was under Roman assault, believers[16] were persecuted by both Jews and Gentiles. The Roman Empire was on the brink of collapse, and even nature seemed to convulse in turmoil. To illustrate this, the Jewish historian, Josephus, reflecting on the times leading to Jerusalem's fall, wrote:

> "For there broke out a prodigious storm in the night, with the utmost violence, and very strong winds; with the largest showers of rain; with continual lightnings, terrible thundrings, and amazing concussions and bellowings of the earth that was in an earthquake. These things were a manifest indication that some destruction was coming upon men, when the system of the world was put into this disorder; and any one would guess

---

[15] Peter never would have considered himself a 'Christian'. He was a Jew through and through who had embraced the long-awaited Messiah of his people. The judgement he speaks of is in reference to he and his fellow Jews, and the 'house of God' Temple. The Aramaic, baytā ʾĕ/alāh reflects the Hebrew בֵּית יְהֹוָה, "house of Yahweh," a phrase found several times in the OT; Psalms 23:6; 27:4; 42:4; 55:14; 122:1; Isaiah 2:3; etc., *always* in reference to the Temple in Jerusalem.
[16] Throughout this book, I will use the word 'believers' in place of 'Christians' as often as possible. The word Christian today is often used as a distinction between Jews. This was not the case in the first century, as a great deal of Christians then *were* Jews. Hence, to avoid this mental hurdle, 'believers' will be used.

that these wonders foreshewed some grand calamities that were coming."[17]

Tacitus, the Roman historian, also wrote regarding the years of chaos in the late 60's AD:

> "The history on which I am entering is that of a period rich in disasters, terrible with battles, torn by civil struggles, horrible even in peace. Four emperors fell by the sword; there were three civil wars, more foreign wars, and often both at the same time. There was success in the East, misfortune in the West... Moreover, Italy was distressed by disasters unknown before or returning after the lapse of ages. Cities on the rich fertile shores of Campania were swallowed up or overwhelmed; Rome was devastated by conflagrations, in which her most ancient shrines were consumed and the very Capitol fired by citizens' hands. Sacred rites were defiled; there were adulteries in high places. The sea was filled with exiles, its cliffs made foul with the bodies of the dead."[18]

Much like the inhabitants of Europe during the second World War, all hope seemed lost, as though the end of all things was nigh. Christianity was not a religion nor was it an established and well-known belief system. At times, Ecclesiastical communities hung by a thread. Except for the grace of God, the early believer communities would have dwindled to extinction.

In addition to external threats, there were internal ones as well. In the New Testament, we find evidence of a growing concern amongst Christ's followers regarding His prophecies, which caused many to lose heart:

> *"...in the last days mockers will come with their mocking, following after their own lusts, and saying, 'Where is the promise of His coming? For ever since the fathers fell asleep, all things continue just as they were from the beginning of creation...'*
>
> *"The Lord is not slow about His promise, as some count slowness, but is patient toward you, not willing for any to perish, but for all to come to repentance. But the day of the Lord will come like a thief..."*
> *2 Peter 3:3–4, 9–10 (NASB)*

---

[17] Josephus, *Jewish Wars*, 4:4.5.
[18] Tacitus, *Histories*, 1:2.

By 67 AD, almost a full generation (from 30 AD to 67 AD), had passed since the prophetic words of Jesus concerning His coming to deliver the Saints from oppression and to finalize the end the Mosaic Age through the destruction of the Temple.[19]

FALSE HOPE

Meanwhile, in Judea, the Jewish rebel forces and many religious leaders were twice deceived by two unexpected occurrences. First, in 66 AD, a Roman official stationed in Judea named Gessius Florus provoked the Jews to anger by stealing from the Temple treasury and sending Roman soldiers to slaughter; 3,600 men, women, and children. Understandably, the inhabitants of Jerusalem retaliated. Consequently, a general named Cestius Gallus and his forces from Syria were sent to quell the uprising.

The Jews resisted, and eventually Cestius fell back. Their forces were ambushed in what became known as the Battle of Beth Horon, where 6,000 Roman soldiers were killed. The Jewish rebels considered this a victory from Yahweh God, and their ambitions soared. Under the delusion of this small achievement, the Jewish rebels formed the "Judean Free Government." They elected three new leaders and began to prepare for war against Rome.[20]

> *"Now as to the periods and times, brothers and sisters, you have no need of anything to be written to you.... While they are saying, 'Peace and safety!' then sudden destruction will come upon them like labor pains upon a pregnant woman, and they will not escape."*
> *1 Thessalonians 5:1, 3 (NASB)*

This was the first deception in which the Jewish people pillared their hopes on sand. But Gallus' invasion was just the tip of the iceberg. The Jews had no idea the worst was yet to come. A devastating final blow was coming to the Temple system and the Law of Moses. The contractual obligations of Deuteronomy were left violated and unfulfilled. The window of transition from Moses to Messiah was closing, and the old wineskin was about to burst.

When Nero caught wind of the insurrection in the Roman province of Judea, he was outraged. As Judeans celebrated what they thought to be a new era, Vespasian and Titus prepared to rain down fire and sword upon the

---

[19] See Luke 21; Matthew 23, 24, 25; and Acts 6:14.
[20] Heinrich Ewald, *The History of Israel: The Apostolic Age* (London: Longmans, Green, and Company, 1885) p. 511-514, e-book.

oblivious rebels.

The second deception came during the heat of the Roman campaign in 69 AD. Vespasian worked his way south from Galilee and destroyed town and village, sparing none. Jerusalem was now in his sights. But as the Jews braced for impact, the great beast Rome received another crushing blow when its third emperor in less than twelve months, Vitellius, was assassinated. The Empire subsequently descended into total chaos.

> "The death of Vitellius was rather the end of [civil] war than the beginning of [Roman] peace. The victors [who killed the Emperor] ranged through the city in arms, pursuing their defeated foes with implacable hatred: the streets were full of carnage, the fora and temples reeked with blood; they slew right and left everyone whom chance put in their way."[21]

Both the apostates in Judea—indeed, the whole inhabited world—believed the Roman Empire was about to fall. News of the Empire's dire state, in conjunction with the reprieve of the war at their doorsteps, would have inevitably caused the Jews to believe their day had come.

> "...while [Titus] was assisting his father [Vespasian] at Alexandria, in settling that government [of Vespasian as the new Emperor in Rome] which had been newly conferred upon them by God, it so happened, that the sedition at Jerusalem was revived, and parted into three factions: and that one faction fought against the other... But for the present sedition, one should not mistake if he called it a sedition begotten by another sedition: and to be like a wild beast grown mad, which, for want of food from abroad, fell now upon eating its own flesh."[22]

But General Vespasian could not bear the thought of his beloved Empire's collapse. He saw a small window of opportunity, and acted swiftly.

> "But when Vespasian had overthrown all the places that were near to Jerusalem, he returned to Caesarea; and heard of the troubles that were at Rome... And as this sorrow of his was violent, he was not able to support the torments he was under;

---

[21] Tacitus, *Histories*, 4:1.
[22] Josephus, *Jewish Wars*, 5:1:1.

nor to apply himself farther in other wars, when his native country was laid waste."[23]

When Vespasian briefly paused his assault on the Holy Land, his own soldiers crowned him the new Caesar of Rome. With their support, he left the Judean campaign and marched to Rome to seize the throne.

To the surprise of the Jews and the whole inhabited world, Rome didn't collapse. In fact, the new Emperor Vespasian revived and reinvigorated the beast.

> "But at Rome the senators voted to Vespasian all the honours and privileges usually given the emperors. They were filled with joy and confident hope, for it seemed to them that civil warfare, which, breaking out in the Gallic and Spanish provinces, had moved to arms first the Germanies, then Illyricum, and which had traversed Egypt, Judea, Syria, and all provinces and armies, was now at an end, as if the expiation of the whole world had been completed."[24]

The revival of the beast was indeed just as the prophecies of John the Beloved foretold:

> *"I saw one of his heads as if it had been slain, and his fatal wound was healed. And the whole earth was amazed and followed after the beast…"* Revelation 13:3 (NASB)

If this wasn't enough to make the apostate rebels of Judea sweat, Vespasian then commissioned his son Titus to continue the bloody campaign against the war-torn Judean people.

> "Vespasian's entire government… was now settled, **and upon the unexpected deliverance of the public affairs of the Romans from ruin**; Vespasian turned his thoughts to what remained unsubdued in Judea. However, he himself made haste to go to Rome… but sent his son Titus, with a select part of his army, to destroy Jerusalem."[25]

But the Judeans refused to surrender, and the plans of rebel Jewish forces

---

[23] Josephus, *Jewish Wars*, 4:10:2.
[24] Tacitus, *Histories*, 4:3.
[25] Josephus, *Jewish Wars*, 4:11:5.

to overthrow Roman rule would prove fatal. The ensuing five-month campaign became a battle of attrition, which included the Romans building an eight-kilometer-long wall of circumvallation. Titus' patience waned in the face of unexpected resilience and tenacity of those behind the walls of Jerusalem. He concentrated his efforts on one section of each of the three walls. Once his army was able to penetrate the Antonia Fortress and the third wall, he directed four legions to wage an all-out slaughter on the Jews. And on the 9th of Av, also known as Tisha B'Av (30 August, 70 AD), Jerusalem and the Temple were destroyed. The prophecies of Jesus the Messiah in Matthew 23 to 25 were fulfilled, as were many of the visions of the Apostle John on Patmos Island.

> "Jerusalem... was so thoroughly razed to the ground by those that demolished it to its foundations, that nothing was left that could ever persuade visitors that it had once been a place of habitation."[26]

LET HOPE ARISE

When all hope seemed lost, the God of All Hope (Rom 15:13) sent the Prince of Peace (Isaiah 9:6) to his friend and faithful apostle, John. What an encounter it must have been! The visions and experiences that followed brimmed with symbol, meaning, and significance. The prophet Ezekiel, hundreds of years prior, when Jerusalem and the Temple of Solomon were about to be destroyed for the first time, also received multi-faceted, multi-layered visions and encounters. Yet there was a sense of urgency for both God and Ezekiel, as his prophecies were necessary for the people of Yahweh God at that time. And so, it was with John and the Jews in his time.

John's angelic encounters and prophetic visions were layered with symbolism, weaving in God's grander narratives like covenant, justice, and new creation. But within this beautiful fabric of God's revealed plans were the answers to more immediate questions and solutions to more immediate circumstances. **Much like the prophetic experiences of Ezekiel, Jeremiah, Daniel, and Zechariah, God was addressing the real-time unfolding of Judah's history as the ruling empire destroyed the Holy City and Solomon's Temple.** These books were also filled with messages of the Messianic Age, God's solution for the problem of evil, and His ultimate plan to renew all creation.

---

[26] Josephus, *Jewish Wars*, 7:1:1.

Likewise, John received grand visions of a new heaven and new earth, the obliteration of evil, and the consummation of the wedding of the Bridegroom King. Jesus also provided him with confirmation that His words recorded in Matthew 23-25 (and many others) were about to come to pass. Behold, the Son of Man was coming in glory to drag the closing curtain across the stage of the Age of Moses. The religious stronghold in Jerusalem would be broken, and the Saints of Jesus delivered from the Roman invasion. The Messianic Age would no longer be partially eclipsed by the Mosaic Age but would finally shine in full splendour.

> *"But when that era [of the Law of Moses] came to an end and the time of fulfillment had come, God sent his Son, born of a woman, born under the written law. Yet all of this was so that he would redeem and set free all those held hostage to the written law so that we would receive our freedom and a full legal adoption as his children."*
> *Galatians 4:4–5 (TPT)*[27]

Things were indeed dark, and everything that could be shaken in the known world was shaken (Heb. 12:26–27). Yet Jesus provided insight into the darkness and understanding of all things spoken by Himself and the prophets of old. The darkest hour was upon the Holy Land and the Saints of God, but it was also the last hour before the rising of the new day. The dawn of this age was at hand. John, the beloved friend of Jesus, was given a message of hope to be shared with the people of Israel and the Bride of Christ.

In addition to the new hope, there was also a message of closure and context to the Yahwistic communities of Judea and the diaspora. Jesus goes into great detail throughout Revelation to communicate to those who associated with Abraham and the Law of Moses.

John's revelation was primarily Jewish-centric and Jewish-focused. In the midst of tribulation among the saints and ecclesiastical communities throughout Judea and the Empire, and the tribulation amidst a falling Rome, John was sent to prophecy the same way Ezekiel and Isaiah were before him. During the last years leading up to the fall of Jerusalem, the Temple, and those who chose to defend it, John was given a message of warning and hope.

Hope is the hallmark of John's vision, with present exhortations and comfort at the beginning and a glimpse of the future chapters of God's grand

---

[27] Scripture quotations marked TPT are from The Passion Translation®. Copyright © 2017, 2018 by Passion & Fire Ministries, Inc. Used by permission. All rights reserved. ThePassionTranslation.com.

story of restoration at the end. Nestled between these two hopes we find answers to the Mosaic narrative in traditional Hebrew imagery and literary style. The Jewish people were being alerted to the great transition at hand.

At this point, there was no redemptive value remaining in the religious temple system nor in ritualistic sacrifices. These constructs emphatically needed to cease, and the people of ancient Israel were invited once again to have a new perspective of what Yahweh was doing. To be sure, he was sinking the old vessel and calling the descendants of Abraham to the new vessel, their Messiah, Jesus.

"Come out of her, my people, so that you will not participate in her sins and receive any of her plagues…" Revelation 18:4 (NASB)

And like the great prophets of old, John the Beloved was privileged to see visions of a time yet to come when Satan and his legions are exterminated once and for all. When two realms, God's and mankind's, are united as one and the Bridegroom King receives His beloved bride, the Saints of Jesus, to consummate the marriage. When Heaven and earth become one, and New Eden is born.

"Then I saw a new heaven and a new earth… And I saw the holy city, new Jerusalem, coming down out of heaven from God… And I heard a loud voice from the throne, saying, 'Behold, the tabernacle of God is among the people, and He will dwell among them.'" Revelation 21:1–3 (NASB)

In the darkest hour of Israel's history, in the most dire time of the early church, Jesus the Messiah bursts forth in radiant light. Yeshua (Jesus) is the lens through which we must read and interpret the visions of John. His light is the light that illuminates the pages of John's Apocalypse.

"God is Light, and in Him there is no darkness at all."
1 John 1:5 (NASB)

THE DATING OF REVELATION

"The Revelation which came to John The Evangelist from God in Patmos, the island to which he was exiled by Nero Caesar."

-The Syriac heading of chapter 1 of Revelation, found in the Crawford Manuscript (8th or 12th century AD).

Sir Isaac Newton was not only an inventor, but a major enthusiast of Bible prophecy, especially the books of Daniel and Revelation. His thoughts and conclusions concerning the dating of John's prophetic encounter on Patmos are fascinating. Newton writes:

"Irenaeus introduced an opinion that the Apocalypse was written in the time of Domitian; but then he also postponed the writing of some others of the sacred books, and was to place the Apocalypse after them: he might perhaps have heard from his master Polycarp that he had received this book from John about the time of Domitian's death; or indeed John might himself at that time have made a new publication of it, from whence Irenaeus might imagine it was then but newly written. Eusebius in his Chronicle and Ecclesiastical History follows Irenaeus; but afterwards in his Evangelical Demonstrations, he conjoins the banishment of John into Patmos, with the deaths of Peter and Paul: and so do Tertullian and Pseudo-Prochorus, as well as the first author, whoever he was, of that very ancient fable, that John was put by Nero into a vessel of hot oil, and coming out unhurt, was banished by him into Patmos.

Though this story be no more than a fiction, yet was it founded on a tradition of the first churches, that John was banished by him into Patmos in the days of Nero. Epiphanius represents the Gospel of John as written in the same time of Domitian, and the Apocalypse even before that of Nero. Arethas in the beginning of his Commentary quotes the opinion of Irenaeus from Eusebius, but follows it not: **for he afterwards affirms the Apocalypse was written before the destruction of Jerusalem, and that former commentators had expounded the sixth seal of that destruction.**

With the opinion of the first Commentators agrees the tradition of the Churches of Syria, preserved to this day in the title of the Syriac Version of the Apocalypse, which title is this: The Revelation which was made to John the Evangelist by God in the Island Patmos, into which he was banished by Nero the Caesar...

This opinion is further supported by the allusions in the
Apocalypse to the Temple and Altar, and holy City, as then
standing; and to the Gentiles, who were soon after to tread
under foot the holy City and outward court. 'Tis confirmed also
by the style of the Apocalypse itself, which is fuller of
Hebraisms than his Gospel. For thence it may be gathered, that
it was written when John was newly come out of Judea, **where
he had been used to the Syriac** [Aramaic] **tongue.**"[28]

Why does the approximate date of when John's Apocalypse was written
matter? Because if he wrote it before 70 AD, then his vision was in fact a
prophecy. If he wrote it after, then his vision was a history book with
commentary. The task at hand for the author and the reader is to sift through
early church writings, historical works, and the scriptures to see if they
provide any clues to help us properly date his book.

I do not wish to dismiss the writings of Eusebius (and a few other early
church fathers) who believed John was exiled to Patmos under the Roman
Emperor Domitian towards the end of the first century AD.[29] The challenge
with this notion is they all seem to rely on the opinion of Irenaeus, an early
church leader. Unfortunately, Irenaeus had a track record of inaccurate
dating; the most erroneous example being when he stated that Jesus had died
at age 50.[30] This diminishes his credibility when it comes to his dating of
John's Apocalypse (mentioned in *Against Heresies,* Books III and V).[31]

The church father and historian Eusebius (as well as Jerome) then drew
from Irenaeus and concluded that John was banished under Domitian as
well.[32] The *Travels of St. John in Patmos* also seems to use Irenaeus' time period.
We can see that Irenaeus was a major source from which the notion that John
was banished to Patmos under Domitian was derived. Therefore, dating
accounts found in early church writings are, at first glance, unreliable.

Moreover, it may be that history became mixed with legend as stories

---

[28] Newton, Sir Isaac, *Observations Upon the Prophecies of Daniel and the Apocalypse of St.
John,* www.blueletterbible.org/Comm/newton_isaac/prophecies/apocalypse01.cfm
[29] Eusebius, *Church History,* Book 3:23
[30] Irenaeus, *Against Heresies,* 2:22:4-6
[31] Irenaeus mentions that he drew information from Polycarp, who was mentored
under Apostle John. This source was either a written account that is now lost to us,
or an oral tradition of Polycarp's.
[32] Eusebius, *Church Histories,* 3, 17.

were passed down over the generations. For instance, revisiting *The Travels of St. John in Patmos*, we read of a Roman emperor lashing out against the apostle John for preaching the gospel in Ephesus:

> "John made a large number of people turn to the faith of Christ and show disdain to the worship of idols. However, all this was reported to Domitian, the emperor of Rome, through a statement made by some inhabitants of Ephesus. They informed him that most of the inhabitants were breaking the laws of the emperor and following some magical art of the so-called Christians. And that in contempt of the worship of the great gods they tore down their most important temples. When the emperor was notified he sent ten officers, with military assistance, and the order to exile us to the island of Patmos."[33]

This is a very similar account written by Tertullian, who's dating is earlier than the writing of Prochorus (the pen name of the writer just quoted). Tertullian's account goes as follows:

> "After these things, when the Gospel was increasing by the hands of the Apostles, Nero, the unclean and impure and wicked king, heard all that had happened at Ephesus. And he sent (and) took all that the procurator had, and imprisoned him; and laid hold of St. John and drove him into exile; and passed sentence on the city that it should be laid waste.
>
> "And after three days, believing men of the city assembled, and counselled one another and said: 'Let us assemble at the church, and see what each man is willing to give, and take a bribe, and offer it to this wicked ruler, and he will give up to us this (man), who turned us away from error unto our Lord.' And when they had taken counsel thus, they collected three hundred pounds of gold, and took ten men, and they went on board a ship to go to Nero, the wicked king, and give the bribe, and brought back the

---

[33] Margarita Grillis, *Acts of John, According to Prochorus: An Apocryphal Account of His Journeys, Miracles and Death [translated]*, (BookBaby, 2015) e-book.

holy man [John]."[34]

Tertullian mentions Nero (who reigned from c. 64 to c. 68), while Prochorus mentions Domitian (who reigned from c. 81 to c. 96). If John was commissioned to prophesy to Israel (like Ezekiel) in order to warn them of the coming destruction of Jerusalem, then Tertullian's account better aligns with the Book of Revelation. Emperor Nero was instrumental in initializing the events that led to Jerusalem's fall.

If John wrote Revelation during Nero's reign, then the passages regarding the "beast of the sea" and the "mark of the beast" in chapter 13 also make sense. Taking a hint from the book of Daniel, we know that beasts represented empires. Facing west over the Mediterranean on the shores of ancient Israel, the empire across the sea would have been Rome. It was the beast that arose from the sea.

What about the "mark?" As some of you may already know, the Hebrew alphabet also served as a numbering system. Because John was writing as a prophet to the nation of Israel, and Aramaic was his native tongue, then it would not have been unreasonable for John to refer to Hebrew numbers when he wrote "666." Therefore, "Nero Caesar" in the Hebrew alphabet is נרון קסר (NRON QSR), which, when used as numbers, represent 50, 200, 6, 50, 100, 60, and 200, equaling 666 when added together.

I appreciate Frank Viola's historical sensitivity to an earlier dating of John's Revelation while trying to hold true to the Domitian tradition. Thus, Viola places John's time upon Patmos circa 70, when Domitian held his father Vespasian's throne in Rome (December 69 to October 70), sitting as proxy while his father returned from Judea.[35] This theory is plausible, bearing in mind Mucianus administered all the details of government, and Domitian was only his aid until the arrival of his father Vespasian.[36] This is still, in my view, the best hypothesis to reconcile some of the early church accounts of the historical and literal context of Jesus' prophecies and John's Revelation.

One other idea to consider was that the early church writers were not referring to "Domitian" (Titus Flavius Caesar **Domitianus** Augustus), but

---

[34] Wright, , LL.D., PH. D, *Apocryphal Acts of the Apostles, Volume 2: The History of John, the son of Zebedee, the Apostle and Evangelist*, (London: Gilbert and Rivington, Whitefriars, City, E.C., and St. John's Square, Clerkenwell, E.C., 1871) e-book.
[35] After Nero committed suicide, three men tried to take the throne and died in the process. Vespasian was the fourth and he succeeded. All this took place in the span of one year.
[36] Cassius Dio, *Roman History*, Epitome of Book 65, 66:2.

rather to "Domitius" (Lucius **Domitius** Ahenobarbus, Nero's birth-name). Emperor Nero took the name Nero Claudius Caesar Augustus Germanicus when he was adopted at age 13 by his great-uncle, the emperor Claudius.[37]

However, if we consider the time of Domitian's **stewardship** of the throne (c. 69 to c. 70) as a time-period reference and not an exact date, then we can reconcile historical events, early church writings, and John's Revelation. How? **If the earliest church fathers like Polycarp and Irenaeus used Domitian as an indicator of the Year of Four Emperors—the time between Nero's fall and Vespasian's ascension—then the period being referenced is accurate.**[38]

Any dating later than 70 AD would also diminish the significance of the words given to John in light of the prophetic fulfillment of Jerusalem and the Temple being destroyed that same year. It would also render John's commission in Revelation 10 to prophecy unnecessary. As it is written:

"Surely the Lord God does nothing,
Unless He reveals His secret to His servants the prophets."
Amos 3:7 (NKJV)

Despite the conflicting views from Irenaeus (A.D. 130– 202) and Origen (A.D. 185– 254), there are many early church references that support a pre-70 AD dating of Revelation. These include: Papias, the writer of the Shepard of Hermas, Tertullian, Ephiphanius, Arethas, Theophlact, and Clement of Alexandria. In addition to these, we have early manuscripts like The Muratorian Canon (ca. A.D. 170), which is the fourth-century Syriac (Peshitto) version of the New Testament.[39]

---

[37] This is merely a hypothesis, but one worth exploring. On another note, Jimmy Akin wrote a brilliant article titled, *Domitian and the Persecution That Didn't Happen,* stating that Christians were not persecuted under Domitian, but rather under Nero: online: www.ncregister.com/blog/jimmy-akin/domitian-and-the-persecution-that-didnt-happen

[38] Another theory is that John was on Patmos Island at least twice in his lifetime. Once on a possible missionary journey around the late 60s AD during the reign of Nero, and perhaps another time while in exile in the 80s AD, under the reign of emperor Domitian of Rome. However, I am more confident he was there during Nero's reign.

[39] The title page of the fourth-century Syriac Version, called the Peshitto, says this: "Again the revelation, which was upon the holy John the Evangelist from God when he was on the island of Patmos where he was thrown by the emperor Nero." Jonathan Welton, *The Art of Revelation* (Rochester: Welton Academy, 2017) e-book.

What is undisputed based on early church evidence is that John was headquartered in Ephesus and spent most of his life after Jesus' ascension ministering to the churches in Asia Minor:

> "Afterwards, John, the disciple of the Lord, who also had leaned upon His breast, did himself publish a Gospel during his residence at Ephesus in Asia…

> "Then, again, the Church in Ephesus, founded by Paul, and having John remaining among them permanently until the times of Trajan, is a true witness of the tradition of the apostles."[40]

> "Each of [the apostles] then went to such country and region as he was charged by the grace (of God). And it happened that when this holy virgin [chaste], namely John, the son of Zebedee, went forth, the grace (of God) accompanied him through the Spirit of holiness, that it might lead him to the country of the Ephesians, where the head and power of idolatry was dominant. And when he had parted and gone forth from Jerusalem, he set his face to go to Ephesus."[41]

In light of the aforementioned, my conviction is that John's prophetic encounter took place while Nero was still alive (hence Revelation 13:18), and before Nero summoned Vespasian and Titus to crush the Jewish Revolt, which led to the destruction of the Temple. Given that Vespasian was dispatched in late 66 or early 67 AD, **I place the writing of the Book of Revelation sometime in 66 or early 67 AD.**

---

[40] Irenaeus of Lyons, *Against Hereisies*, Book 3, Chapter 1, 3.
[41] Wright, , LL.D., PH. D, *Apocryphal Acts of the Apostles, Volume 2: The History of John, the son of Zebedee, the Apostle and Evangelist*, (London: Gilbert and Rivington, Whitefriars, City, E.C., and St. John's Square, Clerkenwell, E.C., 1871) e-book.

2 JESUS IS UNVEILED

"Philip said to Him, "Lord, show us the Father, and it is enough for us." Jesus said to him, "Have I been with you for so long a time, and yet you have not come to know Me, Philip? The one who has seen Me has seen the Father."
— John 14:8–9 (NASB)

Revelation was and is not Plan B for God. Colloquially speaking, Revelation is not God saying, "Well the whole John 3:16 thing didn't work, so now I'm going to give the world the punishment it deserves." The Trinity is not bi-polar. There is not a good cop, bad cop scenario with Jesus and God. Unfortunately, many people believe there is. In both the secular and believing realms there is systemic misunderstanding of the nature and character of God, and it is one that has been shaped by the largely impoverished and legalistic Western theology.

A question to ponder: If you see God as distant, austere, vindictive, then is it possible you have not yet seen The Father?

"The one who has seen Me has seen the Father." John 14:9 (NASB)

JESUS IS PERFECT THEOLOGY

Our understanding of who God is can only come through Jesus, His Son. If we cannot take Jesus at His word then our Faith is futile. To see Him is to see Yahweh God.

*"If you had known Me, you would have known My Father also; from now on you **know** Him, and have **seen** Him."*

Philip said to Him, 'Lord, show us the Father, and it is enough for us.' Jesus said to him, 'Have I been with you for so long a time, and yet you have not come to know Me, Philip? The one who has seen Me has seen the Father; how can you say, 'Show us the Father'?'"
John 14:7–9 (NASB)

All other lenses, including the Old Testament, come secondary to Jesus as the primary revelation of the nature and character of Yahweh God. Speaking of the Old Testament, Paul wrote these opening remarks to his Jewish kinsmen:

"God, after He spoke long ago to the fathers in the prophets in many portions and in many ways, in these last days has spoken to us in His Son, whom He appointed heir of all things, through whom He also made the world. And He is the radiance of His glory and the exact representation of His nature and upholds all things by the word of His power." Hebrews 1:1–3 (NASB)

Pause for a moment and consider what you just read. Jesus is the exact representation of God's nature! In two other places we have Paul making similar statements:

"Jesus is the image of the invisible God." Col 1:15

"Jesus is the image of God." 2 Cor 4:4

Moreover, let us ponder the words of our Lord Jesus when he said, "Truly, truly, I say to you, the Son can do nothing of Himself, unless it is something He sees the Father doing; for whatever the Father does, these things the Son also does in the same way." (John 5:19). And, "Believe Me that I am in the Father and the Father is in Me." (John 14:11).

The implication here is that God was also the One who stooped down to meet the woman caught in adultery, and raise her from her sin and shame.[42] God was also the One who, when asked if He was willing to heal, said, "I am willing, be healed." God was also the One who forgave those who, fully knowing what they were doing, crucified His Son.

Hence, the good cop, bad cop paradigm must be checked at the proverbial door before one enters into the house of Revelation. We must abandon the notion of a Plan B. Jesus and His revelation of God our Father must be the anchor and the plumb line by which we measure and weigh everything we read in the Apocalypse. If we can't see it in Jesus-Made-Flesh, then we have to re-evaluate our conclusions.

GOD'S GRAND LOVE STORY

Before God spoke creation into being, the Godhead looked ahead and saw everything possible for Them to do, including creating all of creation itself. But more specifically, they saw humans, and They saw the fall and the pain and suffering that would afflict creation as a result. God, Jesus, and the Holy Spirit also saw what it would cost to create mankind. For this reason, it was written:

"[The] Lamb was slain from the creation of the world."
Revelation 13:8 (NKJV)

But the Godhead not only saw the cost, they also saw the tremendous value of humans as well. We humans were worth the Blood of Jesus; therefore, God was willing to pay the highest price before creation ever took place.[43] One only pays a high price for something that has a high value!

"[God] has saved us and called us with a holy calling, not according to our works, but according to His own purpose and grace which was given to us in Christ Jesus before time began." 2 Timothy 1:9 (NKJV)

God was not surprised by the fall of Adam and Eve. Genesis chapter 3 was not "plan B." His foresight and provision were already in place before He ever created mankind.

"For whom He foreknew, He also predestined to be conformed to the image

---

[42] "You empower me for victory with your wrap-around presence. Your power within makes me strong to subdue, and by stooping down in gentleness you strengthened me and made me great!" Psalm 18:35 (TPT)
[43] See also 1 Corinthians 7:23.

19

of His Son...
He made the riches of His glory known to the vessels of His mercy, whom
He prepared in advance for glory." Romans 8:29, 9:29 (NKJV)

Jesus has placed such a high value on your life and mine! He looked ahead and considered all that it would cost Him to create us, and decided we were still worth the cost because here we are today![44]

*"For he chose us in him before the creation of the world to be holy and blameless in his sight, **in love**." Ephesians 1:4 (NKJV, emphasis mine)*

Love cannot remain alone. Love is only fully expressed in the context of community. This is why God was not alone from the beginning. Yet Their love burned and longed for greater expression, and so They sought to create, "a chosen people, a royal priesthood, a holy nation, a people for God's own possession." (1 Pet 2:9). Thus, it was settled in eternity past, in the loved-filled community of Father, Son, and Holy Spirit, that people would be made in Their likeness, **which is love**. These created beings would have the essence and breath of the Divine, and a calling to share in and manifest Their selfless love. This community of love would be given the mandate to fill the earth so that the Trinitarian expression of *hesed* and *agape*[45] would fill it.

The final and most mind-blowing piece of this divine masterpiece is that God would dwell and infuse Himself within and through these created beings. "Christ in us" would become our "hope of glory." This too was "according to the purpose of the ages, which He purposed in Christ Jesus our Lord," (Eph 3:1-13).

Paul called all of this 'the secret of the ages' (Rom. 16:25; Col. 1:26; Eph. 3:4–5, 9). This mystery was not only veiled from mortals, it was also hidden from angels as well. Gabriel and Michael didn't know it. Neither did Lucifer, nor his demonic hosts (1 Cor. 2:7–8; Eph. 3:9–10). Paul, along with other apostles and prophets in First Century AD, became "stewards of the divine mystery," (1 Cor. 4:1; Col. 1:25–26; Eph. 3:2–9).

Moreover, God would weave a grand love-story in the narrative of creation: with His Son as the protagonist playing the role of a Bridegroom and mankind as the bride. And in the same way that it was not good for man to be alone (Gen 2:18), so too it would not be good for the Son of Man to be alone.

---

[44] See Luke 14:25-33. Jesus counted the cost!
[45] The Hebrew word חֶסֶד (hesed, Strong's H2617) is even richer than the Greek ἀγάπη (agape).

"For no man ever hated his own body, but he nourishes and cares for his own, just as The Messiah does also for his church. Because we are members of his body and we are of his flesh and of his bones. Therefore, a man should leave his father and his mother and should cleave to his wife, and the two of them shall be one flesh. **This is a great mystery, but I am speaking about The Messiah and about his church.** *"*[46]
Ephesians 5:29–32 (Aramaic)

God would create a bride from Jesus' side and creation would be re-created through the Son of Man.[47] **It was at this point that God then said, "Let there be light."**

JOHN: THE LAST OLD TESTAMENT PROPHET?

"What did you go looking for? A prophet? I tell you, yes, more than a prophet… Amen I say to you, there has not arisen among them born of women one more significant than John the Baptizer; but the least in the kingdom of heaven is greater than he."
Matthew 11:19, 21 (Aramaic Text)

Now I'd like to shift focus to John the Revelator's prophetic office. I will then connect this to God's love story later in this chapter.

The cousin and herald of the Messiah (the other John) was considered more significant than any other prophet in Israel by Jesus Himself. Why? Because of the significance of His message.

Deuteronomy 13 made it clear that a false prophet was to be put to death. John was no false prophet. And if we were to lump him together with the major and minor Prophets of the Old Testament, John would have the shortest book. But his simple message was also the most significant; for it ushered in the greatest moment, the greatest Being, and the greatest epoch season of all time.

---

[46] Bauscher, David. *The Holy Peshitta Bible Translated*, Lulu.com. Kindle Edition, p. 2374-2375.
[47] John 19:34 is being symbolically compared here to Genesis 2:22. Blood and water are symbols of birth and new life. We are born anew through Christ and from Christ, a new creation (1 John 3:2).

John the Baptist was undoubtedly the most *significant* Old Covenant prophet because he had the most significant message. But that does not mean he was the *last* Old Covenant prophet. In Matthew 11, Jesus continues to speak of John, saying, "For all the prophets and the Law prophesied until John ..." Matthew 11:13 (NASB).

In other words, Moses and the Elijah, the Law of the Prophets, were still testifying to the coming of Jesus and the transition of covenant seasons. John the Baptist was being counted amongst the "Prophets" (נביאים Nevi'im) by Jesus at that point in time, roughly 30 AD.

I submit that one *last* prophet, of the order of the "Prophets" (נביאים Nevi'im), arose after 30 AD, many years after Jesus had ascended. His message was not *as* significant as John the Baptist's, in the sense that he had the best sermon of all time, but the last prophet's message was significant, nonetheless. This prophet, brothers and sisters, was John the Apostle, aka, John the Revelator.

Now, how can I draw such a conclusion? Well, perhaps before we get to the conclusion we can simply ask: is it possible that John the Revelator was an Old Testament prophet? I believe the answer is yes... sort of. Let me explain.

My conclusion is based both on a technicality and a presumption. The technicality is that John happened to receive a divine revelation (vis-à-vis Ezekiel) from Yahweh God during a time when the Mosaic Covenant was still in force. (If you read my first book in this series, you may recall the forty-year overlap between the Mosaic and Messianic Covenants that I referred to).

We must also understand that John was prophesying[48] almost exclusively to the people of Israel and to those bound by the Mosaic Law. Revelation is not a handbook placed in a time capsule to help believers survive a pre or post-rapture divine reckoning. It is a time-sensitive, Jewish-centric prophetic illustration on the destruction of Jerusalem and the Temple at the hands of the Romans (vis-à-vis Ezekiel, once again). It is also a framework to help us see and understand the transition of covenant seasons and the renewal of all things. It is a prophecy, not a commentary, because it took place prior to the fall of Jerusalem in 70 AD.[49]

---

[48] Revelation 1:3; 10:11; 19:10; 22:7; 22:10; 22:18, 19.
[49] See the last chapter in book I of this series for an extensive look at the dating of John's Revelation.

The presumption is that John was prophesying to those bound under the Law, during a time when the Law was still technically in effect. Therefore, he is likely concluding the order of "Prophets" to some degree. When we combine the aforementioned points, it is clear John the Revelator was the *last* Old Covenant prophet. Moreover, after the Apostle John, no other person with divine revelation (a throne-room encounter of some sort), whose writing was given Scriptural (canonical) authority, emerged and prophesied to those under the Law.

JOHN'S PROPHETIC OFFICE

Based on the Ephesians 4 model of leadership, we know Scripturally that John was commissioned as an apostle, but also held the office of a prophet (Revelation 10:11; 22:9). In light of this, let us consider the Lord's command to John in Revelation 10:11:

"Prophesy again for a season concerning Gentiles, and races and tongues, and many who rule," (Aramaic Text).

From this we can deduce John would have needed time to prophesy to the Jewish people and warn them. Hence, in the Aramaic we find "for a season" (*zbn*), which indicates a defined time period. It makes no sense for John to have been given a short timeframe to prophecy concerning events that would occur 2,000 years after his death. Also note that he is told to prophecy "again," meaning he (and/or Jesus and the Apostles) had already prophesied about things that concerned the Gentiles (Rome at this point in time) and races (Jew and Greek).

Therefore, it would not have made sense for John to have been given the same commission as Ezekiel but denied the chance to carry it out. Ezekiel spent 430 days warning the Jewish people after eating the scroll he was given by an angel. Thus, it is reasonable to say since John experienced the same supernatural commissioning of Ezekiel (Revelation 10:10), he would have been afforded some measure of time to prophesy as well.

There are in fact, "extensive parallels between the prophecy of Revelation and the prophecy of Ezekiel:

1. The Throne Vision (Rev. 4; Ezek. 1)
2. The Book (Rev. 5; Ezek. 2–3)
3. The Four Plagues (Rev. 6:1–8; Ezek. 5)
4. The Slain under the Altar (Rev. 6:9–11; Ezek. 6)
5. The Wrath of God (Rev. 6:12–17; Ezek. 7)

6. The Seal on the Saint's Foreheads (Rev. 7; Ezek. 9)
7. The Coals from the Altar (Rev. 8; Ezek. 10)
8. No More Delay (Rev. 10:1–7; Ezek. 12)
9. The Eating of the Book (Rev. 10:8–11; Ezek. 2)
10. The Measuring of the Temple (Rev. 11:1–2; Ezek. 40–43)
11. Jerusalem and Sodom (Rev. 11:8; Ezek. 16)
12. The Cup of Wrath (Rev. 14; Ezek. 23)
13. The Vine of the Land (Rev. 14:18–20; Ezek. 15)
14. The Great Harlot (Rev. 17–18; Ezek. 16, 23)
15. The Lament over the City (Rev. 18; Ezek. 27)
16. The Scavengers' Feast (Rev. 19; Ezek. 39)
17. The First Resurrection (Rev. 20:4–6; Ezek. 37)
18. The Battle with Gog and Magog (Rev. 20:7–9; Ezek. 38–39)
19. The New Jerusalem (Rev. 21; Ezek. 40–48)
20. The River of Life (Rev. 22; Ezek. 47)

The reality of this parallel is confirmed by the historical fact that the destruction of Jerusalem in 586 BC and the destruction of the temple in AD 70 happened on the same day in the Jewish calendar—the ninth day of Av."[50]

OLD TESTAMENT PROPHECIES AND THE LOVE OF JESUS

"And the rest were killed with the sword which came from the mouth of Him who sat on the horse, and all the birds were filled with their flesh."
Revelation 19:21 (NASB)

Now we can connect John's prophetic office to God's love story. It is imperative that we learn to reconcile both the character of God, as revealed through Jesus, and John's role as a prophet at the end of the Mosaic age to a Jewish audience. If we don't, then verses like the one just quoted above will immediately overshadow the whole notion of the goodness of God being revealed through the enfleshment of Jesus.

To most of us (like myself), who were raised in the traditional ways of Christianity passed down through Western Civilization, ignorant of the intricacies of Jewish Law, the tone of Apocalyptic Literature (such as the Dead Sea Scrolls), and the blatant fact that John wrote to a Jewish audience, helps us understand how one could easily miss the reference to Ezekiel 39 in the Scripture quoted above (Revelation 19:21).

---

[50] Welton, Jonathan. *The Art of Revelation*, Welton Academy: 2017, e-book.

Now, where I am *not* going with this line of reasoning is to the land of Universalism. Nor will I water down hard passages or difficult points in history. The Romans invaded Judea and destroyed Jerusalem and the Temple in 70 AD as a fulfillment of the prophecies of Old.[51] Jesus said it would happen in Matthew 23 and 24 (and much more plainly in Luke 19 and 21). To grasp the full truth, we must walk a tightrope, with God's love pulling on one end, and Old Testament prophecies (with all their hyperbole and symbolism) pulling the other.

In our modern age, we face a tug-of-war between 21st century Western culture and values—which preaches love is a "feel good" thing—and ancient Semitic culture and values. The Biblical truth is, just because something doesn't "feel good" (like Jesus whipping merchants out of the Temple courts) doesn't mean it isn't rooted in love. I will go so far as to say that as a society, 21st century Westerners perhaps have the poorest definition and understanding of what love is.

Those who have been deceived into believing love is a "feel good" thing can easily put God on trial and charge Him with being "unloving." But they have based their idea about love on something outside of God. They haven't yet come to see that they are merely inheritors of a Biblically illiterate worldview. Jesus' words to the religious leaders in Matthew 23 ("you brood of vipers!") are jarring, but were still rooted in love. In summary, how things or people make us "feel" often have little to do with authentic, self-sacrificial love.

> *"Greater love has no one than this, that a person will lay down his life for his friends." (John 15:13)*

The cross didn't feel good. It was bloody. It was violent. It was love.

> *"You have forgotten the exhortation which is addressed to you as sons,*
>
> *"My son, do not regard lightly the discipline of the Lord,*
> *Nor faint when you are punished by Him;*
> *For whom the Lord loves He disciplines,*
> *And He punishes every son whom He accepts."*

---

[51] Including, but certainly not limited to, Deuteronomy 28:15–68, 29:22–30:10, 31:14–22, and 32:1–43.

It is for discipline that you endure; God deals with you as with sons; for what son is there whom his father does not discipline?

... For the moment, all discipline seems not to be pleasant, but painful; yet to those who have been trained by it, afterward it yields the peaceful fruit of righteousness." (Hebrews 12:5–7, 11)

My point is this: As we work our way through Revelation and encounter difficult passages (wrath, woes, etc.) we must resist:

1. The urge to fall back into old inherited mindsets that have led many to believe that things will get worse, and God is going to dish out major wrath on us.
2. The urge to put God on trial when we come across difficult passages, accusing Him of not being loving because what we read goes against what we think love should be.
3. The urge to dismiss those difficult passages altogether because we don't think they fit within the parameters of what we believe a "loving God" must operate within.

"The thing molded will not say to the molder, 'Why did you make me like this,' will it? Or does the potter not have a right over the clay?" (Rom. 12:20–21)

POSTSCRIPT: THE 1 CORINTHIANS 15 FRAMEWORK

Initially, I wasn't sure where to place the scripture below. I only knew it should appear early on, and not in a place where it could be easily skipped (like the introduction, which I hope you will read). So here it is:

"Then comes the end, when He hands over the kingdom to our God and Father, when He has abolished all rule and all authority and power. For He must reign until He has put all His enemies under His feet. The last enemy that will be abolished is death."
1 Corinthians 15:24 – 26 (NASB)

If you gain nothing else from your eschatological endeavours other than this one scriptural point, you are still coming out miles ahead. My point is this: if you want simple, sound, undisputed eschatology (the part of theology concerned with death, judgment, and the final destiny of humankind), you need not look further than Paul's summation in 1 Corinthians 15. It is literal and to the point. In fact, I highly recommend reading 1 Corinthians 15 entirely and slowly. You can hang your hat on what Paul says about "end times," and walk away feeling hopeful and optimistic.

To close this chapter, here are some highlights from Paul's discourse in 1 Corinthians:

"But the fact is, Christ has been raised from the dead, the first fruits of those who are asleep. For since by a man death came, by a man also came the resurrection of the dead. For as in Adam all die, so also in Christ all will be made alive.

But each in his own order: Christ the first fruits, after that those who are Christ's at His coming, then comes the end, when He hands over the kingdom to our God and Father, when He has abolished all rule and all authority and power. For He must reign until He has put all His enemies under His feet. The last enemy that will be abolished is death...

But someone will say, "How are the dead raised? And with what kind of body do they come?" You fool! That which you sow does not come to life unless it dies; and that which you sow, you do not sow the body which is to be, but a bare grain, perhaps of wheat or of something else...

Just as we have borne the image of the earthy [Adam], we will also bear the image of the heavenly [Jesus]...

Behold, I am telling you a mystery; we will not all sleep, but we will all be changed, in a moment, in the twinkling of an eye, at the last trumpet; for the trumpet will sound, and the dead will be raised imperishable, and we will be changed...

then will come about the saying that is written: "Death has been swallowed up in victory. Where, O Death, is your victory? Where, O Death, is your sting?" The sting of death is sin, and the power of sin is the Law; but thanks be to God, who gives us the victory through our Lord Jesus Christ."
1 Corinthian 15 (NASB)

3 THE VEIL IS TORN: REVELATION CHAPTER 1

"Whenever someone turns to the Lord, the veil is taken away."

— 2 Corinthians 3:16

John's Revelation; the Hisgalus (Hebrew), the Apocalypse (Greek), both mean the same thing in their respective native language: "to unveil." However, the true impact of these opening words of John's letter to his congregations in Asia Minor (modern day Turkey) and his brethren in Jerusalem was not to reveal mysteries and secrets (not to say he didn't), but rather to proclaim what was accomplished on the Cross at Calvary and that the end of the transition of covenant eras had come. Having written "The revelation [unveiling] of Jesus the Messiah," indicates Jesus was being revealed as the One who was about to take away the veil of the Old Covenant.

"For [Jesus] is our peace who made the two one, and he destroyed the wall that was standing in the middle. And he has canceled the hatred by his flesh and the law of commands in his commandments, that for the two, he would create in his Person one new man, and he has made peace."

Ephesians 2:14–16 (Aramaic) [52]

To wit, in book 1 of this trilogy, I spoke at length concerning the transition of epoch seasons, from Moses to Messiah. More specifically, I spoke to how God used 40-year periods repeatedly in Israel's history to mark transition. Thus, from the Cross to the Fall of Jerusalem there is a 40-year period in which the Mosaic Era ends, and the Messianic Era comes into full light.

What does this epoch transition have to do with unveiling? For the answer, let us turn to Matthew 27:51, and witness how Paul uses the notion of 'the veil' when speaking of the Mosaic Covenant:

> *"Therefore, having such a hope, we use great boldness in* our *speech, and* we are *not like Moses,* who *used to put a veil over his face so that the sons of Israel would not stare at the end of what was fading away. But their minds were hardened; for until this very day at the reading of the old covenant the same veil remains unlifted, because it is removed in Christ. But to this day whenever Moses is read, a veil lies over their hearts; but whenever* someone *turns to the Lord, the veil is taken away. Now the Lord is the Spirit, and where the Spirit of the Lord is,* there *is freedom." 2 Cor 3:12-17 (NASB)*

The Messiah removes the veil. In this passage, Paul uses a double meaning for veil. First, he states the Old Covenant blinds like a veil, then he states the Old Covenant *is* a veil, one that only Jesus the Messiah can remove from the people of Israel.

Now, this point is key: only to those circumcised under the Law of Moses is there a veil, meaning if you're a gentile like me, this doesn't apply to you! But to the Jews and proselytes of John's day, the veil remained so long as the Temple system and the sacrificial offerings were still in operation.

Subsequently, John, as the trumpet blower sounding the alarm to alert the people that the destruction of Jerusalem, the Temple, and the sacrificial system, was about to take place, opens his letter by saying, "The revelation [unveiling] of Jesus the Messiah." By this he means Jesus was unveiled as the One who was about to remove the veil of the Old Covenant!

---

[52] Bauscher, David. *The Holy Peshitta Bible Translated*, Lulu.com, Kindle Edition. p. 2367.

LET THE COMMENTARY COMMENCE

א *(v 1 – 3) "The unveiling[53] of Yeshua the Messiah, which God gave unto Him, to symbolize[54] it to His royal subjects, what has been permitted to occur in haste;*

and He knew when to send it in the hand of his angel to His royal subject John, who bore witness to the word of God and to the testimony of Jesus the Messiah — everything that he saw.

Blessedness to the one who reads aloud and to the one who hears the words of this prophecy, and attentively watches for the things which are written in it; for the epoch season is at hand." (Aramaic Text)

The destruction of Israel, Jerusalem, and the Temple will take place very quickly ("hastily"). Verse 2 reads as if it was meant for public oration: "Blessed is he (singular) who reads, and those (plural) who hear." Lastly, we read that the "specific time" (zbn in Aramaic), meaning an "instance" or "season" was immediately upon them.

א *(v 4 – 5) "John, to the seven messianic communities[55] in the province of Asia:*

Grace unto you, and shalom, from the One who is, who was, and who is coming, and from the sevenfold Spirit before his throne, and from

---

[53] "The root word here 'reveal,' 'wave,' is stated in the plural form. And then the suffix in Aramaic can mean 'our', or alternatively, in Aramaic (& Hebrew) it is used to express intense emotion (the likely reading here), with a prime example being 'Hosanna' from Matthew 21:15, or 'mighty' from Revelation 5:2. However, on the Crawford Codex there are no Seyame markings over this word to indicate the scribe read it as a plural noun. Even still, the grammar in the verse (see comments below) strongly indicate the reading is plural." Glaser Translation Notes, pp. 1.

[54] "'He symbolized' – *Shooda* in Aramaic is an important key for unlocking the meaning of Revelation. Symbolic language and imagery is used throughout to represent eternal realities and future events, very similar to the prophesies of Daniel and Ezekiel and the visions Joseph had interpreted in Genesis." Baucher, David. The Aramaic Interlinear Peshitta Holy Bible, pp. 182.

[55] 'Idoto', is one word, literally meaning "an assembly of witnesses." In Greek, ecclesia, what we call "church" today. I have chosen to add context to the translation: these were assemblies or communities of believers who bore witness, or testified, to the fact that Jesus was the Messiah. They were communities *of* the Messiah, hence, messianic communities.

Yeshua the Messiah;

the faithful witness, the firstborn from the dead, preeminent over the rulers of the earth. Him who burns with love for us, and unfettered us from our sins through His blood." (Aramaic)

The early church was founded and mostly comprised of Messianic Jews; Jewish people who had embraced Jesus as their Messiah. John's letter was clearly written to a Jewish audience, as I will point out often.

THE JEWISHNESS OF THE EARLY CHURCH

While the Bible is timeless, it was written over a period of several hundred years by different people in different circumstances. Revelation is no different. Western culture has become obsessed with taking this book and repackaging it to fit Western culture and theology. To separate John's Apocalypse from its Jewish roots is to take the Epistle to the Hebrews and say it was written for Gentiles. Therefore, my effort here is to restore Revelation to its proper context in order to set a proper foundation from which we can launch our exegesis.

"You worship what you do not know; we worship what we know, for salvation is from the Jews." John 4:22 (NASB)

It is important that I preface this section by clarifying my intention. There is no subversive plot to lead the reader to conclude any sort of dualism or tiered status between Jew and Gentile. Nor is it my intention to lead the reader to conclude they must adhere to the Law of Moses and embrace a legalistic lifestyle. Far from it. Rather, my approach here is a historical one to provide an accurate social-historical awareness of the text. My hope is that it will be edifying and lead to greater understanding.

Let us now move into the topic at hand with this truth:

> The Jewish Christians instinctively regarded their new faith as but a further expression of their national religion; the Temple continued to be the central shrine at which they worshipped and many of their members became distinguished for their zealous observance of the Law. To such men the tradition of Israel's unique status with God was a matter of fervent belief, and we have seen something of the grudging and qualified consent which they gave to the admittance of certain favoured

Gentiles to participation in the privileges of their new faith."[56]

As noted, it wasn't until after Jesus ascended that His own followers finally got the memo: God's Grand Love Story, the Eternal Gospel, was not exclusively for the descendants of Abraham (see Acts 10:9-16). But how could this be? Perhaps because they failed to pivot from the initial mission:

> *"These twelve Jesus sent out after instructing them: "Do not go in the way of the Gentiles, and do not enter any city of the Samaritans; but rather go to the lost sheep of the house of Israel." Matthew 10:5–6 (NASB)*

But we do see a gradual shift from Israel-only to Judea, Samaria, and the ends of the earth—albeit long after the Great Commission and Ascension (Matthew 28:18–20 in light of Acts 10:9-16). Nevertheless, the first followers of Yeshua were predominately Jewish. In fact, although Paul was the "Apostle to the Gentiles," preaching abroad in the Roman Empire, his primary strategy was to go into cities and towns that had a Jewish presence, and preach first in their local Synagogues.[57]

Below are some Scriptures that remind us of the fact that the early church was not a Gentile majority led by a handful of Jewish Apostles. It was in fact a Jewish majority led by Jewish Apostles. While it seems this phenomenon did not last past the fall of Jerusalem in 70 AD, it is still an important factor that anchors our interpretation.

> *"...Those who were scattered because of the persecution that occurred in connection with Stephen made their way to Phoenicia and Cyprus and Antioch, speaking the word to no one except to Jews alone. But there were some of them, men of Cyprus and Cyrene, who came to Antioch and began speaking to the Greeks also... [And] news about them reached the ears of the church at Jerusalem." Acts 11:19–22 (NASB)*

> *"After we [Paul and Luke] arrived in Jerusalem, the brethren received us gladly... And when they heard it they began glorifying God; and they said to him, "You see, brother, how many thousands there are among the Jews of those who have believed, and they are all zealous for the Law; and they have been told about you, that you are teaching all the Jews **who are***

---

[56] S. G. F. Brandon, M.A., D.D., *The Fall of Jerusalem and the Christian Church, A Study of the Effects of the Jewish Overthrow of A.D. 70 on Christianity* (London: S.P.C.K, 1951) p. 71.
[57] See, Viola, Frank. *The Untold Story of the New Testament Church: An Extraordinary Guide to Understanding the New Testament* (Destiny Image, Kindle Edition), p. 74.

among the Gentiles…" Acts 21:17, 20, 21 (NASB)

"Therefore, remember that previously you, the Gentiles… were at that time separate from Christ, excluded from the people of Israel, and strangers to the covenants of the promise, having no hope and without God in the world. But now in Christ Jesus you who previously were far away have been brought near by the blood of Christ…

"For this reason I, Paul, [am] the prisoner of Christ Jesus for the sake of you Gentiles… by revelation there was made known to me the mystery, as I wrote before briefly… which in other generations was not made known to mankind, as it has now been revealed to His holy apostles and prophets in the Spirit; to be specific, that the Gentiles are fellow heirs and fellow members of the body, and fellow partakers of the promise in Christ Jesus through the gospel." Ephesians 2:11–13, 3:1, 3, 5–6 (NASB)

"Now if [the Jewish] transgression is riches for the world and their failure is riches for the Gentiles, how much more will their fulfillment be! But I am speaking to you who are Gentiles…

"But if some of the branches were broken off, and you, being a wild olive, were grafted in among them and became partaker with them of the rich root of the olive tree, do not be arrogant toward the branches; but if you are arrogant, remember that it is not you who supports the root, but the root supports you. You will say then, "Branches were broken off so that I might be grafted in." Quite right, they were broken off for their unbelief, but you stand by your faith. Do not be conceited, but fear; for if God did not spare the natural branches, He will not spare you, either…

"For I do not want you, brethren, to be uninformed of this mystery—so that you will not be wise in your own estimation—that a partial hardening has happened to Israel until the fullness of the Gentiles has come in; and so all Israel will be saved…"
Romans 11:12, 13, 17–21, 25–26 (NASB)

Despite all that we have just read, it was still to my surprise that I discovered that Revelation was written to a Jewish audience concerning life-altering Jewish issues: the end of the Mosaic Age, the destruction of the Holy Temple, the end of the sacrificial system, and the heart-breaking demise of the Temple priesthood. All of these things took place historically in 70 AD. Revelation seeks, therefore, to help the Jews make sense of *why* these things happened from a theological perspective.[58] I did not think this way when I set out to write this book. But the analysis of the Aramaic text itself presented these findings. I would liken my experience to the romanticized notions many of us have of archeological adventure and discovery seen in the *Indiana Jones* movies!

    א *(v 6) "And He has made us the priestly kingdom to His God and Father—to Him be glory and dominion to the age of ages. Amen."*

The priestly kingdom echoes the Torah: "'and you shall be to Me a kingdom of priests and a holy nation.' These are the words that you shall speak to the sons of Israel" (Exodus 19:6). Peter also reminds us of this truth: "But you are a chosen race, a royal priesthood, a holy nation, a people for God's own possession, so that you may proclaim the excellencies of Him who has called you out of darkness into His marvelous light" (1 Peter 2:9).

    א *(v 7) "Behold! He comes with clouds, and every eye will see Him, but especially those who pierced Him, and all the generations of the Land will mourn over Him. Yes and amen."*

Jesus spoke words similar to these in John's presence approximately 37 years earlier, saying:

"Upon you will fall the guilt of all the righteous blood shed on earth… Truly I say to you, all these things will come upon this generation.

Jerusalem, Jerusalem, who kills the prophets and stones those who are sent to her! How often I wanted to gather your children together, the way a hen gathers her chicks under her wings, and you were unwilling. Behold, your house is being left to you desolate! For I say to you, from now on you will not see Me until you say, 'Blessed is He who comes in the name of the Lord!'" Matt 23:37–39 (NASB)

Revelation 1:7 is charged with prophetic language, echoing Daniel 7:13 and Zechariah 12:10–14. Both prophets, and specifically the chapters quoted, spoke to the transition of epoch seasons that took place during the 40-year period from 30 to 70 AD. Now, Jesus comes to John to say that the transition period was about to reach its climactic ending.

The coming of the Lord Jesus to bring about an end to the Mosaic Age

---

[58] This theme is discussed at length in my book, *Revelation: Dawn of This Age.*

in 70 AD is the only context in which the final interaction between Jesus and his disciples in John 21 makes sense.

"Peter turned around and saw the disciple whom Jesus loved following them—the one who also had leaned back on His chest at the supper and said, 'Lord, who is the one who is betraying You?' So, Peter, upon seeing him, said to Jesus, 'Lord, and what about this man?' Jesus said to him, "'If I want him to remain until I come, what is that to you? You follow Me!' Therefore, this account went out among the brothers, that that disciple [John] would not die; yet Jesus did not say to him that he would not die, but only, 'If I want him to remain until I come, what is that to you?'
John 21:20–23 (NASB)

John was literally the only one who remained until Jesus came. By the time the Mosaic Age came to an end via the destruction of the Temple, all the other disciples had been killed, save for John. And to be clear, Jesus didn't cause the destruction; He brought about the time for contractual obligations of the Law to be requisite. **Jesus' return signaled the day of fulfilment of Moses' prophecies in Deuteronomy 28:15–68, 29:22–30:10, 31:14–22, and 32:1–43.**[59]

This was after a 40 year period of grace, where through the disciples of Jesus, God pleaded with Israel to turn from their sins (from 30 to 70 AD), just as He did in the days of Moses. During those 40 years, an entire generation died in the wilderness, and a new generation crossed over the River Jordan under Joshua (Yehoshua, a type of Yeshua, Jesus).

Now in Revelation 1:7 (above) where it reads, "all the tribes of the Land," most translations will instead have, "all the tribes of the earth." But this is misleading. One major error with most translations is the rendering of the word "land" as "earth." The Complete Jewish Bible accurately translates verse 7: "all the tribes of the Land will mourn him." From a literary perspective, both the Greek and Aramaic here agreed that "land" is the proper word choice, not "earth" or "planet." Most of the events in Revelation were an isolated incident.

Here is another example:

*"Listen to the word of the Lord, you sons of **Israel**,*
*Because the Lord has a case against the inhabitants of **the land**,*

---

[59] Please take time to read through them, as they will greatly increase one's understanding of why the fall of Jerusalem in 70 AD took place.

For there is no faithfulness, nor loyalty,
*Nor knowledge of God **in the land**...*
*Therefore **the land** mourns,*
And everyone who lives in it languishes." Hosea 4:1–3 (NASB)

I've already made a case for "The Land" meaning "The Land of Israel" in book 1 of this series, so I will only add a brief refresher here. Whenever you read, "The Land," to the Jewish reader (then and even today—see the modern Israeli newspaper, *Haaretz,* literally, "The Land"!) it was a given that it was in reference to the Land of Israel.

From an inter-textual perspective, Revelation 1:7 also alludes to Zechariah 12–14. That text had to do with the Holy Land exclusively, since it focused on Jerusalem. Now, those chapters of Zechariah may be hard to interpret. But I believe one interpretation is that they span the entirety of the Messianic Age we are currently in. Several times between chapters 12 and 14 there are references to the destruction of Jerusalem and the transition period from the Mosaic to Messianic Era. At other points in chapters 12 to 14 of Zechariah, God reveals what He will do at the end of the Messianic Era, which coincides with what John saw in Revelation 20:8–10.

ALPHA AND OMEGA – א ALEPH AND ת TAV

א *(v 8) "I am the Aleph and the Tav," says Yahweh[60] Elohim, "who is and who was and who is coming, the Almighty."*

It is interesting to note that the earliest manuscripts lack "the Beginning and the End" here. It is possibly an addition from later copies for the purpose of fluidity, since Revelation 22:13 states, "the Beginning and the End" in early manuscripts. So, sticking with the Aramaic, verse 8 reads, "I am the Aleph and the Tav," which in Greek translates to Alpha and Omega.

Now, John's native tongue was Aramaic. This was the language he spoke growing up and the language he would have conversed with Jesus during the Messiah's earthly ministry. Therefore, I will venture to suggest that John would have heard words of his encounter with Jesus and the angels in Aramaic as well (either audibly or in his heart). If you are bilingual like me, you know that you will often think in your native tongue. Whatever languages

---

[60] Yahweh is not found in the Greek texts. The Aramaic, 'Marya,' is 'Yahweh' in Hebrew (See The Comprehensive Aramaic Lexicon, G2962). This word is used several times in the Aramaic New Testament, often in reference to Jesus!

you learn after your native tongue, you are still likely to think and have self-talk in your native tongue, depending on how much you use it. So even if John's Revelation was later translated for a Greek speaking audience, I propose that he received and interpreted the information in his native tongue.

Why does this matter? Because the richness of the Gospel is revealed on a whole new level through the lens of ancient Aramaic/Hebrew! The words Alpha and Omega are Greek. But if John were to have heard them in Aramaic/Hebrew, Jesus would have said, "I am the Aleph and the Tav." And that reality makes things interesting, as I will illustrate.

The Hebrew letter pictography for א Aleph is representative of God Himself. The roots of this are based on the image of an ox, representing power, strength, and authority. The letters that make up the word Aleph enhance the imagery. The ל represents both a shepherd's staff and a sceptre of authority. Combined with the א (ox), it was seen as a yoke of an ox. This is where we find deeper meaning of Jesus' words in Matthew 11:29-30,

> *"Take My yoke upon you and learn from Me, for I am gentle and lowly in heart, and you will find rest for your souls. For My yoke is easy and My burden is light."*

It was customary for the elder oxen to be yoked to a younger one so the apprenticing bull would learn from the experienced one. I find this to be mind-blowing in the context of being yoked with Christ.

The last letter, ף, is often omitted from pictography since Aleph is based on the root אל. Nevertheless, ף is part of the final word. In my opinion this is significant. Pey (ף) represents the mouth and the power of the spoken word. This is why John wrote a few verses later that he saw proceeding from the mouth of Jesus, "a sharp two-edged sword," (Revelation 1:16).

So, Jesus is the Alpha, or the Aleph in Hebrew, which still means that He is the beginning in the sense that He is the Creator and the I AM. But in addition to this, etymologically He is the God of all authority, the shepherd who has yoked Himself to us in order to guide and teach with the word of his mouth so His will is accomplished. How amazing is that!

We also know that He is the Omega, which in Hebrew is ת Tav. Tav in ancient Hebrew has a multi-layered meaning. First, its most basic meaning is that of a sign or mark (see Ezekiel 9:4 and Job 31:35 in a translation that supports earlier manuscripts). The significance to be derived from Ezekiel is that the mark represented Passover, or salvation. A mark was placed over the door posts of the Hebrews that told the angel to "pass over" their house.

And the meaning we derive in Job for the word Tav is that it is a binding agreement of a legal document, such as a covenant. Furthermore, the inscription of the letter itself in early Hebrew was simply an upright cross, our modern day "*t*." It is quite likely that the mark Ezekiel was instructed to place upon foreheads in chapter 9 of his book was in fact the sign of the cross!

So, Jesus is also the Omega, or the Tav, which means he is the One who brings to completion, as in the author and finisher of our faith (Hebrew 12:2). Additionally, He is the One who signed with his seal our New Covenant of salvation, a binding marriage agreement. And this legal document was inscribed with the mark of the cross upon which he was crucified. One could summarize as follows: As the Aleph and the Tav, Jesus is the supreme and eternal ruling shepherd and the God who forged an eternal covenant, which He signed with His seal. That is worth a selah!

One final note on Aleph, which will plant a seed for later discussion when we visit chapter 20 of Revelation. In addition to Aleph being the first letter of the Hebrew alphabet, the consonants of the word also denote the number 1000, "Eleph" (see Strong's: #0441 and #0505). When we dive into chapter 20, we will unpack this further and discover the significance of the 1000 years reign of Christ.

א   *(v 9) "I, John, your brother and forthwith your companion in the affliction and in the perseverance which are in Jesus, was on the island called Patmos because of the testimony of Yeshua the Messiah."*

The word most translations substitute for "affliction" here is "tribulation," and this word is the source of much debate and confusion in our present Western culture. But it merely means calamity or affliction. The same word is found in 1 Thessalonians 1:6 and James 5:13. The "pre-trib" vs "post-trib" jargon that has prevailed in the 20th century is completely foreign to the text and proper eschatology in general. **The questions every reader must ask are: what was afflicting the first-century Jewish church and what were they persevering towards?**

> "There is now the reference to persecution in the First Thessalonian Epistle to be considered. In this Paul draws a parallel between the sufferings of his converts at the hands of their compatriots and those of the members of the Judaean churches at the hands of the Jews. This statement and its

immediate sequel, in which, after making some condemnatory observations about the persecuting activity of the Jews, he includes himself, or his party, among the objects of this persecution, would clearly constitute evidence for believing that the Jewish Christians in Palestine notably suffered for their faith at the hands of their countrymen."[61]

John was on the receiving end of the same affliction as his flock. And John and his Jewish brethren were patiently waiting for something to take place in *their* lifetime. This affliction was the same thorn Paul spoke of that was in his flesh: persecution from the "Judaizers." Those who sought to undermine the apostolic work taking place in the Holy Land and the Empire.

Consider the following Scriptures:

- *"Do not go in the way of the Gentiles, and do not enter any city of the Samaritans; but rather go to the lost sheep of the house of Israel...*

  Behold, I [Jesus] send you out as sheep in the midst of wolves; so be shrewd as serpents and innocent as doves. But beware of men, for they will hand you over to the courts and scourge you in their synagogues; and you will even be brought before governors and kings for My sake, as a testimony to them and to the Gentiles...

  "Brother will betray brother to death, and a father his child; and children will rise up against parents and cause them to be put to death. You will be hated by all because of My name, but it is the one who has endured to the end who will be saved.

  "But whenever they persecute you in one city, flee to the next; for truly I say to you, you will not finish going through the cities of Israel until the Son of Man comes."
  Matt 10:5–6, 16–18, 21–23 (NASB)

- *"For nation will rise against nation, and kingdom against kingdom, and in various places there will be famines and*

[61] S. G. F. Brandon, M.A., D.D., *The Fall of Jerusalem and the Christian Church, A Study of the Effects of the Jewish Overthrow of A.D. 70 on Christianity* (London: S.P.C.K, 1951) at 92.

earthquakes. But all these things are merely the beginning of birth pangs.

"Then they will deliver you to tribulation, and will kill you, and you will be hated by all nations because of My name…

But the one who endures to the end, he will be saved. This gospel of the kingdom shall be preached in the whole [known] world as a testimony to all the nations, and then the end will come.

"Therefore when you see the abomination of desolation which was spoken of through Daniel the prophet, standing in the holy place (let the reader understand), then those who are in Judea must flee to the mountains." Matt 24:7–9, 13–16 (NASB)

- *"A great persecution began against the church in Jerusalem, and they were all scattered throughout the regions of Judea and Samaria, except the apostles." Acts 8:1 (NASB)*

Twice in Matthew, Jesus connects the preaching of the Gospel to the Jews in Judea and the Jews spread abroad (the Diaspora, the "Ten Lost Tribes") to the end of the Mosaic Age, culminating in the destruction of the Temple (hence, "flee to the mountains" to escape the Roman invasion in 70 AD). The Messianic followers of Jesus were patiently enduring the hardship He had warned them about. If they could persevere until the end of this transition period, they would be delivered.

As for John being on Patmos, toward the end of book 1 I wrote of this at length. In short, we don't know for sure why he was there. It could have been banishment, but that doesn't imply imprisonment. Or it may be that he was preaching the Gospel there and trying to establish a new community of believers.

א *(v 10 – 11) "And I was in the Spirit on the first day of the week, and I heard from behind (me) a great voice, like a shofar, Who said, 'That which you are seeing, write in a book and send to the seven messianic communities: To Ephesus, and to Smyrna, and to Pergamum, and to Thyatira, and to Sardis, and to Philadelphia, and to Laodicea.'"*

Why does Jesus pick these churches out of all the ones He could have chosen from? Perhaps we will never know fully, but here are some of my thoughts as to the intentionality of Jesus in addressing these communities of Jewish followers:

1. John's flock: As I already stated, John was the last prophet of the Mosaic Age. The message came to him first. It would make sense then that his congregations would become co-labourers in the spreading of this message throughout Judea and the Diaspora.

2. No apostles: If John did in fact receive this visitation from the Lord circa 66–67 AD, then there may have been few (if any) surviving Apostles (the original 11), as many of the others had been martyred. John was perhaps the only remaining original disciple with a large network of followers. Others were too remote, like Thomas for example, who was likely in India at the time. In fact, it was the Jews from this region who were ultimately responsible for Paul's Roman imprisonment (see Acts 21:27).

   > "Tradition holds that 11 of the Twelve Apostles were martyred. Peter, Andrew, and Philip were crucified; James the Greater and Thaddaeus fell to the sword; James the Lesser was beaten to death while praying for his attackers; Bartholomew was flayed alive and then crucified; Thomas and Matthew were speared; Matthias was stoned to death; and Simon was either crucified or sawed in half. John—the last survivor of the Twelve—likely died peaceably, possibly in Ephesus…"[62]

3. Location: Anatolia (Western Asia Minor) was the gateway between the West (Rome) and the East (Israel). John and his followers were strategically located along a major trade route that began at the Hellespont (known today as the Dardanelles) and traversed longitudinally all the way through Antioch of Syria and beyond. Roman Jews on pilgrimage to Jerusalem for one of the feasts would have had to pass through the seven cities of Revelation. Another person who rode through this trade road was Vespasian enroute from Greece to Israel after Nero dispatched him to destroy the Holy Land.

---

[62] Andrew Todhunter, *In the Footsteps of the Apostles,* National Geographic Magazine, March 2012 Issue.

"The Jews also obtained honours from the Kings of Asia, when they became their auxiliaries. For Seleucus Nicator made them citizens in those cities which he built in Asia... and gave them privileges equal to those of the Macedonians and Greeks...

We also know, that Marcus Agrippa was of the like disposition towards the Jews. For when the people of Ionia were very angry at them, and besought Agrippa that they, and only they might have those privileges of citizens, which Antiochus, the grandson of Seleucus, who by the Greeks was called the God, had bestowed on them; and desired that if the Jews were to be joint-partakers with them, they might be obliged to worship the gods they themselves worshipped: but when these matters were brought to the trial, the Jews prevailed, and obtained leave to make use of their own customs."[63]

4. Spiritual Location: Anatolia was once the kingdom of Gyges of Lydia, with Sardis as its capital. Gyges of Lydia is the Greek name for the same man who in Assyria was known as Gugu Ma-Gugu, which in Hebrew is rendered Gog of Ma-Gog. The historical king who became synonymous with Jewish lore of long-standing antagonists of God's people was used by Ezekiel and John to illustrated God's sovereign plan to stay the opponents of His people once and for all (much more on this subject in book three).

5. **The New Epicenter: Lastly and most importantly, the location of the central-hub of the Jesus movement would experience a radical shift in the first century AD.** The Jerusalem Church was the undisputed headquarters of the Messianic Jews, with James, Peter and John as the resident leaders (Acts 15; Gal 2). After the fall of Jerusalem in 70 AD, Asia Minor grew in influence for 1000 years until the Great East-West Schism of 1054 AD.

    The Roman Empire was not the first to adopt Christianity. It was the nations of Armenia in 301 and Georgia in 327, both situated in Asia Minor. The First Christian Council outside Jerusalem was held in Nicaea (of the Nicaean Creed fame), which is in Asia Minor, in 325

---

[63] Josephus, *Antiquities of the Jews,* By William Whiston, M.A. (London: University of Cambridge, 1737) p. 3:1–2.

AD. Another Council was held in Constantinople in 381 (Asia Minor), followed by subsequent Councils in Ephesus in 431 (Asia Minor), and Chalcedon in 451 (Asia Minor).

> "The Church at Caesarea after A.D. 70 would probably have been the chief centre of Christianity in Palestine, being composed mainly of Gentiles, who would certainly have constituted the more influential party after the Jewish national disaster. As such the Caesarean Church is likely to have inherited certain traditions of the original Jerusalem Church and a considerable respect for its memory."[64]

Caesarea and Antioch were well known centres for followers of Jesus. But it was the churches of Ephesus and Smyrna that grew in renown[65] and thus tilted the centrality of our Faith from the Levant to Asia Minor after Jerusalem was destroyed. **Perhaps this is why John, the last surviving leader of the Jerusalem church, was sent to Asia Minor to tend to the work Paul began there.**[66]

> "[After] A.D. 70 the Church of Jerusalem disappears completely from the life and concern of the Church… In the period before we see the Church strongly centralized around the mother community of Jerusalem, whose authority and prestige are unchallenged, even by the daring Paul. From this period, which is so well illumined by the writings of Paul and the narrative of Acts, we pass on in our survey to find the life of the Church [in Jerusalem] disappearing into obscurity..."[67]

---

[64] S. G. F. Brandon, M.A., D.D., *The Fall of Jerusalem and the Christian Church, A Study of the Effects of the Jewish Overthrow of A.D. 70 on Christianity* (London: S.P.C.K, 1951) p. 43.

[65] See Ignatius' letters to the Ephesians and the Smyrnaeans.

[66] The soil upon which Jerusalem stood did not remain void. History tells us that a Roman city named Aelia Capitolina was built on top of Jerusalem's ruins. It had a church community in it, and early church father, Hegesippus, was a part of it.

[67] S. G. F. Brandon, M.A., D.D., *The Fall of Jerusalem and the Christian Church, A Study of the Effects of the Jewish Overthrow of A.D. 70 on Christianity* (London: S.P.C.K, 1951) p. 183.

THE PRIESTLY DESCRIPTION OF JESUS

It is one thing to read Hebrews 8 and to know theologically that Jesus is our High Priest. But it is a whole different level to know it experientially! John *saw* Jesus adorned as the High Priest in a mesmerizing encounter with his beloved friend and Messiah.

א *(v 12 – 17) "And I turned to intimately know that voice who spoke with me, and when I turned around, I saw seven menorahs of gold;*

And in the midst of the menorahs as the likeness of a man, and he wore an ephod and he was girded around his chest with a golden sash.

His head and his hair were white like wool and like snow, and his eyes were like flames of fire. And His feet were in the likeness of the brass of Lebanon[68] which is heated in a furnace, and his voice was like the voice of many waters.

And there exists in his right hand seven stars, and a sharp sword[69] proceeding from his mouth, and I saw Him[70] like the sun radiating in its intensity."

In Revelation chapters 1 to 3, there are five major references to the priestly garments of Aaron the Priest. This is important because it helps us understand the office of the High Priest was the most honored and esteemed with all the Jews. He was a big deal. He was the only one who was permitted by God to go into the Temple once a year and offer sacrifices for the atonement of Israel's sins. Jesus then became the ultimate, super-human, super-natural High Priest.

---

[68] "The Greek of Westcott & Hort's edition has 'Burnished brass' - neuter noun, dative case matched with 'Burning' - feminine noun, genitive case; this is a grammatical 'no, no' in Greek. Both case and gender should agree with these two words. The Greek seems also to be an invented word not occurring elsewhere in Greek literature. It appears a translator made a compound Greek word out of two Aramaic words 'Brass' and 'Lebanon,' which did not exist before and confused all the translators. Most translations of the Greek have 'Burnished brass' as the meaning." Bauscher, David, *The Aramaic English Interlinear Peshitta Bible*, Lulu.com, p. 2744.
[69] "Sword" can also be translated as "spear" or "lance." See Jennings', pp. 205.
[70] "From the Aramaic Crawford reading, "and I saw Him.""

"Now the main point in what has been said is this: we have such a high priest, who has taken His seat at the right hand of the throne of the Majesty in the heavens, a minister in the sanctuary and in the true tabernacle, which the Lord set up, not man...

But now He [Jesus] has obtained a more excellent ministry, to the extent that He is also the mediator of a better covenant, which has been enacted on better promises...

When He said, 'A new covenant,' He has made the first obsolete. But whatever is becoming obsolete and growing old is about to disappear."
Hebrews 8:1–2, 6 (NASB)

Jesus was seen in the heavenly tabernacle, and Moses made a copy of what already existed in heaven (Hebrews 8:5–6). He stood beside the Menorah, the golden lampstand (Exodus 25:31–40), and alluding to Aaron, the first High Priest, Jesus, was seen in a sacerdotal ephod, the priestly garment.

"Aaron shall enter the Holy Place with this: with a bull as a sin offering and a ram as a burnt offering. He shall put on the holy linen tunic, and the linen undergarments shall be next to his body, and he shall be wrapped about the waist with the linen sash and the linen turban wound around his forehead (these are holy garments)." Leviticus 16:3–4 (NASB)

And in Exodus we read,

"And you shall make holy garments for Aaron your brother, for glory and for beauty... make Aaron's garments to consecrate him, that he may serve as priest to Me. And these are the garments which they shall make: a breastplate, an ephod, a robe, a tunic of checkered work, a turban, and a sash." Exodus 28:2–4 (NASB)

If Aaron's ephod was made for glory and beauty, how much more Jesus'! There are even more priestly garment descriptions in chapters 2 and 3 of Revelation. Now, the vision of Jesus as High Priest would have immediately resounded with a first century Jewish audience. And as Hebrews 8:6 points out, the Messianic Covenant made the Mosaic Covenant obsolete; now it was time for that covenant to disappear.

א *(v 17 – 18) "And when I saw him, I fell at his feet as one dead, and he laid his right hand upon me saying,*

'Fear not! I am the First and the Last; and am he who lives, but

became dead, and behold! I am alive unto the age of ages, amen.

And I have the key of Death and of Sheol.'"

In the Aramaic Jesus states that He has authority to bind and loose, open and shut (hence "keys"; see Matthew 16:17–19) Death and Sheol.[71] This statement has profound theological implications—especially since both Death and Sheol will be destroyed *prior* to heaven and earth being renewed. I explore this more in chapter 20 of Revelation in the third book of this series.

א *(v 19) "Write henceforth what you have seen, and things that are and prepared to come to pass after these."*

This breakdown is significant to helping us understand the chronology of John's visions. The Aramaic agrees with the above translation, where the connective "and" links three timeframes: past, present, and future. Here is a simple framework for Revelation's order of events by chapter:

- Past (what John beheld): 4, 5, 12
- Present (what is): 1–3, 6–11, 13–20a, 22
- Future (after these things): 20b, 21

The key thing to remember here is that these timestamps are relative to when John was receiving the vision (say 67 AD), not when you are reading his vision 2,000 years later!

א *(v 20) "The mystery of the seven stars which you saw upon my right hand and the seven menorahs: seven stars are the angels[72] of the seven messianic communities, and the seven menorahs of gold which you saw are the seven messianic communities."*

---

[71] Hades is a foreign concept to Jewish theology, and the word does not exist in the Old Testament or Aramaic New Testament. Greek translations replaced Sheol with Hades because Greek readers would have not had context for Sheol; hence a Greek proxy for a realm of the dead. Unfortunately, Hades was part of the Greek pantheon as the brother of Zeus and Poseidon. As you can see, it becomes problematic when you try to fit Hades into the Jewish narrative of Yahweh God.

[72] In almost every other instance this word is used in the NT, it is translated as "angel." There is no reason to deviate here by translating the word to "messenger." The Hebrew and Aramaic are the same: the word angel and messenger are one. Context determines translation. For instance, Matt 11:10, John the Baptist is a messenger (same word here).

Every time you read "lampstand" in Revelation, replace it in your mind with "menorah." The Aramaic specifically uses the word menorah.[73] This again illustrates Jesus was speaking primarily to a Jewish audience who would be receiving grave news concerning their homeland, their symbolic place of worship (Temple), and their kinsmen: the ~1,000,000 Jews slaughtered and 97,000 enslaved[74] by Vespasian and Titus in 70 AD. John's Revelation was as primary to the people of Israel as Paul's Corinthian letters were primary to the Gentiles in Corinth.

[73] Strong's G3087.
[74] According to Josephus, Jewish Wars, 6:9:3.

4 BEGIN WITH THE END – PART 1: CHAPTER 20a

"The Judge was seated and scrolls were opened I was seeing that this beast was killed and its body was destroyed, and it was given to the burning of fire. And the rest of the beasts were taken away from their authority, and length of life was given to them until a time and a season...
Because the kingdom and authority and the greatness and the kingdom under Heaven is given to the holy people of The Highest."

— *Daniel 7:10–12, 27, David Bauscher, The Holy Peshitta Bible Translated, p. 1683*

I know, you were expecting me to move from chapter one of Revelation to chapter two. And that was the plan. But I have received an overwhelming unction that I believe is from the Lord to follow chapter 1 and transition directly to chapter 20a. Many people ask *where* we citizens of this age fit into the book of Revelation. If we correctly conclude that much of Revelation was written to Messianic Jews in the first century AD, this question is an important one. Chapter 20a is the answer.

In book 3 we will discuss at length the climactic buildup to chapter 20b, which is preceded by a semi-crescendo in chapter 19 with the fall of Apostate Jerusalem (articulated by John in an Ezekiel- and Jeremiah-like fashion). The great tragedy is that Apostate Jerusalem turns out to be all the things she was supposed to be the antithesis of: Sodom, Egypt, and Babylon.[75] Revelation chapter 19 and the first 6 verses of chapter 20 took place when Solomon's Temple was destroyed in 70 AD.

DEUTERONOMY 28 FULFILLED

At the 'end of days,' the power of the "Law of sin and death" (Romans 8:2) was broken once for all. The Law was the "power of sin" (1 Corinthians 15:56), and the wrath that the Law brought (Romans 4:15) was the "ministry of death" poured out upon the old sacrificial system (2 Corinthians 3:7). It brought about a curse for all who were under it (Galatians 3:10), just as Moses prophesied in Deuteronomy chapters 28 to 32: "for all have sinned and fallen short of the glory of God" (Romans 3:23). Jesus Himself echoed Moses' prophetic words, saying, "upon you [religious leaders] will fall the guilt of all the righteous blood shed on earth, from the blood of righteous Abel to the blood of Zechariah... Truly I say to you, all these things will come upon this generation," (Matthew 23:35–36).

As I mentioned before, these things will be discussed in great detail in book 3. For now, suffice to say that the realities listed above are the anchor points for much of chapters 6 to 19 of Revelation. These points are illustrated in vivid Hebraic prophetic style, filled with hyperbole and shrouded in mysterious language.

With the Mosaic Age now concluded, it having eclipsed the Messianic Age for 40 years (which began when Jesus was resurrected, ~30 AD), the age of the Messiah we're all now in could shine all the brighter. As J.R.R. Tolkien so beautifully wrote at the coronation of Aragorn:

"Now come the days of the king! May they be blessed."[76]

---

[75] See Revelation 11:8; 1 Peter 5:13; Ezekiel 16; Jeremiah 3:8. And if you have time, check out "Who Is This Babylon?" by Don K. Preston.
[76] Tolkien, J.R.R., *The Lord of the Rings: The Return of the King.*

REGARDING SATAN

The last order of business to conclude the Mosaic Age was to deal with Satan. Having first usurped the throne of Adam (Genesis 3; Luke 4:6), Satan was given a dominion during the Mosaic Age as well.

"Now is the judgment of this Age.
Now is the ruler of this Age cast out.
And I, when I am lifted up upon The Land [of Israel],
will be drawing everyone unto me." John 12:31 (Aramaic Text)

"The ruler of this Age comes, and in me he has nothing...

'The ruler of this Age has been judged."
John 14:30; 16:11 (Aramaic Text)

So when Jesus burst onto the scene, it is no surprise that Satan would scramble to maintain his authority. But Daniel, John, and of course, Jesus, saw prophetically that Satan's days of dominion were numbered. Consider the following passages from Scripture:

- "And a fourth kingdom will be mighty as iron, and like iron that hammers and pounds everything, so also it shall break up and tread on everything...

  And in the days of those [Roman] kings, the God of Heaven shall raise up the Kingdom that is for an age that shall not be destroyed, and the kingdom shall not be left to another people, but it shall pulverize and it will consume all these kingdoms, and it shall be established for ages."

  "And he shall speak words against the Most High and treachery against the Holy Ones of The Highest, and he will think to change times and laws, and they shall be given into his hand for a season, seasons, and half of a season. And the Judge sat and they took his authority away from him that they would ruin him and would destroy him until the end. Because the kingdom and authority and the greatness and the kingdom under Heaven is given to the holy people of The Highest."

Daniel 2:40, 44; 7:25–27[77]

- "And the great Dragon was cast down, that Chief Serpent, which is called The Devil and Satan, which deceives all The Earth, and it was cast down unto The Earth and its Angels were cast down with it. And I heard a great voice from Heaven that said,

  'Now is the deliverance and the power and The Kingdom of our God, for The Accuser of our brethren is cast down, which accused them night and day before our God,'

  "And they were victorious by the blood of The Lamb and by the word of His testimony and they did not love their lives unto death.

  'Therefore Heavens, celebrate, and those who dwell in them; woe to The Earth and to the Sea, for The Devil, who has great fury, has descended to them, as he knows that he has little time.'" Revelation 12:9–12[78]

- "I was beholding Satan himself who fell like lightning from Heaven." Luke 10:18[79]

Paul summarized as follows:

"For He rescued us from the domain of darkness, and transferred us to the kingdom of His beloved Son." Col 1:13 (NASB)

And,

"When He [Jesus] had disarmed the rulers and authorities, He made a public display of them, having triumphed over them through Him [on the cross]." Col 2:15 (NASB)

These Scriptures provide us with the context to now read and interpret the following verses in Revelation 20a.

---

[77] Bauscher, David. *The Holy Peshitta Bible Translated*, Lulu.com. Kindle Edition, p. 1684-1685.
[78] Ibid, (pp. 2539-2540).
[79] Ibid. (pp. 2017).

REVELATION 20

א *(v 1) "And behold! I saw another angel descend from heaven, having the key of the depth, and a great chain in his hand." (Aramaic Text)*

The key here representing divine authority to bind or loose (see Matthew 16:19). The Aramaic word for depth matches the Hebrew, tehom תְּהוֹם). The most famous use of this word is in Genesis 1:2, where the Spirit hovered over the deep. The Biblical imagery of tehom is often associated with deep waters and sometimes as a gateway to the underworld.[80]

א *(v 2) "And he arrested the dragon, the serpent of old, who is the accuser, and the adversary, and restrained him a thousand years..."*

The two main things to consider here are the nature of the restraint and who was and wasn't restrained. The nature of the restrained will be discussed in verse 3. So as for who, the vision doesn't depict demons or the whole kingdom of darkness being restrained—only Satan. Demons were not restrained. This is an important distinction.

א *(v 3) "And he threw him down to the depth, and took hold of him and submerged him from above, that he no longer cause the whole of the Gentiles to be deceived. After this, he will be given unrestraint for a short time."*

As for the nature of the restrained, most translations depict Satan being thrown in prison and the angel locking him up and throwing away the key. Surprisingly, the Aramaic paints a different picture. Because of the use of tehom (depth—think Mariana Trench), the imagery is more like deep waters in the middle of the sea (like the deep blue of the Mediterranean).

Therefore Satan is thrown *down,* and the angel holds Satan and submerges him (the word also means, "to drown"), pushing him down to the depths of the sea. Remember, this is figurative language. A spiritual being wouldn't be affected by water! And in the depths, Satan is held there for a thousand years (more on this "thousand years" bit later).

And what is the nature of Satan's restraint? He is no longer able to cause widespread deception of the nations of the world. The word "deception" also

---

[80] For example, Genesis 7:11; Ezekiel 31:15.

means "to cause to forget" or "wander away." How fitting! Satan caused Adam to forget who he was and his created value in the Garden. Following the voice of the serpent caused him to wander away from God. Am I saying that people stopped walking in deception after 70 AD? Far from it. But much of human deception comes from a result of the Fall and what was inherited through Adam.

> *"That which comes out of the person, that is what defiles the person. For from within, out of the hearts of people, come the evil thoughts, acts of sexual immorality… All these evil things come from within and defile the person." Mark 7:20–23 (NASB)*

> *"To the pure, all things are pure; but to those who are defiled and unbelieving, nothing is pure, but both their mind and their conscience are defiled." Titus 1:15 (NASB)*

And this deception continued to be perpetuated by dark spiritual beings, even after Satan's restraint: "you previously walked according to the course of this world, according to the prince of the power of the air, of the spirit that is now working in the sons of disobedience" (Ephesians 2:2 NASB).

But this legal right to cause widespread deception was stayed during the inauguration of the Messianic Age. "How can anyone enter the strong man's house and carry off his property, unless he first ties up the strong man? And then he will plunder his house," (Matthew 12:29). From the day Jesus uttered those word until now, Satan's house has been repeatedly plundered and an increasing number of captives set free (Luke 4:18). As a result, the early Messianic community of Jesus grew from a few thousand to over 2 billion today (one third of the global population). It expanded beyond the Eastern Mediterranean to the far reaches of the Gentile world. This is exactly what Paul spoke of in Romans 9 to 11: "a partial hardening has happened to Israel until the fullness of the Gentiles has come in; and so all Israel will be saved" (Romans 11:25–26).

The early church fathers also understood that the binding of Satan was something that had already taken place, rather than a future event:

- "Our Lord Jesus Christ himself said, 'No one can enter the strong man's house and plunder his goods, unless he first binds the strong man.' By 'strong man' he means the devil, who was able to hold the human race in bondage. By his 'goods' that Christ was to 'plunder,' he means God's future faithful ones whom the devil was keeping for himself because of their ungodliness and various sins. It was for the purpose of binding this strong man that John, in the Apocalypse, saw 'an angel coming down from heaven... who bound [the ancient serpent] for a thousand years.' The angel, that is, checked and repressed his power to seduce and possess those destined to be set free."[81]

- "[Jesus] visited the region of those who are mortal, for as one who is stronger he wished to bind the strong one, so that he might make vessels of mercy out of those who had earlier been vessels of wrath. And he accomplished this through that work that he had promised before when he said, 'No one can enter a strong man's house and plunder his wares, unless he first binds the strong man,' that is, the devil."[82]

- "For through his passion the one who is stronger than [the devil], namely Christ our God, bound him who seemed to be strong and freed us, who were his spoils, from his hands and condemned him by throwing him into the pit. This is shown by those demons who pleaded that he not send them into the pit. The demonstration that the devil is bound is the disappearance of idol worship, the destruction of pagan temples, the abandonment of the defilement of altars, and the knowledge of the will of God throughout the world."[83]

- "Possessing the power of the Father, the Lord came down into the flesh, for he was going to wage war upon the leader of the world, and when he had been bound, he was going to free his captives."[84]

- "Therefore, both by the cross of Christ and by the authority of the cross he bound the enemy of the world who deceived

---

[81] William C. Weinrich, eds. *Revelation*. vol. 12 of Ancient Christian Commentary on Scripture. ICCS/Accordance electronic ed. (Downers Grove: InterVarsity Press, 2005), p. 321. Quoting St. Augustine (c. 354 – 430).

[82] Ibid. Quoting Primasius (c. 550–560). Bishop of Hadrumetum in North Africa (modern Tunsia).

[83] Ibid. Quoting Andreas of Caesarea (c. 563 – 637).

[84] Ibid. Quoting Bede The Venerable (c. 673 – 735).

those who dwell upon the earth."[85]

- "At this time, the time of the incarnation of the Lord, the devil was bound, not being able to resist the marks of the Saviour's deity. And, therefore, when they sensed that they were spiritually bound, the wicked demons cried out, 'What have you to do with us, O Son of the living God? Have you come here to torment us before the time?' And the Lord also made clear their bondage when he said, 'Or how can one enter a strong man's house and plunder his goods, unless he first binds the strong man? Then indeed he may plunder his house.'"[86]

א *(v 4 – 6) "And behold! Thrones, and they were seated upon, and judgement was given to those souls that were slain because of the testimony of Jesus and for the word of God. And they worshipped not the beast, nor its image, nor did they receive his mark between their eyes (forehead) or upon their hands. And they lived and they reigned with their Messiah a thousand years.*

This is the first resurrection.

Blessed are those and holy are those who take part in the first resurrection. Upon these the second death has no dominion. Rather, they become priests of God and their Messiah, and they shall reign with him a thousand years."

In order to see what is happening here, we need to understand the notion of first and second resurrection, and first and second death. This is John's theology, so you will only find it in his writings.

THE FIRST DEATH, THE FIRST RESURRECTION

First things first. After Adam, everyone was considered dead, even while they walked the earth: "From the tree of the knowledge of good and evil you shall not eat, for on the day that you eat from it you will certainly die."

---

[85] Ibid. Quoting Apringius of Beja (c. 6th century AD).
[86] Ibid. Quoting Oecumenius the Rhetor (c. 6th century AD). Not the same as the 10th century bishop of Tricca in Thessaly.

(Genesis 2:17). Did anyone notice that Adam and Eve did not drop dead the day they ate in Genesis 3? Did God lie? No! So who died? The beings they were created to be. This is what Jesus meant when he said, "Another of the disciples said to Him, 'Lord, allow me first to go and bury my father.' But Jesus said to him, 'Follow Me, and let the dead bury their own dead,'" (Matthew 8:21–22).

Paul clarified in Romans 5: "Therefore, just as through one man sin entered into the world, and death through sin, and so death spread to all mankind, because all sinned... For if by the offense of the one, death reigned through the one, how much more will those who receive the abundance of grace and of the gift of righteousness reign in life through the One, Jesus Christ," (Romans 5:12, 17). Did you notice the "reign in life" part? Sounds like Revelation 20:6! The first death has existed from the beginning. Anyone outside of Christ was and is already dead.

> *"And you were dead in your offenses and sins... even when we were dead in our wrongdoings, [God] made us alive together with Christ (by grace you have been saved), and raised us up with Him, and seated us with Him in the heavenly places in Christ Jesus, so that in the ages to come He might show the boundless riches of His grace in kindness toward us in Christ Jesus." Ephesians 2:1, 5–7 (NASB).*

The "ages" to come is plural. In the Age of Messiah (now), and the Age of All Things New (still to come), we live and reign with Christ. The Ephesians were first dead, then made alive!

This helps lead us to understanding of the first resurrection. In juxtaposition to the first death, which takes place while people are still alive (outside of Christ), the first resurrection takes place while people are alive—in Christ.

> *"Truly, truly, I say to you,* **the one who hears My word, and believes Him who sent Me, has eternal life, and does not come into judgment, but has passed out of death into life.**
>
> *Truly, truly, I say to you, a time is coming and* **even now has arrived,** *when the dead will hear the voice of the Son of God, and those who hear will live...*
>
> *Do not be amazed at this; for a time is coming* **when all** *who are in the tombs will hear His voice, and will come out: those who did the good deeds*

to a resurrection of life, those who committed the bad deeds to a resurrection of judgment." John 5:25, 28–29 (NASB)

This is where John first introduces the notion of two resurrections. The first resurrection comes through Jesus. "And this is eternal life, that they may know You, the only true God, and Jesus Christ whom You have sent," (John 17:3). When he said, "a time is coming and even now has arrived," he was speaking of the first resurrection. And in John 5:28, where he said, "a time is coming when <u>all</u> who are in tombs," he was referring to the second resurrection. Not only was Jesus claiming he would provide the spirit with life, but that he has the power and authority to even fulfill the prophecy of Ezekiel 37, bringing dead and rotting flesh back to life!

But going back to the first resurrection, the prophet Daniel saw the time where the Age of Moses would end:

> "At that time Mikaeil, the Great Angel, shall stand, who is commanded concerning the children of your people, and there will be a time of suffering, like to which has never been from the days of the world, and in that time some of the children of your people shall escape, everyone who is found who is written in The Scroll. And the many who sleep in the dust shall be awakened, these to the life of [an age], and those to loss and to the shame of their companions for [an age]." Daniel 12:1–2[87]

Daniel was speaking of the great distress that came over the Holy Land when the Romans slaughtered one million Jews and destroyed the Holy Temple. Spiritual slumber, an ongoing theme in the Old Testament[88], and picked up by Paul a few times (Ephesians 5:14; 11:8; Romans 13:11), was something that the inhabitants of Judea were awoken from; in either a good way or a bad way. Some went from death to life through Jesus, and others fell into the Gehenna experience,[89] slain by the sword of their oppressors (first it was the Babylonians, next it was the Romans). Those who found the resurrection lived throughout the Age of Messiah even after their bodies died. Those who remained in darkness fell asleep during this same age, awaiting even until this day, the second resurrection.

---

[87] Bauscher, David. *The Holy Peshitta Bible Translated*, Lulu.com. Kindle Edition, p. 1696. The author incorrectly used "eternity" for alam, the Aramaic word that most commonly means "age" or "generation" (olam in Hebrew).

[88] Isaiah 51:17; Isaiah 52:1; Isaiah 60:1; Malachi 4:2

[89] I discuss this at length in book 1. See also Jeremiah 7:31, 19:2–6.

The first resurrection begins with knowing Jesus, and that relationship continues even when our current bodies die ("fall asleep" as Paul would say). "If Christ has not been raised, your faith is worthless; you are still in your sins. Then also those who have fallen asleep in Christ have perished," (1 Corinthians 15:17–18).

Those in Christ, even if the body dies, never skip a beat! They continue to live and reign with Christ. "Jesus said to her, 'I am the resurrection and the life; the one who believes in Me will live, even if he dies, and everyone who lives and believes in Me will never die,'" (John 11:25–26). Jesus plainly explains that bodily death is not death to the spirit.

> *"But he [Stephen], being full of the Holy Spirit, looked intently into heaven and saw the glory of God, and Jesus standing at the right hand of God;* [56] *and he said, "Behold, I see the heavens opened and the Son of Man standing at the right hand of God." …They went on stoning Stephen as he called on the Lord and said, "Lord Jesus, receive my spirit!" …Having said this, he fell asleep." Acts 7:55, 59, 60 (NASB)*

Understanding the first resurrection, verses 4 to 6 of Revelation 20 are now crystal clear: Those who were persecuted and martyred for their faith in Christ did not die in vain. In fact, they never died at all! Their bodies fell asleep but their souls (or spirits) remained with Christ and in Christ. John's vision served as a witness to those still awake; a testimony that there was in fact life after death and glory and honour for those who are faithful even unto death.

> *"Now if Christ is preached, that He has been raised from the dead, how do some among you say that there is no resurrection of the dead?*
>
> *… But someone will say, 'How are the dead raised? And with what kind of body do they come?' You fool!'" 1 Cor 15:12 35, 36 (NASB)*

The fact that Paul had to dedicate an entire section in his letter to explaining once again that there is a real resurrection and life after death helps us understand that for many people in the early church, it was a hard truth to accept. And it wasn't just a Gentile issue. "For the Sadducees say that there is no resurrection." (Acts 23:8). John's vision then silences unbelief and teaches us that in death those in Christ are still reigning with him, even today!

Reigning with Christ isn't a future event. It happens the moment you are delivered from the kingdom of darkness and brought home into the kingdom of the Messiah.

- *"The one who overcomes, I will grant to him to sit with Me on My throne, as I also overcame and sat with My Father on His throne."* Revelation 3:21

- *"But you are a chosen generation, a royal priesthood, a holy nation, His own special people, that you may proclaim the praises of Him who called you out of darkness into His marvelous light."* 1 Peter 2:9

- *"You have made them to be a kingdom and priests to serve our God, and they will reign upon the earth."* Revelation 5:10

- *"Blessed be the God and Father of our Lord Jesus Christ, who has blessed us with every spiritual blessing in the heavenly places in Christ."* Ephesians 1:3

- *"If we are children, heirs also, heirs of God and fellow heirs with Christ, if indeed we suffer with Him so that we may also be glorified with Him."* Romans 8:17

- *"This is a trustworthy saying: If we died with Him, we will also live with Him; if we endure, we will also reign with Him."* 2 Timothy 2:11–12

One last thing: The first death and first resurrection are temporary. They both have an end. It is the second death and second resurrection that are everlasting.

"For He [Jesus] must reign until He has put all His enemies under His feet. The last enemy that will be abolished is death… We will not all sleep, but we will all be changed… and the dead will be raised imperishable, and we will be changed. For this perishable [body] must put on the imperishable, and this mortal must put on immortality.

But when this perishable puts on the imperishable, and this mortal puts on immortality, then will come about the saying that is written: Death has been swallowed up in victory. Where, O Death, is your victory? Where, O Death, is your sting?" 1 Corinthians 15:25–26, 51–55 (NASB)

The abolition of the first death is the trigger event for the second resurrection. "For in the [second] resurrection they neither marry nor are given in marriage, but are like angels in heaven," (Matthew 22:29). As for the second resurrection and second death, these will be explored later when it is mentioned in Revelation 20:12 and 20:14.

A final thought on the first and second resurrection pertains to the Aramaic versus the Greek in verse 5. As written above, it reads, "This is the first resurrection." The Greek adds, "The rest of the dead did not come to life until the thousand years were completed. This is the first resurrection." My thought is that those who made copies of the book, translating from Aramaic to a Greek audience in the Greek tongue, at some point felt compelled to insert commentary into the verse.[90] To wit, those closer to the time and culture of Jesus already understood that we in Christ have the first resurrection *now*, while those further away in both region (culture) and chronology (future centuries) from Jesus needed further explanation.

א *(v 7) "And after the thousand years are accomplished, the adversary was given unrestraint from his captivity."*

Let us now turn our attention to the thousand year time period.

---

[90] This is not a unique instance. See for example Matthew 6:13, where some translations have ""For thine is the kingdom, and the power, and the glory, forever," and others do not.

5 BEGIN WITH THE END – PART 2: CHAPTER 20a

*"**It is now** the age of the kingdom of God and His Messiah; and He shall reign from age to ages."*
— *Revelation 11:15 (Aramaic Text)*

THE THOUSAND YEARS

I am so excited to dig into this! In book 1 I wrote at length concerning the transition of epoch seasons, from the Age of Moses to the Age of Messiah. In that volume the focus was on the words of Jesus. Now we shall discuss the same event through the eyes of John. Revelation 20 introduces us to the third and final age of mankind:

> *"Of the Sabbath He spoke in the beginning of the creation; And God made the works of His hands in six days, and He ended on the seventh day, and rested on it, and He hallowed it. Give heed, children, what this means; He ended in six days. He means this, that at six thousand years the Lord shall bring all things to an end; for the day with Him signifies a thousand years." The Epistle of Barnabas, 15:3–5*

John recounts the heavenly proclamation he witnesses. At the time of his writing (1st century AD), the age of the kingdom and of the Messiah has begun. To elucidate this, in book 1 I covered the concept of epoch seasons, or ages, and how they are ingrained in the Jewish worldview:

> "Six thousand years is the duration of the world. Two thousand of the six thousand years are characterized by chaos; two thousand years are characterized by Torah, from the era of the Patriarchs until the end of the Rabbinic period; and two thousand years are the period of the coming of the Messiah."
> Sanhedrin 97a:14

But if the epoch seasons of mankind have lasted roughly 2,000 years, why did John write of a 1,000 year period? John's terminology was relevant to his day, where apocalyptic literature abounded and an expectation of an imminent golden era was prolific, especially in the Essene community (the 'Dead Sea Scrolls' people). Let's look at some examples:

- "They shall keep apart from every uncleanness according to the statutes relating to each one, and no man shall defile his holy spirit since God has set them apart. For all who walk in these (precepts) in perfect holiness, according to all the teaching of God, the Covenant of God shall be an assurance that they shall live for thousands of Generations." The Damascus Document, The Exhortation, sect. 7

- "And I saw written in them that one generation after another will do evil in this way, and evil will last [until] generations of righteousness [arise] and evil and wickedness shall end and violence shall cease from the earth and un[til good shall come on the earth] on them." 4Q204=Enoch (1Enoch 106, 19-107, 2)

- "God has chosen them for an everlasting Covenant, and all the glory of Adam shall be theirs...

  "Those who hold fast [to the sure house of Israel] are destined to live forever and all the glory of Adam shall be theirs...

  "Thou wilt keep thine oath and wilt pardon their transgressions; thou wilt cast away all their sins. Thou wilt cause them to inherit all the glory of Adam and abundance of days…

"To the penitents of the desert who, saved, shall live for a thousand generations and to whom all the glory of Adam shall belong, as also to their seed forever." Various Qumran scrolls: 1QS 4.22-23; CD 3.19-20; 1QH 17.14-15; 4QpPs.37 3.1-2. Translation from Vermes 1987.

- Then they shall say: 'The days of the forefathers were many (even), unto a thousand years, and were good; but behold, the days of our life, if a man has lived many, are three score years and ten, and, if he is strong, four score years, and those evil, and there is no peace in the days of this evil generation.'

"…And a great punishment shall befall the deeds of this generation from the Lord, and He will give them over to the sword and to judgment and to captivity, and to be plundered and devoured.

"And He will wake up against them the sinners of the Gentiles, who have neither mercy nor compassion, and who shall respect the person of none, neither old nor young, nor any one, for they are more wicked and strong to do evil than all the children of men."

"This concerns the Teacher of Righteousness, to whom God made known all the mysteries of the words of His servants the Prophets. For there shall be yet another vision concerning the appointed time. It shall tell of the end and shall not lie.

Interpreted, this means that the final age shall be prolonged, and shall exceed all that the Prophets have said; for the mysteries of God are astounding. If it tarries, wait for it, for it shall surely come and shall not be late." 1QpHab VII in Vermes 1997

- "And the days shall begin to grow many and increase amongst those children of men till their days draw nigh to one thousand years. And to a greater number of years than (before) was the number of the days…

And they shall know that it is the Lord who executes

judgment…

And shows mercy to hundreds and thousands and to all that love Him…

And do thou, Moses, write down these words; for thus are they written, and they record (them) on the heavenly tablets for a testimony for the generations forever." Jubilees 23

While the language of the day was similar,[91] they were all drawing from the same ancient promises found in the Law of Moses:

"Know therefore that the Lord your God, He is God, the faithful God, who keeps His covenant and His faithfulness to a thousand generations for those who love Him and keep His commandments." Deuteronomy 7:9 (NASB)

"You shall not worship them nor serve them; for I, the Lord your God, am a jealous God, inflicting the punishment of the fathers on the children, on the third and the fourth generations of those who hate Me, but showing favor to thousands, to those who love Me and keep My commandments." Exodus 20:5–6 (NASB)

The notion of a thousand years in Revelation and a thousandth generation in Exodus coincide even further in light of a simple text analysis. In Revelation, the Aramaic root word for "year" can also mean "age" or "era"[92], while the Hebrew root word for "generations" can also mean "age" or a "period" of time.[93]

Jewish sages also seemed to blend figurative dates found in Scripture with actual timespans in the story of mankind.

"Six thousand years is the duration of the world, and it is in ruins for one thousand years. The duration of the period during which the world is in ruins is derived from a verse, as it is stated: "And the Lord alone shall be exalted on that day" (Isaiah 2:11), and the day of God lasts one thousand years. Abaye says: It is in ruins for two thousand years, as it is stated: "After two days

---

[91] See also: 1 Enoch 1:9; 10:11–15; 18:14-16; 21:6; The Epistle of Enoch (Book 5), 93:1-3; 2 Enoch 33:1; Sanhedrin 97a:2, 12.
[92] See J. Payne Smith's Syriac Dictionary, p. 587.
[93] See Brown Driver Brigg's Hebrew and English Lexicon, p. 189.

He will revive us; in the third day He will revive us, and we shall live in His presence." Sanhedrin 97a:12, from Hosea 6:2

"Six eons for going in and coming out, for war and peace. The seventh eon is entirely Shabbat and rest for life everlasting." Midrash, Pirkei De-Rabbi Eliezer

Jewish mysticism maintained this similar notion of epoch seasons and a thousand-year period:

"There are two general stages in time; This world and the World to Come. This world will endure six millennia... The era of Moshiach [Messiah] ushers in the periods of a transitional stage. It will begin during the latter part of the sixth millennium (and will conclude with the resurrection of the dead). The seventh millennium marks the beginning of the world to come... During this stage the world ceases to exist in its present form and will be in a state of desolation for 1000 years, as scripture states "A song for the day of Sabbath". That is, a Sabbath of eternal rest."[94]

R.I. Burns also has an interesting hypothesis with respect to what a 1,000-year reign symbolized to the Jewish reader:

"After a careful examination of the Book of Enoch another 1,000-year period of earthly rule does in fact come jumping off the pages for the reader. The world before the flood was ruled by the Watchers and by their offspring for 1,000 years. In this light, the 1,000-year rule of Christ does seem to have a corollary. The millennial reign of Christ can now be viewed juxtaposed to the earlier millennial rule of the Watchers and their children... According to Enoch's book the descent of the Watchers occurred 'in the days of Jared.' Referring to the genealogy included in chapter 5 of the Book of Genesis, Jared was born about 1,194 years before the flood, and his son, Enoch, was born about 1,033 years before the flood... This

---

[94] *Kabbalah: The Beginning of Wisdom*, chapter 8, trans. by Rabbi Amiram Markel and Michoel Tzvi Wolkenfeld, 2004-2006, from Sefaria.org. Please note that in no way am I promoting Kabbalah in a religious sense. Rather, I reference it because it is a long-standing Jewish tradition of mystical interpretation of the Bible.

means the domination and rule of the Watchers and their children in the realm of humankind would have lasted for at least 1,000 years."[95]

From this framework we can apply Paul's language to our understanding of the three epoch seasons of mankind:

> "Six thousand years is the duration of the world. Two thousand of the six thousand years are characterized by chaos; two thousand years are characterized by Torah… and two thousand years are the period of the coming of the Messiah." Sanhedrin 97a:14

> "These are in accordance with the working of the strength of His might which He brought about in Christ, when He raised Him from the dead and seated Him at His right hand in the heavenly places, far above all rule and authority and power and dominion, and every name that is named, **not only in this age but also in the one to come**." Ephesians 1:19–21 (NASB)

Recapping the events of history and cross-referencing them with the Biblical narrative, here is how we can make sense of Revelation 20:1-7:

- Jesus came at the tail end of the Age of Moses (which lasted ~2000 years).
- Between His Resurrection and the destruction of Jerusalem and the Temple was a 40 year period (a generation), where both the Age of Moses (since sacrifices were still being offered in the Temple) and Age of Messiah were in effect and overlapping.
- At the end of this transition heaven abolished the sacrificial system, and Satan was restrained.
- The Age of Messiah would now take off in full radiance, no longer shadowed by the Age of Moses.

At the end of the Age of Messiah (which will have lasted ~ 2,000 years), Satan would be given the ability to deceive the nations one last time. Now let that sink in for a bit. Give it some thought. What you just read would suggest that we today are most likely living in the time where Satan has been

---

[95] Burn, R. I., *The Book of Enoch Messianic Prophecy Edition: Time-Capsule to the Last Generation* (SageWorks Press: San Francisco, 2017), p. 202.

unrestrained and is at work deceiving the nations. Wait... what? Yes, if we follow the framework of the text, that is what it appears to suggest to us who happen to be living in the 21st century.

"And after the thousand years are accomplished, the adversary was given unrestraint from his captivity." Revelation 20:7 (Aramaic Text)

Because we find ourselves to be alive, it just so happens that **we seem to be living at the tail end of the figurative 1000 years—the third epoch season, the Messianic Age.** At the beginning of this chapter I stated Revelation 20 would answer the question of where we find ourselves today in relation to the book. This is what I meant.

I don't like the term "last days." It has been misused and misunderstood for far too long. I won't be trying to fearmonger, as there is nothing to fear in the real last days. Almost every instance where a notion of "last days" is mentioned in the New Testament, it was in reference to the last days of the Mosaic Age. In contrast, when the Bible speaks of "latter days" (Deuteronomy 31:29, Ezekiel 38–39) or the "last *day*" (John 6:39, 6:40, 6:43, 6:54, 12:48) it is referring to the end of this current age: the age of ages.[96]

LIVING IN THE LAST DAYS – FOR REAL THIS TIME

As I alluded to earlier, the 21st Century is prophesied about in Revelation 20:7. When we compare Revelation to Ezekiel (which are remarkably similar in structure and themes), we observe a few interesting things. First, Ezekiel was prophesying about the first time Jerusalem fell as well as imminent events. Second, his prophecy regarding distant future made up only a small part of the overall book.

Out of the 48 chapters in Ezekiel, only the last 10[97] spoke of the very end of human history (the end of the Messianic Age). Similarly, Isaiah, who prophesied concerning the fall of the Northern kingdom of Israel (the Southern kingdom was Judah and Jerusalem), had a similar pattern: out of 66 chapters, only the last 10 spoke of the distant future. Like Ezekiel and Isaiah, John also prophesied about imminent events, namely the second and prolonged fall of Jerusalem and the destruction of the Temple. The sections

---

[96] The phrase עָלַם עָלְמַיָּא "age of ages," the literal reading found in places like Daniel 7:18, Ephesian 3:21 and Revelation 10:6, may even suggest a three-stage period of mankind. Olam/Alam singular (one) and olam/alam plural (two) equals three ages.
[97] or 12: either 36 to 48, or 38 to 48, depending on your interpretation.

that speak of distant future events (Revelation 20:6 and onward) only make up a small percentage of the overall narrative.

And both Ezekiel and John provide vivid, elaborate, and symbolic descriptions of the fall of Jerusalem (see Ezekiel 15, 16, 19, 23, and Revelation 17–19), and the legal consequences for her contractual infractions. Both prophets also describe the agents of Law-enforcement at length (Babylon, Rome) in incredible detail. But when they switch from looking at what is immediately before them to looking across the plain of time into the distant horizon, the details become sparse.

For instance, Ezekiel's vision of God restoring all creation (undoubtedly one of the most important events of all time, found in Ezekiel 47:6–12), there are only 6 verses describing this event, in a book of 48 chapters and 1,273 verses! Likewise, when John's vision shifts from what is in front of him to what lies ahead, there are only 8 verses vaguely depicting the climactic end of this great story of God and mankind.

WILL THERE REALLY BE AN "END" TO THIS AGE?

Next, I would like to share a few thoughts regarding the idea of an indefinite end and the two main competing ideas that stem from it. One view suggests the age we are in right now will continue for hundreds, if not thousands, of years, and how things unfold hinges on our contribution as believers. Meanwhile, the other view maintains that all of Revelation has already ended, and there is nothing more to the story.

Speaking of the first view, I'm all for the notion of co-labouring with Christ; especially when it comes to advancing the kingdom of God, influencing society, praying for healing, all of it. But what about the Great Resurrection of all who have ever died (1 Corinthians 15), or the renewal of all creation (Romans 8:20–25)? I do believe that miracles have continued from the Apostles even till this day, including raising the dead—these are signposts of the time that is to come, where mortal bodies will no longer die. And God has empowered us to solve temporal issues of planetary (environmental) decay.

But when God says in both Isaiah and Revelation, "Behold! I make all things new!" it's clear He alone is the one who is able to make that happen. And when Jesus, Ezekiel, Paul and John (among others) speak of all the dead being raised and given the same flesh that Jesus currently wears, only He can accomplish such a feat.

70

Shifting now to the idea that all of Revelation has been fulfilled, the main issue is that people still die. Yet the future hope is that death will be defeated, and our mortal bodies will no longer decay (1 Corinthians 15). If physical death is forever part of the plan, then we make heaven the goal and still fail to resolve the Genesis 3 problem. Further, to suggest that Revelation has been fulfilled (or, "heaven is now") is to say to those in China, Iran, Sudan, Somalia, Pakistan, and so many other places where Christians are persecuted: "This is as good it as gets. Enjoy God's New Creation!" This also implies that their current state is what it looks like when God wipes away every tear from their eyes, and that what most would call hell is somehow supposed to be heaven for them.

This is a imperialistic, Western, First-World ideology that only makes sense to those who have never suffered austerity or real persecution. It is an abhorrent theology for this reason alone. What's more is this line of thinking again puts the future hope of a renewed cosmos on mankind, taking us back to the fallacies of the first view. The final defeat of death (not just spiritual, but physical), the Great Resurrection, the renewal of the cosmos, the complete and total eradication of all evil; these things have been destined to come about by the power and might of God alone. And they will take place at the consummation of this Age.

EFFECTS OF SATAN'S RELEASE

With those thoughts now clarified, I'll dovetail on the reality of modern-day persecution and end this section with a final thought. One can't help but marvel at Christianity's growth from the 500 people that Jesus revealed Himself to (1 Corinthians 15:6) to the 2.7 billion who profess His name today. Now, we should refrain from judging who is a "real Christian" and who isn't; the Judgement Seat has one name written on it, and it God's, not ours! And over the centuries, believers have been able to impact culture (education, politics, charity, hospitals, etc.) and indeed, entire nations, and God's kingdom expanded to the far reaches of the planet.

In the midst of this growth, moderate persecution against Christians and Jews has been a constant these past two thousand years (as Jesus said it would[98]). Then something unimaginable took place: In the early 20th century, the Ottoman (Turkish) Empire directly persecuted and exterminated over 2

---

[98] See John 15:20; Acts 5–8; Gal. 3:4; Philippians 1:29, 3:8; 1 Thessalonians 2:14; 1 Peter 2:19, 4:12; 2 Corinthians 11:23–29; 2 Timothy 1:8, 3:12, 4:5.

million Christians—1,000,000 Armenians, 750,000 Greeks, and 300,000 Assyrians. The Armenians, the Greeks, and the Assyrians (Syrians) were the first Christians outside of Judea, and it was the Armenians (who spoke Aramaic), not the Romans, who were the first nation to declare Christianity their official religion. Then after the Ottoman-German alliance, Germany persecuted and killed over 6 million Jews (some suggest that number was even higher) just years after the Christians' genocide. **As we will discover later on in this book, the Ottoman Empire (modern-day Turkey) was the same geographic location once referred to as Magog, where the seven churches of Revelation were.** Coincidence?

From that point on persecution of Christians and Jews went from moderate to extreme, relatively speaking. While Jews have been dealing with anti-Semitism for centuries, since 1948 tensions with neighbouring countries and abroad have been increasing. As for Christians, one expert suggests that "more Christians have died for their faith in this current century than all other centuries of church history combined... [having] documented cases in excess of 26 million martyrs"[99] In Sudan alone, over 1.3 million Christians were killed in just a 6–year period in recent years.

Now my goal here isn't to instill fear. If you look at China and Iran, where persecution is intense, so is the growth of the Church. As Isaiah prophesied, "to the degree that the darkness increases, so does God's glory," (Isaiah 60:1–2, paraphrased). Nevertheless, this reality can't be ignored. It *means* something.

Additionally, another phenomenon that is increasing over the earth is **mass deception**. All that we know to be true is being challenged; wrong is now right, and right is now wrong. The degree in which this has affected every level of government and society is unprecedented, as is the rate of speed in which assimilation of the masses is taking place. Indeed, I propose, this can only be **supernatural:**

"And after the thousand years are accomplished, the adversary was given unrestraint from his captivity. And he will set out to cause them to be deceived, the whole of the Gentiles in the four corners of the land of Gog and Magog, and will gather them to war, those whose number is as the sand of the sea." Revelation 20:7–8 (Aramaic Text)

---

[99] *Modern Persecution*, Dan Wooding, 2010,
https://www.christianity.com/church/church-history/timeline/1901-2000/modern-persecution-11630665.html

For most of the Messianic Age, Satan was hindered from causing world-wide deception. Suddenly, two trigger events take place: the land of Magog annihilates millions of Christians and Jews at a scale never seen before, and a deception has gone out in the nations that is unprecedented.

Lastly, we can deduce from Scripture that at the advent of a Messianic figure's ultimate mission, there was a genocide of infants as sort of a precursor. For instance, in the early days of Moses' ministry, the lives of every first-born in Egypt was taken overnight. Similarly, when Jesus was born, Herod had every male child under two years of age and younger slaughtered. Today, one cannot fail to notice that there has been a genocide of infants on a global scale in recent years. Most of it government sponsored. Is it possible that this phenomenon is the ultimate precursor to the advent of the Bridegroom King?

In my view, the events we have witnessed from the turn of the 20th century until now fit the text of Revelation 20a from a historical and theological perspective. Combining these factors with the ones I stated earlier, **I believe the transition from what *has* happened in Revelation to what *will* happen in Revelation is found in chapter 20:7–8.** That said, I don't believe we have seen all of verse 8 come to pass, and we certainly haven't hit verse 9 yet.

Yet, the reader must understand that this exposé of what Satan is now doing is for exegetical purposes only. By no means do I intend to focus on what the enemy is up to. He doesn't deserve the attention! We should not afford him even a glance. **Eyes on Jesus at all times—He is where our attention must remain.** Whatever we focus on we magnify. So *who* is magnified in your mind— a defeated being, or the LORD and Ruler of the entire universe?

> *"You will keep in perfect peace*
> *those whose minds are steadfast,*
> *because they trust in you.*
> *Trust in the Lord forever." Isaiah 26:3–4 (NIV)*

WE ARE STILL WINNING

I understand some readers might be wondering if there is anything we should be doing, or anticipating, if in fact verse 8 is in play. In short, no, because immediately following verse 8, God says in verse 9: "and fire came down from heaven and devoured them." Life is very easy when we aren't chasing after conspiracy theories—no supreme evil overlord, no One World Order, no 666s embedded into technology. Such narratives are foreign to early church fathers and have only come about in the 19th and 20th centuries.[100]

The greatest conspiracy that ever took place was the plan that Satan, Judas and the religious leaders executed against Jesus. And the Gospels (especially John) remind us constantly that Jesus was aware of this plot at all times, and could clearly see into the realms of darkness. **So how did Jesus handle the conspiracy?** Was he on a witch hunt, or keeping tabs on the conspirators? Was he up late at night waging spiritual warfare against the demonic realms? He washed Judas' feet, healed the ear of one who came to arrest him, and publicly forgave all his conspirators on the cross. Selah.

We cannot afford to lose sight of the plans and purposes of God. There is nothing to fear, and there is no reason to hide. The Great Commission is still our mission. And the enemy is still beneath our feet (Romans 16:20). Eyes on Jesus! Therefore allow me to provide you with anchors in truth so that you will not be tossed about by every wind of doctrine or conspiracy theory (Ephesians 4:14):

"For unto us a child is born, unto us a son is given, and the government will be upon His shoulders. And He will be called Wonderful Counselor, Mighty God, Everlasting Father, Prince of Peace. Of the increase of His government and peace there will be no end. He will reign on the throne of David and over his kingdom, to establish and sustain it with justice and righteousness from that time and forevermore. The zeal of the LORD of Hosts will accomplish this." Isaiah 9:6–7

"Then the sovereignty, dominion, and greatness of the kingdoms under all of heaven will be given to the people, the saints of the Most High. His kingdom will be an everlasting kingdom, and all rulers will serve and obey Him." Daniel 7:27

"The Son of God appeared for this purpose, to destroy the works of the devil." 1 John 3:8 (NASB)

"'Lord, even the demons are subject to us in Your name!' And He said

---

[100] Via John Nelson Darby and friends. Perhaps as a result of the wide-spread deception mentioned earlier?

to them, 'I watched Satan fall from heaven like lightning. Behold, I have given you authority to walk on snakes and scorpions, **and authority over all the power of the enemy,** *and nothing will injure you.'"*
Luke 10:17 (NASB)

"Every spirit that does not confess Jesus is not from God; this is the spirit of the antichrist, which you have heard is coming, and now it is already in the world. You are from God, little children, **and have overcome them;** *because greater is He who is in you than he who is in the world."*
1 John 4:3–4 (NASB)

"These signs will accompany those who have believed: in My name they will cast out demons, they will speak with new tongues; they will pick up serpents, and if they drink any deadly poison, it will not harm them; they will lay hands on the sick, and they will recover."
Mark 16:17–18 (NASB)

"Then the end will come, when He hands over the kingdom to God the Father after He has destroyed all dominion, authority, and power. For **He must be continually reigning until He has put all His enemies under His feet.** *The last enemy to be destroyed is death."*
1 Cor 15:24-26 (Aramaic Text)

*"**All authority** in heaven and on earth has been given to Me. Go, therefore, and make disciples of all the nations, baptizing them in the name of the Father and the Son and the Holy Spirit, teaching them to follow all that I commanded you; and behold, I am with you always,* **to the end of the age."** *Matthew 28:18–20 (NASB)*

"IT IS NOW the AGE of the kingdom of GOD and His Messiah; and He shall reign from age to ages." Revelation 11:15 (Aramaic Text)

MOVING ON TO REVELATION CHAPTER 2

Hopefully this section scratches your "what does Revelation say about today?" itch. I know we can't help ourselves; I too have been very curious about this question. Because of Revelation 20:9+ is yet to come, commentary for the rest of chapter 20 will resume in book 3 of this series.

Having discussed where we are today, we can now focus on John's prophetic word to his churches in Asia Minor (Turkey, aka Magog) and his Jewish kinsmen in the Holy Land without the distraction of "will this verse happen to me?" looming in the back of our minds. Next, we will continue unraveling the texts that describe the fulfillment of Old Testament Law and prophecies through the fall of Jerusalem. We'll also discover how God's redemptive narrative prevails even in the midst of difficult passages.

6 SEVEN MESSIANIC COMMUNITIES

*"The festival of Shavu'ot [Pentecost] arrived, and the believers all
gathered together in one place... They were all filled with the Ruach
HaKodesh [Holy Spirit] and began to talk in different languages, as the
Spirit enabled them to speak.*

*Now there were staying in Yerushalayim [Jerusalem] religious Jews from
every nation under heaven... Totally amazed, they asked... "How is it
that we hear them speaking in our native languages? We are Parthians,
Medes, Elamites; residents of Mesopotamia, Y'hudah [Judea],
Cappadocia, Pontus, Asia [Minor], Phrygia, Pamphylia, Egypt, the
parts of Libya near Cyrene; visitors from Rome; Jews by birth and
proselytes [converts]; Jews from Crete and from Arabia..."*
— Acts 2:1, 4, 5, 7–11 (CJB)[101]

The place names provided above encompassed most of the Roman
Empire.[102] Included in the list we see that Jews from Asia Minor were present.
The Torah legally required all Jews to make three annual pilgrimages to

---

[101] Taken from the Complete Jewish Bible by David H. Stern. Copyright © 1998.
All rights reserved. Used by permission of Messianic Jewish Publishers, 6120 Day
Long Lane, Clarksville, MD 21029. www.messianicjewish.net.

[102] Notice the exaggeration, "every nation under heaven." This is why we can't take
everything you read in the Bible literally! We must understand the intended poetic
meaning, and not become hung up on literal analysis.

Jerusalem: in spring for Pesach [Passover], in summer for Shavuot [Pentecost], and in the fall for Sukkot [Tabernacles]. On this one historic day, pilgrims from cities like Ephesus, Smyrna, Pergamum, Thyatira, Sardis, Philadelphia and Laodicea would have been present.

> "For no one country can contain the whole Jewish nation, by reason of its populousness; on which account they frequent all the most prosperous and fertile countries of Europe and Asia, whether islands or continents, looking indeed upon the holy city as their metropolis in which is erected the sacred temple of the most high God... (circa 1st century AD)."[103]

The Spirit planted seeds, and men like Paul, Barnabas, Apollos, Sopater of Berea, Aristarchus, Secundus, Gaius of Derbe, Timotheus, Tychicus, Trophimus (Acts 20:4), Timothy, and John watered and nurtured them. Contextually, the seven churches mentioned in Revelation are not random or unknown (save for Ephesus). They were thoroughly evangelized by the Apostle Paul and his team (see Acts 19–20). Then, at some point, these communities of believers came under John's oversight, perhaps out of necessity following the martyrdom of Paul.

> "There was the Church at Jerusalem and churches in Judaea [Galatians 1:17, 18; 1 Corinthians 16:3; Galatians 1:22]... According to the Galatian Epistle a Church already existed at Antioch in Syria, and the Epistle to the Romans witnesses to the existence of a Church of non-Pauline foundation in the capital city of the Empire. The fact that these churches at Rome and Antioch were established by Christians other than Paul and his companions indicates that there was successful missionary effort beyond the confines of the Pauline mission-field...
>
> Christianity was essentially a product of Judaism, and it was primarily carried to the Gentiles by men who were by birth and upbringing Jews, generally of a very zealous type. Their whole interpretation and presentation of the new faith was essentially based on Jewish concepts and permeated by the influence of

---

[103] Philo, *In Flaccum,* as published in Vol. IV of The Works of Philo Judaeus, translated from the Greek by C. D. Yonge, B.A. (London: Henry G. Bohn, 1855) 7:45–46.

Jewish practice and outlook. Paul himself supplies significant illustration of this. Although he is so vividly conscious of his role of Apostle to the Uncircumcision… he seeks to instruct, or exhort, or to demonstrate a point to his readers, by some quotation from the Old Testament, employed in a thoroughly rabbinical manner, without any kind of explanation…

[Paul] assumes that they will appreciate the significance of the examples of Abraham and Isaac, of Sarah and Hagar, and, even more remarkable, that they will understand such recondite Judaistic ideas as the Spiritual Rock, the Mosaic Tablets of Stone, the Covenant, the Sin of Adam, the Stumbling Stone, and Rock of Offence…

We may rightly conclude, therefore, that the Gentile Christians were thoroughly dominated in all essential matters of the faith by their Jewish brethren, and that even in the case of those who had been converted by Paul and his companions there was a natural predisposition to subservience to Judaistic influence."[104]

It is to these thoroughly Jewish communities that our Lord and Saviour manifests Himself in a series of visions thoroughly charged with Jewish symbolism, Jewish prophecy, and a key link to the Jewish narrative in God's grand story. Were Gentiles a part of these fellowships? Of course they were. Am I advocating for some sort of tiered or elite status between the two groups? Of course not. What I am overemphasizing is the fact that this vision was directed specifically to the Jews of that day, with a timely message that was crucial to their understanding of what God was about to do in their midst. The Apostles never called themselves "Christians."[105] They would have considered themselves to have been enlightened Jews.[106]

"Thus in each local Church it would appear that there was an original nucleus of Jewish believers, and the attention of the Gentiles to the new faith was usually attracted in the first

---

[104] S. G. F. Brandon, M.A., D.D., *The Fall of Jerusalem and the Christian Church, A Study of the Effects of the Jewish Overthrow of A.D. 70 on Christianity* (London: S.P.C.K, 1951) p. 17, 21, 22.
[105] It was a name given to early followers of Jesus by Greeks. See Acts 11:26.
[106] See Acts 22 and 23.

instance through the controversy caused in the synagogue by the Christian exegesis of the Jewish scriptures to prove the unique status and vocation of Jesus [Acts 13:43-48; 14:1-4; 17:10-12; 18:5-8]. [We] shall do well to notice also that the author of the Acts in his presentation of the tradition of Christian Origins never gives any indication that the numbers of the Gentile converts were large, while he makes several statements about the considerable numerical strength of the Jewish Christians in Palestine [Acts 2:41, 47; 4:4; 6:1, 7; 9:31; 21:20; 1 Corinthians 15:6]."[107]

Revelation is the continuation of the discourse Jesus began in Luke 19, and Matthew 23 and 24. He picks up where he left off, addressing the same audience and fulfilling the very prophecies he spoke to them. The 40-year window was closing, and everything he prophesied concerning their nation was about to come to pass.

Moreover, Abaddon (Aramaic for "destruction"; Revelation 9:11), along with the son of Abaddon (lit. "son of destruction" in Aramaic; 2 Thessalonians 2:3), the instruments of their great calamity, were about to start their voyage toward their Holy Land right near where the seven churches were located. Across the Aegean Sea, once Nero had dispatched Vespasian and his son Titus from Greece to destroy Jerusalem, the seasoned general rode from Achaea in Greece, across the Hellespont, and through the cities of Asia Minor towards Judea.[108] The seven churches under John's care were perhaps the proverbial canaries in the mine, serving as the first warning signal to the inhabitants of the Holy Land.

TURKEY, ASIA MINOR, MAGOG

The plot of ground where the seven churches of Revelation dwelt upon (modern-day Turkey) has seen many empires rise and fall from the time after Noah's flood until now. Starting with the most recent, some notable ones included:

---

[107] S. G. F. Brandon, M.A., D.D., *The Fall of Jerusalem and the Christian Church, A Study of the Effects of the Jewish Overthrow of A.D. 70 on Christianity* (London: S.P.C.K, 1951) p. 28.
[108] Josephus, *Jewish Wars*, 2:20:1; 3:1:3.

- **Ottoman Empire**
- **Seljuk Empire**
- **Byzantine Empire** (this one is really important to Christians. They reigned for a literal 1,000 years. It is worth looking up online and learning about their history.)
- **Asia Minor**
- **Anatolia**
- **Magog** (cue the ominous music)
- **Hittite Empire** (Uriah, David's top soldier and husband of Bathsheba, was a Hittite.)

Yes, Magog is a part of the list. In Greek, Magog would have been known as the Lydian Kingdom (1200 BCE to 546 BCE).

"The prophetic biblical formula "Gog and Magog" links the name of Japheth's second son to Gyges king of Lydia, that land of Asia Minor that once belonged to the Persian Empire...

Gaels of Christian times asserted firmly that they descended from Magog... Their "invasions" of Britain invariably refer to maritime routes from Asia Minor to Britain. The Phoenician "ships of Tarshish" became an immediate dimension of this Japhethite dispersion."[109]

Gog, or Gyges, once reigned right where all the seven churches were. This guy was somewhat infamous, in a bad way, because he was evil.

"Magog could easily be identified as a war god but only after the Uruk-Aratta war, not in the pre-colonization period. In the Uruk-Aratta war Magog undoubtedly led one of the griffin armies including ancestors of the Egyptians as well as Semites. Anhur was conceived as spiritual leader of the Egyptian army. We have now seen Magog in the role of three different Egyptian gods--- Anubis, Shu and Anhur."[110]

---

[109] Pilkey, John, Noah's Family Speaks: Postdiluvian History from Noah to Abraham, Genesis 10-11 Studies Book 2 (Anacortes: R. S. Marshall, 1984). Kindle Edition.
[110] Ibid.

GOG, GYGES, GUG: IT'S ALL THE SAME

Make no mistake, Gog/Gyges was a real person. Because Gog/Gyges reigned in Lydia (Western part of Asia Minor, where John's churches were) he was commonly known as Gyges of Lydia, or Gug of Ludu.

> "[Magog's brother] Gomer (Ezekiel 38:5 - Cimmerians) was an enemy of the Assyrians that invaded ancient Asia Minor by coming down from the north around the 8th century BC. The Assyrians called the barbarous invading Cimmerians (Gomer) "creatures of hell."
>
> These nations all coexisted in Asia Minor (modern Turkey) at a time when Magog (also known as Ludu or Lydia in both the Bible and the Assyrian texts) was led by a militant leader called Gog (685-652 BC), about 100 years before the Book of Ezekiel was written. Gog is the Hebrew spelling for the name of this militant leader from western Asia Minor, who was known as Gyges of Lydia to the Greeks. This same leader was known as "Gugu, king of Ludu" and "Gugu, King of Lydia" to the Assyrians...
>
> In the Assyrian language "the land of Gugu" is rendered as Ma-gugu, just as "the land of Zamua" is rendered as Ma-zamua. The Hebrew spelling of Magugu is "Magog," and thus, "Magog" simply means "the land of Gog." When Ezekiel 38:2 refers to Gog from the land of Magog, as the chief prince of Meshech and Tubal, scripture refers to a specific geographic area – Asia Minor; to a specific time period- when Magog (Lydia), Meshech, and Tubal were coexistent; and to a specific ruler – Gog (Gyges to the Greeks) – who led the defensive efforts of Magog, Meshech and Tubal against invading Gomer (the Cimmerians)."[111]

If you check out this cool document called "The Ancient Records of Assyria", or the "Assyrian Royal Court Records," these records dating back

[111] Goodman, Jeffrey. *The Comets of God - New Scientific Evidence for God: Recent archeological, geological and astronomical discoveries that shine new light on the Bible and its prophecies* (Tucson: Archeological Research Books, LLC., 2011), p. 338-339, Kindle Edition.

to 700 BC also mention Gyges of Lydia/Gog of Magog:

> "Guggu (Gyges), king of Lydia, a district of the other side of the sea, a distant place, whose name, the kings, my fathers, had not heard, Assur, the god, my creator, caused to see my name in a dream. "Lay hold of the feet of Assurbanipal, king of Assyria and conquer thy foes by calling upon his name,"

> On the day that he beheld this vision, he dispatched his messenger to bring greetings to me [King Assurbanipal]…

> He sent his forces to the aid of Tushamilki, king of Egypt, who had thrown off the yoke of my sovereignty. I heard of it and prayed to Assur and Ishtar, saying: "May his body be cast before his enemy, may (his foes) carry off his limbs." The Cimmerians, whom he had trodden underfoot, by calling upon my name, invaded and overpowered the whole of his land. His son seated himself upon his throne, after him (i.e., his death)"[112]

Now, Greek historians and philosophers like Herodotus, Plutarch and Plato also wrote of Gog/Gyges/Guggu. In short, Japheth bore a son who, from the little history we can gather, was known as a military leader, and according to Greek legend, an usurper who assassinated his king to seize the throne. Also worth noting is that the capital city of the Gog/Gyges/Guggu kingdom in Lydia was *Sardis* (Revelation 3:1).

WHY THIS REGION?

If Asia Minor had such a dark history, why would God come to the Messianic communities in this region and bestow upon them such a powerful message from Jesus through John? Here are some thoughts:

Though the land of Canaan was cursed (Genesis 9:25), God sent Abraham anyway. And in this cursed land, God established the people of Israel, the city of Jerusalem, and the Holy Temple. So isn't it just like God to take a land like Asia Minor, plant his church there, and make it the new epicenter of the early church?

In case you didn't know, Constantinople (modern-day Istanbul,

---

[112] Luckenbill, Daniel David. *Ancient Records of Assyria and Babylnia Volume II* (Chicago: The University of Chicago Press, 1927) p. 297–298, e-book.

previously called Byzantium), which was in Asia Minor, could be likened to Jerusalem in the sense of religious authority and significance in the early church. Have you heard of the Council of Nicaea or the Nicaean Creed? That all took place in Asia Minor! As Westerners, when we think of early church we think of Rome. But this is not the case. After Jerusalem fell, it was Asia Minor, not Rome, that became the central hub for 1,000 years.

Since God took the cursed land of Canaan and established His people there, it stands to reason He would do the same with Asia Minor, establishing it as the center for religious leadership and thought. Now, I am not suggesting that Constantinople replaced Jerusalem, or Asia Minor replaced Israel. ABSOLUTELY NOT! Romans 9 to 11 will still come to pass. Although it's important to state that though Asia Minor was a *launch pad* for a new chapter in God's grand love story, it was not the final destination. But for a season, it served a purpose.

With that said, let us turn our attention to each of the seven cities mentioned in Revelation.

7 SEVEN LOVE LETTERS: CHAPTERS 2 – 3

"The things which will soon take place."
— *Revelation 1:1*

EPHESUS

Paul's letter to the Ephesians refers to the famous church of Ephesus! To the Ephesians Paul wrote, "[I have] heard of the faith in the Lord Jesus which exists among you and your love for all the saints." (Ephesians 1:15). This theme of love is one that Jesus picks up on below. For context, you may liken Ephesus to Boston, Massachusetts. It was a major port city, a large center for trade, and boasted massive agoras (shopping malls). Ephesus even superseded Pergamum as the Roman capital of Asia Minor in the mid-first-century AD. It was also home to the goddess Artemis, the "goddess of love." Her temple was huge, and idol-worshippers came from all over to pay homage and employ the services of the temple harlots.

One textual note before we begin. At the start of each letter you will read, "To *the messenger (or angel) of the congregation*," which is the literal Aramaic translation. Historically, we know this was a direct reference to the Jewish assemblies of their day. In the synagogues, "there was the *Sheliach Tsibbur* or 'messenger of the congregation,' who read the prayers."[113] This messenger could also be known as the "angel of the assembly."[114] Bottom line: Jesus was originally addressing a predominately Jewish audience.

REVELATION 2:1–7

"And to the messenger[115] who is in the messianic community[116] of Ephesus write: 'Thus says he who holds the seven stars in his hand, he who walks amongst the menorahs of gold:

'I know your works, and your toil, and your patience, and that you are not able to tolerate evil, and you have tested those who say to themselves that they are Apostles, and they are not, and you have found them false. And you have patience and you have endured because of my name and you have not grown weary.

'Except there is this that concerns me about you:[117] That first love of yours, you abandoned it. Cause yourself to remember where you stepped away from it, and do the first works.

---

[113] De Witt Burton, Ernest. *The Ancient Synagogue Service*, Vol. 8, No. 2 (Aug., 1896), p. 143-148 Published by: The University of Chicago Press.
[114] See, *Palestine: The Physical Geography And Natural History Of The Holy Land*, by Kitto, John, London: Charles Knight & Co., Very Good. 1841, p. 806; Samuel Burder, *Oriental Customs*, Michigan: University of Michigan, 1923, p. 387;
[115] Identical to the Hebrew, malak (Strong's H4397), messenger is the same word for angel. It carries a missional or occupational sense. Context determines if we use angel or messenger. Because Jesus is speaking to John, it wouldn't make sense for John to then relay the Lord's words to heaven's angels. Rather, the first century Jews are being commissioned to share with one another these exhortations.
[116] As noted earlier, 'Idoto', is one word, literally meaning "an assembly of witnesses." In Greek, ecclesia, what we call "church" today. I have chosen to add context into the translation: these were assemblies or communities of believers who bore witness, or testified, to the fact that Jesus was the Messiah. They were communities *of* the Messiah, hence, messianic communities.
[117] "That concerns me about you" is the most literal translation. The word עַל (Strong's G5228) matches the Hebrew, and can mean upon, over, unto, against, toward, or concerning. Context is king. See Matthew 4:6, "He will command His angels *concerning* thee.," not *against* thee. I can't imagine Love-Incarnate coming *against* His beloved who is suffering for His namesake. Rather, I see compassionate advice, so that the enemy is not able to find a foothold and gain leverage against them.

'If however you don't, I will come for your sake,[118] and I will cause a shaking[119] of your menorah, if you don't restore yourself. Except you have this to your credit: That you are detesting the works of the Nicolaitans,[120] those things which I myself am also detesting.

'He who has ears, let him hear what the Spirit is speaking to the messianic communities. And to he who is in victory[121] I will give from the tree of life to eat, which exists in the Paradise of God.'"

SMYRNA

Smyrna could be likened to Miami, Florida. It is situated on the Aegean coast, and enjoys a favorable climate. The region had a large Jewish population, leading to hostility towards those among them who embraced Yeshua as their Messiah. Smyrna was also home to Polycarp, an incredible

---

[118] "For your sake" is the same word, עַל (Strong's G5228), "concerning," as above. However a literal translation, "I will come concerning you," misses the meaning. "For your sake" stays true to the root work, but is smoother in English.

[119] It is impossible for the word to imply that Jesus will "remove" the church. The Aramaic root is based on trembling, like an earthquake. So the image is that of something being shaken, stirred, or be moved about.

[120] The seventh-century Western Church Father Isidore of Seville wrote in *Etymologies, Book 8, The Church and Sects*: "The Nicolaites (Nicolaita) are so called from Nicolaus, deacon of the church of Jerusalem [Acts 6:5], who, along with Stephen and the others, was ordained by Peter. He abandoned his wife because of her beauty, so that whoever wanted to might enjoy her; the practice turned into debauchery, with partners being exchanged in turn." Stephen A. Barney, W. J. Lewis, J. A. Beach and Oliver Berghof (ed.), *The Etymologies of Isidore of Seville* (Cambridge University Press, 2006), p. 175.

[121] This is mind-blowing: the root word means clear, guiltless, righteous, deserving, or worthy (see Marcus Jastrow's, pp. 397) in Talmudic and Midrashic literature. But in the Peshitta, it seems to have carried an implication that to be righteous was to be victorious or to have overcome (see J. Payne Smith's pp. 115). In short, the victory is a theological one, afforded vicariously through the death and resurrection of Jesus. We are living *from* victory, *His* victory, which affords us right standing. An amplified translation might read, "to he who is living from Christ's victory." Hence, "in victory" (the Aramaic has a participle, but -ing would be awkward, so I've added "in" at the front of "victory" to reflect the concept that we are constantly in Christ's victory).

early church father who was a direct disciple of John the Apostle. He, and several other believers, faced great persecution and death in Smyrna.

REVELATION 2:8–11:

"And to the messenger who is of the messianic community of Smyrna write: 'Thus says the First and the Last, he who was dead and lives.

'I know your hardship and your poverty – except you are rich! – and of the blasphemy of those who say to themselves, "Judaic! Judaic!"[122] when they are not, except they are of the synagogue of Satan.

'Do not fear at any point that which is being schemed for you to experience. Behold! The Devil is scheming[123] to have you thrown into the jail house; he will be testing you, and there will be suffering to you for ten days – be faithful unto death, and I will give to you a crown of life.

'He who has ears, let him hear what the Spirit is speaking to the messianic communities. He who is in victory will not be litigated[124] by a second death.'"

PERGAMUM

Pergamum was to its region what Hollywood is to us; but celebrities back then weren't movie stars, they were the gods. In Pergamum you would have found temples and shrines dedicated to all the major deities of the day: Zeus, Dionysius, Demeter, Asclepius, Trajan, Isis, Athena, and so on. People

---

[122] BFBS has "Jewish," or "Judeans." But the Crawford "Judaic" makes more sense.

[123] The Syriac adds two instances of the same verb, "Schemed" and "Scheming." This is fascinating. The text seeks to make clear that plans of evil come from Satan, not God! See 1 John 1:5 and James 1:17.

[124] The Aramaic נֶהַר (Strong's G2873) has a legal sense, and can mean to dispute, to wrong, or to litigate. While I understand translators who take this to mean a suffered wrong or harm, it is more theologically accurate to maintain the legal tone, since Jesus has manifested Himself as High Priest to those who were once under the curse of the Law, and stand to watch their country suffer litigation from the Law.

flocked from all over the Roman Empire to consult with mediums, ask for healing powers to overcome illnesses, and participate in rituals. Hence, Pergamum was Satan's throne.

REVELATION 2:12–17

"And to the messenger who is in the messianic community of Pergamum write: 'Thus says he who has the sharp sword of two edges of His mouth.[125]

'I know where you dwell, a region where Satan has his throne. But you are holding tight in my name, and have not denied my faith, and in the days when you and my faithful witness contended for the sake of all my faithful witnesses, he was murdered among you,[126] and was made a spectacle where Satan dwells.[127]

'Except there is a small thing that concerns me about you, that there are those who are holding tight to the doctrine of Balaam, him who taught Balak to throw a stumbling block before the children of Israel: to eat sacrifices of idols and to commit fornication.[128]

---

[125] "Of his mouth" is found in the Syriac, but not in BFBS.

[126] "And in the days... among you." This translation is from David Bauscher. He comments, "Greek has 'of Antipas.' 'Antipas' in Aramaic would be opytna, opyjna or oapytna. Frankly this does not look like any Aramaic word in the text, so I don't see the explanation for the Greek reading based on word similarity in Aramaic. I do see that the Aramaic verse speaks of 'My witness' and does not name him. This may have presented a problem to a Greek translator who also played the role of editor as well. A second phrase – 'for the sake of all My witnesses' is missing in the Greek texts. After careful inspection, I saw that 'for the sake of all' – 'Mettul d'col' was probably translated as the Greek name Antipav – 'Antipas,' which strange to say, means 'For the cause of all,' from two Greek words, anti – 'for, instead of, for the cause of' + pav – 'all, every'. So, may the Greek translator have put a name to 'My witness' as 'Antipas.'" *The Aramaic English Interlinear Peshitta Bible*, p. 2745.

[127] "Was made a spectacle where Satan dwells" is found in BFBS.

[128] This fornication equals idolatry formula takes place twice in Revelation (here, and 2:18-29), and is a clearly Hebraic allusion. The Israel story, time after time, depicts the children of Abraham being led into idolatry by way of fornication. Solomon is perhaps the greatest illustration of this. Moreover, citing Jewish sources, Pseudo-Philo's recounting of the Balaam narrative follows this fornication equals idolatry pattern: "And then Balaam said to him 'Come let us plan what you

'There are also those of you who are holding tight to the doctrine of the Nicolaitans, in like manner.[129]

'Repent therefore, but if not, I will come for your sake, immediately, and I will cause them to have an encounter[130] with the sword of my mouth.

'Now he who has ears, let him hear what the Spirit is speaking to the messianic communities. To he who is in victory, I will give of the manna that is hidden, and I will give him a small white stone, and upon the small stone, a new name,[131] whose inscription no man knows but he who receives it.'"

THYATIRA

You can think of Thyatira as a blue-collar city, much like Detroit. And in the same way blue-collar cities are known to have strong unions, Thyatira had several trade guilds. But these guilds came with spiritual practices associated with them (i.e. Freemasons), and the worship of Apollo, the local deity, was customary. Lydia, from Acts 16:14, was from Thyatira, and she was a textile trader.

---

should do to them. Pick out the beautiful women who are among us and in Midian, and station them naked and adorned with gold and precious stones before them. And when they see them and lie with them, they will sin against their LORD and fall into your hands; for otherwise you cannot fight against them'" (Ps-Philo 18:13-14 [Harrington, OTP]).

And the Testament of Reuben suggests that fornication leads to idolatry: "So then, my children, observe all the things that I commanded you, and do not sin, for the sin of promiscuity is the pitfall of life, separating man from God and leading toward idolatry, because it is the deceiver of the mind and the perceptions, and leads youths down to hell before their time" (Test. Reub. 4:6-7 [Kee, OTP]).

[129] As the footnote in the letter to the Ephesians indicated, the practices of the Nicolaitans was linked to fornication and spiritual practices ("doctrine").

[130] Most Bible's read, "make war." This is poor theology and a misuse of the text. The word means "to join, to come near, to touch." See Marcus Jastrow's, p. 1410. The Aphel Imperative denotes causative verb, hence, "cause them to encounter."

[131] This mention of a small stone with a name upon it would have easily reminded the Jewish reader of God's blueprints for Aaron's priestly garments in Exodus 28:6-14: "Take two onyx stones and engrave on them the names of the sons of Israel." But here the stones are no longer black (onyx), but they are white, since they are no longer guilty of sin, but washed clean by the blood of Jesus.

REVELATION 2:18–29

"And to the messenger who is in the messianic community which is in Thyatira write, 'Thus says the Son of God, he who has eyes like flames of fire and his feet like the brass of Lebanon.[132]

'I know your works, and your love, and your faith, and your servanthood, and your perseverance; and your latter works are greater than the first.

'Except there is a great thing that concerns me about you, because you condone your wife[133] Jezebel[134] who says concerning herself that she is a prophetess,[135] and she teaches and causes my servants be deceived,[136] to be fornicating[137] and

---

[132] The Greek has "burnished brass," likely in an attempt to explain the metaphor rather than translate it literally. Residents and descendants of the Fertile Crescent and surrounding regions would not have needed the explanation.

[133] The Byzantine Greek mss. (Majority text) agrees with the Aramaic, "your wife," instead of "that woman." Note also that this is of **great** concern.

[134] Who was Jezebel? This passage needs to be understood in light of Rev 3:10, that an hour of testing was to come (at that time) upon the Known World and the Land of Israel. Jezebel was mostly likely a personification of Israel, as John's prophecy was for a Jewish audience and in the spirit and tradition of his prophetic forerunners: See Isaiah 50:1; Ezekiel 16:1-63; Jeremiah 3:1-25; Zechariah 5:5-11; Hosea 1:3 (and also Galatians 4:21–31). John does this again in Revelation 17–19, personifying Israel as a great harlot. **"Jezebel" here may also be a specific reference to the religious leadership within the Holy Land** and their relationship to the rulers (like king Ahab) over Judea and surrounding regions, as they were Roman puppet kings. This led to compromises of the Law (offering Roman sacrifices in the Temple) and a hardness of heart (see John 19:6–15).

[135] Another juxtaposition is presented here: Jezebel in the OT tried to violently silence the voice of the prophets in Israel. Here, presuming Jezebel is apostate Israel, is attempting to silence the prophetic voices of Jesus' followers by imposing her "prophetic" voice and deceptive Law-based doctrine (see Galatians 3).

[136] This is the exact same verb used to describe the deception that Satan was restrained from causing in Revelation chapter 20. Another translation could be, "causes my servants to forget/wander in err."

[137] Fornication here is "less likely a literal charge than a metaphor describing her positive relations with Greco-Roman society" (*The Jewish Annotated New Testament, Second Edition*, ed. Amy-Jill Levine and Marc Zvi Brettler), Accordance electronic ed. (New York: Oxford University Press, 2017), p. 544). Adultery is often also a metaphor for idolatry. See Jeremiah 3.6–11. This may also hint at systemic hypocrisy. Take for instance the infamous story in the Mishnah of Rabban Gamliel,

eating the sacrifices of idols.[138]

'But I gave her time for repentance,[139] and she did not desire to return from her fornication.

'Behold! I will throw her down[140] onto a death bed[141], and those

---

who visited a bathhouse in Acre (west of Galilee) which featured a nude statue of Aphrodite, the goddess of sexuality. "Idolatry thus is no longer about the actual making and worshipping of idols. It is, rather, a metaphor for what happens whenever a Jew loses his or her focus upon the tenets and ideals of the covenant with God." Avery-Peck, Alan J., "Idolatry in Judaism", in: Encyclopedia of Judaism. Consulted online on 11 May 2018.
http://dx.doi.org.proxy.lib.umich.edu/10.1163/1872 9029_EJ_COM_0080
[138] While Jesus walked the earth, the Temple rulers had instituted daily sacrifices to the Roman Emperors, who were considered to be divine. As Josephus recounts, "Petronius then quieted them, and said to them, 'Will you then make war against Caesar?' The Jews said, 'We offer sacrifice twice every day for Caesar, and for the Roman people'" (Wars; 2:10:4). This was most likely a Zevach Sh'lamim, a Peace Offering, since it was political tokenism between Rome and Judea. **Peace Offerings were eaten by the priests and their families**. The seduction then, seems to be a societal easing toward Roman culture and religious practices (Lev 17.10–14). The mix between Judea and Rome is further illustrated in Revelation 17 to 20.
[139] This time of repentance was the forty-year window, from 30 to 70 AD, where the New Covenant and Old Covenant periods overlapped. The end of the Old Covenant period was marked by the destruction of the Temple in Jerusalem, causing animal sacrifices to literally cease from that day forward. I speak of the forty-year transition period at length in my book, *Revelation: Dawn of This Age*.
[140] Same verb used in Revelation 20:3. But here, Jesus is not "throwing down" in anger. He is the same yesterday, today and forevermore. He is the one who raised the woman caught in adultery (John 8:2–11). He is the one who could have extinguished the life of Saul of Tarsus because he killed the first followers of Jesus. Yet Jesus instead came to Saul in love, and loved covered over a multitude of sin. And even though Israel was subject to the consequences of violating the Law of Moses, Romans chapters 9, 10 and 11 reminds us of God's grand love story; "all Israel shall live" (Aramaic text, Romans 11:26).
[141] The Aramaic here is "bier," a mobile cot for the dead (see Luke 7:14). The Greek uses κλίνη (Matthew 9:2, Luke 5:18), a cot for the lame and sick. But the context clearly prefers the Aramaic. The word image is that Jezebel is to be carried on a bier to a funeral pyre, a place of burning the dead. This metaphor may also be an illusion to the Gehenna fire of Jeremiah (Jeremiah 7:31–32, 32:35, 19:2–6, 19:11–14), which is echoed by Jesus (Matthew 23:33), which became a symbol of Jerusalem being burned to the ground by a foreign power (Babylon, then Rome) as a result of the fires of idolatry lit within the hearts of God's covenant people.

who commit adultery with her into great oppression,[142] except that they repent of their works.[143]

'And her sons I will have executed by a penalty of death[144], and all the messianic communities will know that I search the reins and the hearts, and I will give to every one of you according to your works.[145]

'I say to you and to the rest who are in Thyatira, all of those who do not have this doctrine, those who have not "known the depths of Satan," as they say, I won't throw down, concerning you, another burden.

'That which you have, therefore, be holding fast until I come.

'Now to him who is in victory and practices my works, I shall give authority over the peoples,

'to shepherd them with a staff of iron[146], and like the vessels of a potter you will shape[147] them in the same manner I have also

---

[142] Referring to the Roman invasion of Judea from 67 to 70 AD, resulting in the massacre of (according to Josephus) over 1,000,000 Jews, and the enslavement of tens of thousands. The oppression did not come because Jesus ran out of patience. Rather, it was a prophetic fulfilment based on the words of Moses and the contractual obligations of the Law, outlined in Deuteronomy 28:15–68, 29:22–30:10, 31:14–22, and 32:1–43.

[143] This repentance is explained in Galatians 3:10 and 4:21–31, and was specific to a Jewish audience.

[144] This is a difficult passage to translate. The root word is from the Hebrew, "to cut," in the sense of using a sword on an enemy. But word here אֶקְטוֹל has a judicial sense, like a judge finding someone guilty of the death penalty (see William Jennings' Lexicon pp. 102, and Marcus Jastrow's p. 1349). What is emphatic here is that we do not have Jesus slaughtering someone because they did not repent. Rather, it is a judicial action based on the covenantal obligations of the Law.

[145] Jesus giving according to "their works" can only mean the Law, since Jesus followers stand in accordance with His works by faith. An alternate translation from the Crawford Codex may be: "I search the bride and the heart, and I give to you as women bridal veils, according to your works." Because this is based on Greg Glaser's transcription alone, I don't yet have the confidence to make it official. Nevertheless, it fits the theme of Hagar and Sarah, the Bride and the Whore, prevalent in Jeremiah and Revelation.

[146] Iron means unbreakable authority, whereas wood would be subject to fractures.

[147] The primary definition of this word is to "grind," as one who sharpens a blade or one who crushes wheat in a mill. Given the context of pottery (the word can

received of my Father.[148]

'And I shall give him the Star of the Morning.[149]

'He who has ears, let him hear what the Spirit is speaking to the messianic communities.

SARDIS

The Sardis region was well known for its abundance of gold, much like the Sierra Nevada during the California gold rush. Like all the other regions in the seven love letters, Sardis also had a very large Jewish community and even a prominent synagogue.[150] Sardis was founded by the Lydian king Gyges, which translates to Gog (of Magog) in Hebrew. Interestingly, the Persian King Cyrus II (aka Cyrus the Great) later sacked the city through a hidden entrance, coming unexpectedly, "like a thief in the night."

REVELATION 3:1–6

And to the messenger who is in the messianic community of Sardis write, 'Thus says he who has to Himself sevenfold Spirit[151] of God and seven stars. I know your works and the

---

also mean clay), the implication is the same, to grind or shape in order to make something better and more useful (a sharp blade or flour for bread).

[148] Verses 26 and 27 speak of the Great Commission to disciple nations. And we do this in the manner of Ephesians 4:11–15, the five-fold ministry, "for the equipping of the saints for the work of ministry, for the building up of the body of Christ; until we all attain to the unity of the faith, and of the knowledge of the Son of God, to a mature man, to the measure of the stature which belongs to the fullness of Christ." We shepherd like the Good Shepherd: "As the Father has sent me, so I send you" (John 20:21).

[149] Jesus is the Morning Star (Numbers 24:17; 2 Peter 1:19; Revelation 22;15), and he gives himself to us! "Therefore be imitators of God, as beloved children; and walk in love, just as Christ also loved you and **gave Himself up for us**" (Ephesians 5:1–2). Historically, messianic imagery was often affiliated with celestial object. For instance, the second-century Jewish messianic figure Simeon Bar Kochba ("son of the star").

[150] Josephus, *Antiquities*, 14.235,259–61.

[151] Also found in Revelation 1:4, "sevenfold Spirit" can be translated literally as "seven Spirits." Again, this is thoroughly Jewish language. See 1 Enoch 20.1–8; or

name that you have, and those of you who are alive, and those of you who are dead.

'Now wake up and prop up the remainder of those who are ready to die, [152] for I have not found your works to be made complete before God.[153]

Cause yourself to remember what you heard and received; take heed and return.[154] But if you do not wake up, I will come for your sake as a thief, and you will not know what hour I will come for your sake.[155]

'But I have a few names in Sardis, those who have not stained their priestly garments, and they walk before me in white and they are worthy.

'He who overcomes thusly is clothed with a white priestly garment[156], and I shall not erase his name from the Book of

---

the liturgical text from Qumran Cave 4, 4 QShirShabb (Songs of the Sabbath Sacrifice).

[152] "The one who has found his life will lose it, and the one who has lost his life on My account will find it." Matthew 10:39 (also 16:25). Those who are dead in verse 1 are those who have not been born again. They are still dead in their sins. Those ready to die are those ready to be born again, they put to death the flesh in order to come alive (Romans 8:13). John uniquely develops the notion of a First Death, Second Death, and First and Second Resurrections in both his Gospel and Revelation. I discuss this at length in *Revelation: Dawn of All Hope*.

[153] This is what Paul called "dead works" (Hebrews 6:1; 9:14; Philippians 3:4-9), which is to live an outward life of piety without the inward regeneration of the Spirit (Ephesians 2:8-10; Heb.11:6). See also John 3:35–36.

[154] "what you heard and received." This is almost a direct quote from First John 1:1–3. In other words, "remember all the things John taught you about Me (Jesus)!"

[155] There is a layered implication here: to the immediate audience, Jesus will come much like Cyrus, and will bring a refiner's fire and launder's soap to his people in Sardis, calling them higher and maturing them into His image (Malachi 3:2; Romans 8:29). In broader context, Jesus was coming to oversee the fulfilment of his prophetic words in Matthew 23 and 24 (and Luke 19:28–44; 21:5–24): the fulfillment of Deuteronomy 28:15–68, 29:22–30:10, 31:14–22, and 32:1–43. And the Roman invasion in 67 AD was unexpected, like a thief in the night.

[156] Here and in 3:4 above, the word "priestly" in not in the text, but it is implied, so I have added it ("priestly garment"). When the Sanhedrin, a tribunal in Judea, judged a priest to be fit for service, he was clothed in white. See Samuel Burder, *Oriental Customs*, Michigan: University of Michigan, 1923, p. 387. Thus, when we are

Life,[157] and I shall confess his name before my Father and before his angels.[158]

'He who has ears, let him hear what the Spirit is speaking to the messianic communities."

PHILADELPHIA

Philadelphia, to me, is much like the Philly of the 1970s portrayed in the first *Rocky* movie: a blue-collar region with down-an-out people struggling to recover economically. The Biblical Philadelphia suffered physical and financial devastation caused by a series of earthquakes.[159] The city was also renamed twice: first, to Neocaesarea (New Caesar), and perhaps just months or short years after John wrote these words, to Flavius. The second name was after the new Roman emperor Vespasian, the 'Nebuchadnezzar' who started the campaign against Israel that his son Titus would finish. This "new name" reference will come up again shortly in the text below. Lastly, the "synagogue of Satan"[160] here gives us a clue to the strong adversity Jewish followers of Jesus would have faced from their fellow kinsmen in the region.

---

born anew in Jesus, we become a royal priesthood (Isaiah 61:6; Exodus 19:6; 1 Peter 2:9; Revelation 1:6).

[157] The notion of a "Book of Life" is not unique to John. It is in fact a key symbol of Jewish identity, taking us all the way back to Exodus: "But now, if You will forgive their sin, very well; but if not, please wipe me [Moses] out from Your book which You have written!" However, the Lord said to Moses, "Whoever has sinned against Me, I will wipe him out of My book. But go now, lead the people where I told you. Behold, My angel shall go before you; nevertheless on the day when I punish, I will punish them for their sin" (Exodus 32:32–34). The context of Exodus 32 is the sin of the Golden Calf, and Moses trying to make atonement for their sin (32:30). He was unable, because only Jesus would be able to make atonement for the sin of Israel (read all of Hebrews!).

[158] A reminder of the words of Jesus in Matthew 10:32 and Luke 12:8.

[159] Pliny, Nat. 2.86.200; Strabo, Geogr. 12.8.18; 13.4.10.

[160] In no way does this reference to a "synagogue of Satan" suggest that John became anti-Semitic. John was a Jew through and through. It simply suggests that Jesus was exposing the hearts of a certain group of people in a specific region. For instance, Satan was able to penetrate the heart of Judas because of his hardness of heart, causing Him to betray Jesus (John 13:27). Hardness of heart therefore could have led this group of people to fall under the same deception that blinded Saul of Tarsus, leading him to persecute the Saints.

REVELATION 3:7-13

"And to the messenger of the messianic community of Philadelphia write: 'Thus says the Holy Truth, he who has the key of David, who opens and there is none who shuts, and he shuts and there is none who opens.[161]

'I know your works, and behold! I have given an open door before you which no man can shut, because you have little power, and you have practiced my word and have not denied my name.[162]

'And behold! I have given from the synagogue of Satan, those who say concerning themselves that they are Jews and are not, but they are lying, behold! I will make them come and prostrate themselves before your feet,[163] and they will know that I burn with love for you.[164]

'For the sake of you who keep the word of my perseverance, I will also keep you from the trial that is foreordained to come upon all of the Known World[165], to test the inhabitants of The

---

[161] Quoted from David Bauscher, who comments: "The Crawford text of this verse conforms more closely to The Peshitta reading of Isaiah 22:22 than does the Greek or The Harklean Aramaic text, and also to the Hebrew present participles, "who shuts", "who opens", more closely than the Greek does. Even the Aramaic phrases & there is none who closes & there is none who opens are identical in The Peshitta of Isaiah where the black highlighted letters are shown in bold type, while the Harklean has 'no man shuts' and 'no man opens,' conforming to the Greek readings." *The Aramaic English Interlinear Peshitta Bible*, p. 2745.

[162] It is my belief that Jesus was taking something these Jews had experienced personally; the doors of the synagogue they once attended being shut in their face and their re-entry barred because they could not deny that Yeshua was the Messiah, and uses what the enemy meant for evil to catapult them into destiny.

[163] We have no known historical account of what this looked like. But we do know that God opposes the proud and gives grace to the humble.

[164] This word in Aramaic אַחֲבָת literally means to burn, or to be lit, with passionate love. How beautiful is the love of Jesus towards you and I!

[165] This is the first time in this book that we have come across a reference to a geographical region beyond Israel. Up to now, we have seen "The Land" הָאָרֶץ which typically refers to the Land of Israel. But now we have תֵּבֵל (H8398), the whole inhabitable world, or, the known world. Historically, this would have been synonymous with the Roman Empire, given its vast expanse. For instance,

Land.[166]

'I come immediately. Hold fast whatever you have, that no man take your crown.[167]

'And he who is in victory I will make them a pillar in the Temple of God,[168] and to the outside world he will not go to again[169], and I shall write upon him the Name of my God, and the name of the city – the New Jerusalem – which descends from my God,[170] and my new Name.[171]

Matthew 24:14, "This gospel of the kingdom shall be preached *in the whole world* as a testimony to all the nations, and then the end will come." Or, Colossians 1:5–6, "the gospel which has come to you, just as *in all the world* also it is bearing fruit." Revelation 3:11 picks up on the fulfillment of Matthew 24, as Paul confirms in Colossians 1.

[166] In contrast to the inhabited world, the Roman Empire, we shift back to The Land of Israel, since these prophecies are for them almost exclusively. An amplified translation might read, "I also shall keep you from the trial that is foreordained to come upon all of the Roman Empire, to test the Jewish inhabitants of the Land of Israel."

[167] The destruction of Israel (Judea at the time), known as the Jewish-Roman War, did not only affect the Jews within the Holy Land, but also abroad. Jews in places like Philadelphia would soon be targets of Roman hate as well: "The raising of the standard of revolt against Rome, however, had its repercussions throughout the whole of Palestine and a large part of the Diaspora... The news of the revolt, and especially of the slaughter of the Roman garrison at Jerusalem, had a disastrous consequence for the Jewish population. This bloody act naturally provoked Jewish reprisals. The Gentile cities of **Philadelphia**... were attacked, the neighbouring Syrian villages were laid waste, and without doubt Gentiles throughout Palestine generally perished as victims of Jewish fanaticism." S. G. F. Brandon, M.A., D.D., *The Fall of Jerusalem and the Christian Church, A Study of the Effects of the Jewish Overthrow of A.D. 70 on Christianity* (London: S.P.C.K, 1951) at 158.

[168] Flowing in line with the Roman invasion of Israel (also prophesied by Jesus in Luke 19:28–44 and 21:5–24), which resulted in the beloved Temple being destroyed, Jesus reminds them of a New Temple, his Bride (1 Corinthians 3:16–17; Ephesians 2:19–22; 1 Peter 2:5).

[169] Jesus speaks to both the Diaspora and those forced to leave Judea (either because of the current persecution, or the imminent Roman invasion), as a future hope that when He restores all things (Acts 1:6), they will no longer be displaced.

[170] See Revelation 21. It is important to note that Revelation ends with heaven coming down to this physical earth, and this earth becomes Eden once more!

[171] In the same way the Yahweh God renamed several Old Testament figures, and Jesus likewise with some of His disciples, we too, are given new names – that is to say, a new purpose and destiny as sons and daughters made in His image.

'Now he who has ears, let him hear what the Spirit is speaking to the messianic communities."

LAODICEANS

The Laodicean region was like Manhattan: rife with high rollers and bankers. A major center of commerce and trade, it had five agoras (shopping malls), and a 20,000 person auditorium. Citizens were so wealthy that when an earthquake in 66 AD devastated the city of Laodicea, they refused the Roman relief fund and used their own cash to rebuild the ruined city. Further to this point, you may have noticed that I called this letter, "Laodiceans," not, "Laodicea." This was intentional, and the explanation is in the footnote below.

It should not be a stretch to learn that Laodicea had a strong Jewish community.[172] The region was also known to be a medical hub, specifically for collyrium (eye-salve). Lastly, natural mineral water sources flowed in to Laodicea from Hierapolis (and still does today. Check it out online, it is stunning!), and water from Colossae; one source hot, the other cold. These water sources served as a powerful illustration in Jesus' admonition below.

REVELATION 3:14–22

"And to the messenger of the messianic community of the Laodiceans[173] write, 'Thus says the Amen, the Faithful and True Witness, and the Genesis[174] of the Creation of God.

---

[172] Josephus, *Antiquities*, 12.147–53.

[173] The Aramaic reads Laodiceans, not, Laodicea, referring to the people, not the place. Why? Because Laodicea, Colossae, and Hierapolis were destroyed by an earthquake in AD 66. Meaning there was no city to write to at the time, just the people who once lived in it, until it was rebuilt (see Thayer's Greek-English Lexicon under the entry for "Laodicea", and Bishop Lightfoot, *Colossians and Philemon*, p. 274–300). This supports a date as early as 66 AD for the writing of Revelation.

[174] The Aramaic and Hebrew are the same word, רֵאשִׁית (H7225) "the beginning." But the word goes much deeper than that. The Book of Genesis in the Torah is called בְּרֵאשִׁית "In The Beginning," named after the first words in the first sentence of the book (this is the case for all five books of the Pentateuch). Jesus was the author of creation, and therefore, He *is* the Genesis (John 1:3, 10; Colossians 1:16; Romans 11:36; Hebrews 1:2).

'I know your works; you are not cold and you are not hot. It would be best if you were either cold or were hot,[175]

'but you are lukewarm and neither cold nor hot.[176] I am preparing to be causing you to be restored[177] by my mouth,[178]

'because you said[179] that you are wealthy, and, "I have become powerful, and on account of nothing do I lack,"[180] but you are not knowing that you are weak, and miserable, and blind,[181] and

---

[175] By referring to the uniqueness of each source of water, Jesus ultimately leads his listeners to understanding that they cannot mix covenants (old wine vs. new). The waters from Hierapolis and Colossae were completely different from one another, and each served a purpose. But mixed together, the waters were useless for healing properties (hot mineral water) or for drinking (cold spring water). This mixing here is similar to the teaching found in Matthew 9:17 and Luke 5:35–39, and is powerfully illustrated by Jesus at the wedding in Cana (John 2:10).

[176] They were neither mindful of piety through their upbringing under the Law, nor were they pursuing a deeper relationship with Jesus. Rather, they were caught up in the Manhattan-like lifestyle of "money makes the world go 'round," and lost sight of their identity in Yahweh God through Yeshua.

[177] The Aramaic, מתבָּנָ, is in the Aphel (like the Hebrew Hiphil) Infinitive Construct, a causative action. The word itself means "to return," "to change direction," "to restore," "to answer," or, "to vomit." However, "vomit" has very few lexical examples, while the other translation options have several. Second, the same root word is used again in 3:19, but is translated as repent. So how can one be repent, and the other to vomit? And theologically, it doesn't fit the character of Jesus at all. See verse 19, "whom he has *compassion* for."

[178] Man does not live by bread (or material things), but by the word of life that proceed from the mouth of Jesus (Matthew 4:4; John 6:68). His Word would wash them like the mineral waters that flowed into the region (Ephesians 5:26).

[179] Because calamity came by their mouth, Jesus will restore by his mouth.

[180] Laodicea, a center for banking (think Manhattan), was well known for its affluence. Now, it was common for the Roman Empire to provide a relief fund for cities hit with natural disasters, such as earthquakes. But the Laodiceans were so wealthy that Tacitus, the Roman historian, writing of the effects of the 66 AD earthquake on Laodicea, remarked, "without any relief from us, [Laodicea] recovered itself from its own resources." Tacitus, Annals, 14:27.

[181] The Aramaic does not have both, "and poor, and blind," like the Greek, but just one. Most Aramaic translations opt for "poor" over "bind." But I have chosen "blind" for two reasons. First, as Bauscher notes, "The DSS Aramaic Simkat & Mim (each word has both letters in corresponding places) appear more similar to each other than the Estrangela counterparts s & m, thus making it more likely a translator would confuse the DSS script words than the Estrangela script words. The DSS letters (Yodh and Nun) are also much more similar (Yodh and Kap also) than in the other scripts" (*The Aramaic English Interlinear Peshitta Bible*, p. 2746). So

naked.

'My royal counsel to you:[182] Be buying from me gold proved by fire, that you may become wealthy, and be clothing yourself with white priestly garments, that you not unveil the shame of your nakedness, and be blinded by eye-salve, that you may see.

'I have compassion for those who I admonish and instruct. Be aroused to zeal therefore and return.'[183]

'Behold! I stand at the door and I am knocking. If a man listens to my voice and will open the door, then I will enter and I will dine with him, and he with me.[184]

'And he who is in victory I will grant him to be sitting with me upon my throne, just as I have overcome and I sit with my Father on his throne.

'Now he who has ears, let him hear what the Spirit is speaking to the messianic communities."

---

there is a likelihood of scribal error. Second, there are several synonyms for poverty in verse 17, so "poor" is unnecessary. Especially when Jesus provides the solution to all that hinders them, including sight. Also note that nakedness was a sign of extreme poverty.

[182] The word, מְלֹךְ, is based on the root, "king," or the root verb, "to reign." Thus, the variant, "to counsel," carries with it a monarchal tone, as the advice is coming from the King of Kings.

[183] This is a summons to a first-love encounter with Jesus, much like we read in the letter to the Ephesians. The abiding love that Jesus speaks of at length in John 15 and 17 is the key to maintaining the fires of God's love—stoked and ablaze.

[184] How beautiful is this picture of an invitation to intimate covenant union with Jesus! In the same way he broke the bread and sipped the wine of covenant with His disciples, we are invited to sit at that same table with Him in matrimonial intimacy (See also Exodus 24:1–18).

7 THE TRIUMPH OF THE CROSS: CHAPTERS 4 – 5

"He made you alive together with Him, having forgiven us all our wrongdoings, having canceled the certificate of debt consisting of decrees against us… having nailed it to the cross. When He had disarmed the rulers and authorities, He made a public display of them, having triumphed over them through Him."
—— *Colossians 2:13–15 (NASB)*

Perhaps one of the most beautiful moments I have had with Jesus while studying His Scriptures was back in 2018 when I was reading Revelation 4 and 5. My mind was caught up in imagining what it looked like; what it felt like to see what John saw. Suddenly, the scene in my mind changed, and I was watching John and Mary at the foot of the cross, beholding Jesus' in his final moments before offering up his life.

"Now beside the cross of Jesus stood His mother… So when Jesus saw His mother, and the disciple whom He loved standing nearby, He said to His mother, "Madam, behold, your son!" Then He said to the disciple, "Behold, your mother!" And from that hour the disciple took her into his own household." John 19:25–27 (NASB)

It was at that moment that I realized something: because John, the beloved friend of Jesus, endured until the end and witnessed the triumph of the cross from earth's perspective—which looked as if Jesus was defeated, humiliated, and killed from man's eyes,—years later John was invited to **see the exact same event**, the triumph of the cross, from heaven's perspective!

> *"After these things I looked, and behold, a door standing open in heaven, and the first voice which I had heard, like the sound of a trumpet speaking with me, said, "Come up here, and I will show you what must take place after these things." Immediately I was in the Spirit; and behold, a throne was standing in heaven, and someone was sitting on the throne."*
> *Revelation 4:1–2 (NASB)*

When John was invited to "come up here," his eyes were opened to see from above; a direct contrast to the view he had of the cross from below. While a few dozen men mocked Jesus from earth's perspective, millions upon millions of angels worshipped in heaven. While he was crucified like a criminal here, he was exalted as a king there!

I was in tears as I came to these realizations because I could see what John had first seen when Jesus was on the cross. Yet we know that for the joy set before Him, He endured the cross. You and I were His joy!

> *"Jesus, the originator and perfecter of the faith, who for the joy set before Him endured the cross, despising the shame, and has sat down at the right hand of the throne of God." Hebrews 12:2 (NASB)*

Therefore, I invite you now to not only read but envision the enthronement that followed the enfleshment of our Lord and Saviour, Jesus Christ, Yeshua Messiah. He is indeed the King of all Kings, Lord of all Lords, President of all Presidents, Prime Minister of all Prime Ministers! He is the God of all hope (Romans 15:13), so get your hopes sky high!

> *"For a Child will be born to us, a Son will be given to us;*
> *And the government will rest on His shoulders;*
> *And His name will be called Wonderful Counselor, Mighty God,*
> *Eternal Father, Prince of Peace.*
> *There will be no end to the increase of His government or of peace*
> *On the throne of David and over his kingdom,*
> *To establish it and to uphold it with justice and righteousness*
> *From then on and forevermore.*
> *The zeal of the Lord of armies will accomplish this."*
> *Isaiah 9:6–7 (NASB)*

Let us now behold the triumph of the cross from heaven's perspective.

REVELATION 5

"And one of the elders said to me, "Stop weeping; behold, the Lion that is from the tribe of Judah, the Root of David, has overcome so as to be able to open the scroll and its seven seals."

And I saw between the throne (with the four living creatures) and the elders a Lamb standing, as if slaughtered, having seven horns and seven eyes, which are the seven spirits of God sent out into all the earth. And He came and took the scroll out of the right hand of Him who sat on the throne…

Then I looked, and I heard the voices of many angels around the throne and the living creatures and the elders; and the number of them was myriads of myriads, and thousands of thousands, saying with a loud voice,

"Worthy is the Lamb that was slaughtered to receive power, wealth, wisdom, might, honor, glory, and blessing."

And I heard every created thing which is in heaven, or on the earth, or under the earth, or on the sea, and all the things in them, saying,

"To Him who sits on the throne and to the Lamb be the blessing, the honour, the glory, and the dominion forever and ever."

And the four living creatures were saying, "Amen." And the elders fell down and worshiped." Revelation 5:5–7, 11–14 (NASB)

How beautiful was that? Especially when compared to the suffering of the cross. Remarkably, Jesus wasn't done yet! He didn't ascend and retire. He is still at work:

"For as in Adam all die, so also in Christ all will be made alive. But each in his own order: Christ the first fruits, after that those who are Christ's at His coming, then comes the end, when He hands over the kingdom to our God and Father, when He has abolished all rule and all authority and power. For He must reign until He has put all His enemies under His feet. The last enemy that will be abolished is death."
1 Cor 15:22–26 (NASB)

The Aramaic reads that Jesus must be *continually reigning* until He has put all His enemies under His feet. He is not only on the throne, he is actively ruling from it, and every enemy of God is being crushed by Him, one by one. Because of this, we can co-labour with Christ, yoked to Him in meekness and humility (Matthew 11:28–30), and disciple the nations as he commissioned us to do (Matthew 28:18; Revelation 2:26–27).

This coronation ceremony is the context for everything that takes place in Revelation chapters 4 to 9; it is one long sequence of events. Chapters 10 and 11 then interject, and John shifts from being an observer of the unfolding of the Mosaic judicial system (more on this later) to being commissioned as a participant in the great story that was unfolding.

REVELATION 4: A THRONE ROOM ENCOUNTER

א *(v 1 – 2) "After these things I looked, and behold! A door opened in Heaven, and a voice which I heard like a shofar speaking with me saying, 'Ascend to here, and I shall show you that which is permitted to happen after these things.'*

And suddenly I was in the Spirit, and behold! A throne placed in Heaven, and upon the throne One sat."

One of the key takeaways from this passage are the words, "that which is permitted," as this is significant to our theological framework. Factoring in Deuteronomy 28–32[185], and Matthew 23–24[186], **we must understand that the upcoming legal proceedings of Revelation 5 to 9 are permissive in a legal sense, and are not events that are instigated vindictively.** When Jesus came on the scene, the 'courts of Moses' were adjourned. That adjournment lasted 40 years; a grace period to deliver those bound from the Law of Moses from the legal consequences found in Deuteronomy 28:15–68 for breach of covenant. This was part of the gospel Paul preached to fellow Jews:

"Or do you not know, brothers and sisters (for I am speaking to those who know the Law), that the Law has jurisdiction over a person as long as he lives? For the married woman is bound by law to her husband as long as he is alive; but if her husband dies, she is released from the law

---

[185] Deut. 28:15–68, 29:22–30:10, 31:14–22, and 32:1–43.
[186] Also Luke 19:28–44; 21:5–24.

concerning the husband. So then, if while her husband is alive she gives herself to another man, she will be called an adulteress; but if her husband dies, she is free from the law, so that she is not an adulteress if she gives herself to another man.

"Therefore, my brothers and sisters, you also were put to death in regard to the Law through the body of Christ, so that you might belong to another, to Him who was raised from the dead, in order that we might bear fruit for God... But now we have been released from the Law, having died to that by which we were bound." Romans 7:1–4, 6 (NASB)

Paul ties in the born-anew experience (John 3:3) with contractual freedom from the Law of Moses as the only way of escaping the consequences of Deuteronomy 28:15–68.

"[God] has made us sufficient to be ministers of a new covenant, not of the letter [of the Law] but of the Spirit. For the letter [of the Law] kills, but the Spirit gives life.

"Now if the ministry of death, carved in letters on stone, came with such glory that the Israelites could not gaze at Moses' face because of its glory, which was being brought to an end, will not the ministry of the Spirit have even more glory?" 2 Corinthians 3:6–8 (NASB)

When writing to the Galatians, Paul warns his Jewish kin in that community to beware of the life-threatening decision it is to bind oneself to the contractual obligations of the Law of Moses:

"O foolish Galatians! Who has bewitched you? It was before your eyes that Jesus Christ was publicly portrayed as crucified. Let me ask you only this: Did you receive the Spirit by works of the law or by hearing with faith?... For all who rely on works of the law are under a curse; for it is written, 'Cursed be everyone who does not abide by all things written in the Book of the Law, and do them.'... Christ redeemed us from the curse of the law by becoming a curse for us... Now before faith came, we were held captive under the law, imprisoned until the coming faith would be revealed. So then, the law was our guardian until Christ came, in order that we might be justified by faith."
Galatians 3:1, 2, 10, 13, 23, 24 (NASB)

Now this may have seemed like a long digression, **but to miss this point is to miss the entire book of Revelation.** Look around you today: Where can you go to offer sacrifices in accordance with the Law? Where is the High Priest to offer services in the Temple? It doesn't exist anymore. That is the whole point. All of the warnings in the New Testament were temporal and imminent to the Jewish audience of those days, **those who still had a choice to defect back to the sacrificial system of Moses.** That choice is not available today. That option ceased when Jerusalem and the Holy Temple were destroyed by the Romans in 70 AD. Those who stayed under that system perished with it; over 1,000,000 per Josephus' estimates. That is a big deal.

Taking inventory of the above mentioned items and pondering them carefully, consider now the opening verse of Revelation chapter 4 once again: "that which is permitted to happen." In Galatians 3:10, Paul warns of the curse of the Law (referencing Deuteronomy 28:15-68), and echoes the warnings of Jesus in Matthew 23:35–36, where He warns, "on you may come all the righteous blood shed on earth… Truly, I say to you, all these things will come upon this generation." He is referring to the 40-year period. Jesus' words in Matthew 23 were spoken just days before his crucifixion. From that time to 70 AD (when the Temple fell) was 40 years.

John ascends into the heavenly realm to witness the legal proceedings that took place to permit the contractual obligations of the Law of Moses to be satisfied, thereby ending that covenant once and for all. The "curse of the Law," as Paul said, was to be enabled. The calamities and woes in Revelation are simply the fulfilment of Deuteronomy 28–32, as Jesus and His disciples warned their kinsmen for 40 years. Jesus adjourned the courts of Moses at His advent; now, He alone has legal right to bring the court back into session. He will bring the covenant to a close.

"Christ has obtained a ministry that is as much more excellent than the old [covenant] as the covenant he mediates is better, since it is enacted on better promises. For if that first covenant had been faultless, there would have been no occasion to look for a second [covenant]…

In speaking of a new covenant, he makes the first one obsolete. **And what is becoming obsolete and growing old is ready to vanish away.***"* *Hebrews 8:6, 7, 13 (NASB)*

THE HIGH COURT WAS IN SESSION

"And I saw a strong angel proclaiming with a loud voice, 'Who is worthy to open the scroll and to break its seals?'

... And one of the elders said to me, "Stop weeping; behold, the Lion that is from the tribe of Judah, the Root of David, has overcome so as to be able to open the scroll and its seven seals."' Revelation 5:2, 5 (NASB)

Isaiah, Ezekiel and John each experienced a vision of God on His throne (Isaiah 6, Ezekiel 1, and Revelation 4). Visions are symbolic. Another thing these prophets had in common was that they were each summoned to prophesy the judgement and destruction of those under the Law of Moses: Isaiah to the Northern Kingdom of Israel, Ezekiel to the Southern Kingdom of Judah, and John to the ancient boundaries of both regions combined; which, in the days of John, became Judea, Samaria, and Galilee under Roman rule.

The throne of God represented a reprimand. For Israel, the reprimand consistently came in the form of a foreign super-power being given legal right to set foot on the Holy Land and destroy it. God called Ezekiel to warn of the Babylonian invasion, which led to the destruction of Solomon's Temple and Jerusalem. In Revelation, God calls John to warn of the Roman invasion, which would lead to the destruction of Herod's Temple (the 2nd Temple) and Jerusalem.

The events of Revelation 4 and 5 are the same events that Daniel saw in his vision at the end of the age he was living in:

"As I looked,
thrones were placed,
and the Ancient of Days took his seat;
...a thousand thousands served him,
and ten thousand times ten thousand stood before him;
the court sat in judgment,
and the books were opened.
...and behold, with the clouds of heaven
there came one like a son of man,
and he came to the Ancient of Days
and was presented before him.
And to him was given dominion
and glory and a kingdom,
that all peoples, nations, and languages
should serve him." Daniel 7:9, 10, 13, 14 (NASB)

As we read in Revelation 4 and 5, the Ancient of Days is enthroned, and Jesus, who refers to himself as 'the son of man,' comes to the Ancient of

Days to be crowned. Daniel's vision continues:

> *"[The horn] shall speak words against the Most High,*
> *and shall wear out the saints of the Most High,*
> **and shall think to change the times and the law;**
> *and they shall be given into his hand [see Revelation 2:10]*
> *for a time, times, and half a time.*
> *But the court shall sit in judgment,*
> *and his dominion shall be taken away,*
> *to be consumed and destroyed to the end.*
> *And the kingdom and the dominion*
> *and the greatness of the kingdoms under the whole heaven*
> *shall be given to the people of the saints of the Most High."* Daniel
> 7:25–27 (NASB)

The time had come for the age of Messiah to eclipse the age of Moses.

א *(v 9 – 10) "They praised a new praise[187], and they were saying, 'Worthy are You, Who takes the scroll and loosens its seals. Consider that you were sacrificed and you have bought us by your blood for Elohim from all Tribes, Gentiles, and ethnicities.[188]*

And you have made them to be for our Elohim——a Kingdom, Priests and Kings——and they shall reign upon the earth.'"

Those who wished to transition from the Law of Moses to the Law of the Spirit (Romans 8:2; James 1:25) inherited the first-fruits of the kingdom that Jesus was and still is establishing upon the earth. For those who did not heed the warnings of Moses in Deuteronomy 28 to 32, Jesus in Matthew 23 to 25, or his Apostles (like some of the Pauline Epistles I quoted above), the trial, prosecution, and execution would now commence. This court did not have

---

[187] *New song*, indicating a new beginning or new era; Isaiah 42.10; Ps 33.3; 40.3 (*The Jewish Annotated New Testament, Second Edition*, ed. Amy-Jill Levine and Marc Zvi Brettler, accordance electronic ed. New York: Oxford University Press, 2017, 549).
[188] It is important to see the dichotomy here. John hears the Galatians 3:28 phenomenon coming to pass: through Christ there is no longer Jew or Greek, male or female. All are one in Him. The word "tribes" implies Tribes of Israel, in contrast to the barbarian Gentiles (Greeks and Romans). Lastly, all other nations ("ethnicities") outside of the Roman empire (you and I) are also accounted for.

a judge's gavel, but rather a sealed scroll[189] that would be unsealed:

"Then I saw when the Lamb broke one of the seven seals."
Revelation 6:1a

Again, it must be stated that Jesus is not the one who is instigating. He is permitting the judicial system of the Law to run its course:

"Do not think that I will accuse you before the Father; the one who accuses you is Moses, in whom you have put your hope. For if you believed Moses, you would believe Me; for he wrote about Me."
John 5:45–46 (NASB)

THE TWO-SIDED SCROLL

Revelation 5:1 tells us that the scroll is inscribed on both sides. I believe that this symbolized both sides of the covenantal terms of the Law found in Deuteronomy 28: the blessings and the curses. On one side of the scroll we have the blessings (Deuteronomy 28:1-14), and on the other side the curses (Deuteronomy 28:15–58). The blessings of the Law are for those who inherit them through Jesus' finished work. "For Christ is the end of the Law [of Moses] for righteousness to everyone who believes" (Romans 10:4).

> "For in no way is anything called a "testament," unless those who are about to die make it, and it is sealed until the death of the testator, and after his death, it is opened. And so, after the death of Christ every mystery was revealed."[190]

On the other side of the scroll were the curses of the Law. Moses was the prosecutor (John 5:45). The verdict was sealed. The penalty was death (Hebrews 10:28; Romans 4:15, 8:2; 1 Corinthians 15:56; 2 Corinthians 3:6). "For all who rely on works of the law are under a curse; for it is written, 'Cursed be everyone who does not abide by all things written in the Book of the Law, and do them'" (Galatians 3:10).

> "This book [scroll] signifies the teaching of the Old Testament, which was given into the hands of our Lord, who accepted the

---

[189] Sealed scrolls were legal documents widely used in antiquity.
[190] Caesarius of Arles (468 AD), William C. Weinrich, eds. Revelation. vol. 12 of Ancient Christian Commentary on Scripture. ICCS/Accordance electronic ed. (Downers Grove: InterVarsity Press, 2005), p. 69.

judgment from the Father."[191]

However, this scroll may also be an allusion to the "flying scroll" found in the book of Zechariah 5. An angel revealed to the prophet that the scroll was a "curse that is going forth over the face of the entire land" (Zechariah 5:3). Soon after witnessing this scroll, Zechariah then sees four chariots of war with different colour horses (Zechariah 6:1–9)! If this is the case, it re-enforces the notion that this was an isolated incident, given that the scroll of Zechariah flew over the Land of Israel, and his visions were predominately about Jerusalem and the Holy Land.

What follows in Revelation chapters 6 to 9 are spiritual illustrations of historical calamities that befell the Holy Land. The spiritual illustrations are thematically based on the curses within the Law of Moses. The curses provide vivid language to describe physical events (Roman soldiers, war, famine, etc.), in the same style and prophetic mantle of the First Temple prophets like Ezekiel and Jeremiah.

---

[191] Apringius of Beja (~500 AD), ibid.

8 LAW ENFORCEMENT: CHAPTER 6

"O Jerusalem, Jerusalem, the city that kills the prophets and stones those who are sent to it! How often would I have gathered your children together as a hen gathers her brood under her wings, and you were not willing! See, your house is left to you desolate.
For I tell you, you will not see me again, until you say, 'Blessed is he who comes in the name of the Lord.'"
— Matthew 23:37–39 (NASB)

As the horrors of war and death unfolded before John's spiritual eyes (again, he was witnessing what would soon take place in the Holy Land in those days), it seemed like his visions were constantly answering two major questions:

- **Why** is this happening?
- **Who** will it happen to (and who will it not happen to)?

John answers these questions throughout his prophetic experience. Knowing this helps us understand what would otherwise seem to be odd interjections (like the numbering of the 144,000), and easily misunderstood personifications (like the Bride vs. the Harlot).

The reader must also be mindful that because we are dealing with a pre-existing 2,000-year history of challenges with the Law, and these challenges are well documented in Israel's story (i.e. The Old Testament), the Book of Revelation consistently makes rapid references to events and prophecies throughout. This is sort of like being on the TV show *Jeopardy*, where there is only one theme called "Times where Israel broke the Law." **In order to keep up with all of the references, the reader must contextually think back to the Law, Prophets, and Writings, and not allow one's imagination to conjure up some sort of present or future woe interpretation.**

If the trigger event for the woes was the verdict from the Law of Moses (which led to the physical destruction of the Temple), and if the two questions Revelation constantly answers are, "Why did this happen, and to whom," then it makes sense to conclude Revelation draws from both history and Scriptures (Old Testament) to help those who are associated with it understand the transition from the Old to the New.

> "Therefore, he opens [the scroll] and unseals the testament, which he had sealed. And Moses the lawgiver knew that it was necessary for [the testament] to be sealed and hidden until the coming of his passion, and so [he] covered his face and in that way spoke to the people, revealing that the words of preaching were veiled until the time of Christ's coming... Now the face of Moses is uncovered; now it is revealed, and therefore the apocalypse is called a "revelation"; now his book is unsealed."[192]

FOUR CAVALRYMEN OF WARFARE

א *(v 1 – 2) "And I heard one of the four Creatures (Lion)[193] speaking like the sound of thunder: 'Come!'*

[192] Saint Victorinus of Pettau (304 AD), William C. Weinrich, eds. *Revelation. vol. 12 of Ancient Christian Commentary on Scripture.* (Downers Grove: InterVarsity Press, 2005), p. 77.
[193] Assuming the same order of appearance in Revelation 4:7, I will include that same order here as a hypothetical. However, there are no clear identifiers in Revelation 6:1–7.

And I heard[194], and I saw, and behold! A white horse, and he[195] who sat upon it had a bow, and to him was given a crown, and he went forth victorious, and he blamelessly defeated by overcoming."[196]

At numerous times, the early Jewish historian, Josephus, is careful to point out that neither Vespasian nor his son Titus has any sort of vendetta against the inhabitants of Israel. It was Nero who dispatched them to crush the rebellion in Judaea. In fact, numerous times during the campaign, Titus tried to reason with the Zealots, and did not desire to burn the Temple.

> "But Titus said, that 'Although the Jews should get upon that holy house, and fight us thence, yet ought we not to revenge ourselves on things that are inanimate [the Temple], instead of the men themselves:' and that he was not in any case for burning down so vast a work as that was: because this would be a mischief to the Romans themselves; as it would be an ornament to their government while it continued."[197]

Vespasian and Titus were simply carrying out orders. Perhaps their vocation was to be only *perceived* as the enemies of Israel (compare this notion with Jeremiah 43:10 and Isaiah 45:1). This by no means justifies the atrocities carried out by the Romans; but it is important to keep in mind that their cause did not commence as a malicious one.

א *(v 3 – 4) "And when he opened the second seal, I heard the second Creature (Calf) which said, 'Come!'*

---

[194] "I heard" is not in the Greek texts, only the Aramaic.

[195] This rider is not Jesus. See the visions of Zechariah below. Further, Jesus could not have been "sealed." Nor would Jesus use weapons of war. And as King, Jesus would not have been summoned by his own subjects (the living creatures).

[196] "victorious, and he blamelessly defeated by overcoming," are all the same root word used 3 times. This rapid repetition is a classic Hebrew formula (what Robert Alter calls a "Leitwort;" see, *The Art of Biblical Narrative*, chapter 5). The root is the same as in Revelation 2:7 (see my footnote there), and I have attempted to capture the tri-fold meaning of this word in an amplified way. The striking similarity to Revelation 2:7 suggests a legal righteousness here, since the root word means "to be innocent, righteous, pure." Given the historical context of the Jewish-Roman war, it could be that this victory was to be seen from a judicial sense; whereby an executioner, though they take the life of a person condemned to capital punishment, cannot be found guilty of murder. The executioner was given legal right to take a life, and therefore cannot be stained with that blood.

[197] Josephus, *Wars*, 6:4:3, https://penelope.uchicago.edu/josephus/war-6.html

And a red horse went out, and to him who sat upon it was permitted[198] *to take away shalom from The Land*[199] *and to kill each one, and a significant*[200] *sword was given to him."*

The opposite of peace is war. The Romans would not simply march upon Jerusalem and declare victory. This campaign lasted three and a half years (a time, times, a half time). Vespasian took the old northern kingdom of Israel (Galilee, Samaria) and laid waste to every town and village.

> "[The Romans] destroy the neighbouring villages, and smaller cities. So these troops over-ran the country, as they were ordered to do, and every day cut to pieces, and laid desolate the whole region."[201]

Then, as Vespasian was about to take on Jerusalem, he left for the throne of Rome in the Year of Four Emperors. Titus was left to wage war upon the old southern kingdom of Judah and take Jerusalem. Those who weren't slain in the Holy Land were taken as slaves, as prophesied in Deuteronomy 28:68: "You will offer yourselves for sale to your enemies as male and female slaves, but there will be no buyer," which Josephus confirms:

> "Now the number of those that were carried captive, during this whole war, was collected to be ninety-seven thousand... [The Romans] sold the rest of the multitude, with their wives and children; and every one of them for a very low price: and that because such as were sold were very many, and the buyers very few."[202]

א *(v 5 – 6) "And when he opened the third seal, I heard the third Creature (Human) saying, 'Come!' And behold! A black horse, and he who sat*

---

[198] This same word was used in Revelation 1:3 and 4:1, and speaks to the legal right that precedes the events about to take place.

[199] See my footnote for Revelation 3:10. The translator must decide based on context if the scribe was referring to the Land of Israel, or the Earth. Given the context, I believe the Land of Israel is implied here.

[200] The Aramaic רַבְּתָא can mean large, great, or significant. The size doesn't really matter since this is a spirit-vision, so I have opted for significance as it is more meaningful here.

[201] Josephus, *Wars*, 3:9:4, https://penelope.uchicago.edu/josephus/war-3.html

[202] Josephus, *Wars*, Book 6, https://penelope.uchicago.edu/josephus/war-6.html

upon him had a balance scale in his hand.

And I heard a voice from among the Creatures, saying, 'A measure of wheat for a denarius[203] and three measures of barley for a denarius[204], and don't be amazed[205] by the [extortion of] wine and the oil!'"

Any student of the Jewish-Roman war of 66 AD will tell you that famine and starvation were critical factors that led to the demise of the Jewish people. This is well documented.

> "[Titus was told] that a *medimnus* of wheat, was sold for a talent: and that when, a while afterward, it was not possible to gather herbs, by reason the city was all walled about, some persons were driven to that terrible distress, as to search the common sewers, and old dunghills of cattle, and to eat the dung which they got there: and what they of old could not endure so much as to see, they now used for food."[206]

> "The very wisps of old hay became food to some; and some gathered up fibres, and sold a very small weight of them for four Attick Drachmæ [several days wages]."[207]

> "Nor was there any place in the city [of Jerusalem] that had no dead bodies in it; but what was entirely covered with those that were killed, either by the famine, or the rebellion: and all was full of the dead bodies of such as had perished, either by that sedition, or by that famine."[208]

Josephus even provides us with an example of how extortion of oil was employed in the Holy Land:

---

[203] The measure, a קָבָא (cab), was the amount required to bake a loaf of bread. In Matthew 20:2 and John 12:5 we are told that a denarius was a day's wage. So the literal meaning here is, "a day's wage for a loaf of bread." That's expensive bread!
[204] Wheat and barley were staples for basic food, and units of measurement were part of understanding pricing (see Ezekiel 4:9–11).
[205] The conjugation of תָּהַּ here is "to wonder" or "to be amazed." In the context of the verse, I added the implication of extortion in parentheses as this is implied.
[206] Josephus, *Wars*, 5:13:7, https://penelope.uchicago.edu/josephus/war-5.html
[207] Ibid, 6:3:3.
[208] Ibid, 6:7:2.

"John [of Giscala] contrived a very shrewd trick, and pretending that the Jews who dwelt in Syria were obliged to make use of oil that was made by others than those of their own nation… so he bought four *amphorœ* with money, as was of the value of four Attic *drachmœ*, and sold every half amphora at the same price [an 800% profit]... by sending away great quantities, and having the sole privilege so to do, he gathered an immense sum of money together."[209]

The final point here breaks my heart. I wish it were not so. I've said repeatedly that the curses of Deuteronomy 28 (et al.) befell those who remained under the Law. Here we see to what degree the accuracy of Moses' prophecy in Deuteronomy manifested itself. In verses 56 and 57 of chapter 28 we read:

"The refined and delicate woman among you, who would not venture to set the sole of her foot on the ground because of her delicateness and tenderness will be hostile toward… her children to whom she gives birth, because she will eat them secretly for lack of anything else, during the siege and the hardship with which your enemy will oppress you in your towns."

Compare these prophetic words to the horrific account recorded by Josephus during the Roman siege against Jerusalem:

"There was a certain woman that dwelt beyond Jordan; her name was *Mary*… She was eminent for her family, and her wealth; and had fled away to Jerusalem with the rest of the multitude, and was with them besieged therein at this time… And it was now become impossible for her any way to find any more food, while the famine pierced through her very bowels, and marrow… She then attempted a most unnatural thing: and snatching up her son, which was a child sucking at her breast… she slew her son; and then roasted him; and eat the one half of him; and kept the other half by her concealed... So those that were thus distressed by the famine, were very desirous to die: and those already dead were esteemed happy; because they had

[209] Ibid, 2:21:2.

not lived long enough either to hear, or to see such miseries."[210]

How much more can I emphasize the fact that John was commissioned to prophesy to his Jewish kin, and that his visions were for their emancipation from the curses of the Law? **If one were to pause and just read Deuteronomy 28:15–68, 29:22–30:10, 31:14–22, and 32:1–43, the book of Revelation would be a no-brainer.** The accuracy of Moses' words can only be supernatural.

א *(v 7 – 8) "When he opened the fourth seal, I heard the voice of a Creature (Eagle) saying, 'Come!'*

And I saw a pale horse, and the name of him who sat upon it was Death, and Sheol was cleaved to him.[211] And authority was given to him[212] over a fourth of The Land[213] to kill by the sword, and by starvation, and by Death,[214] and by the animals of The Land."

Josephus explains that in addition to all those slain in Galilee and Samaria, in the third year of the campaign, when Rome surrounded Jerusalem, it just so happened to be during the Feast of Passover. As was customary (see Acts 2:5), Jews and proselytes from all over the Roman Empire went up to Jerusalem to observe the Holy Festivals. Sadly, the city was brimming with people when Titus besieged the city and shut it in.

> "And as for the rest of the multitude, that were above seventeen years old, [Titus] put them into bonds, and sent them to the Egyptian mines. Titus also sent a great number into the provinces; as a present to them: that they might be destroyed upon their theatres, **by the sword, and by the wild beasts**...
>
> Now the number of those that were carried captive, during this

---

[210] Josephus, *Wars*, 6:3:4, https://penelope.uchicago.edu/josephus/war-6.html
[211] This is a bizarre image: Sheol, a spiritual location, is personified. Sheol cleaves, or is "connected," to Death. This picture here is two riders riding "two-up," as they say, on a single horse, with Sheol's arms around Death's waist.
[212] Theologically, we must remember that Jesus holds the keys of Death and Sheol (Revelation 1:18), meaning He is only allowing Death and Sheol to operate within their legal boundaries. Where is Hades? See my footnote on Revelation 1:18.
[213] The Land of Israel.
[214] How can one be killed by Death? The implication is that the spirit of death would also take lives on its own, without human intervention, similar to Exodus 12.

whole war, was collected to be ninety-seven thousand. As was the number of those that **perished during the whole siege eleven hundred thousand [that is, 1.1 million people]**... The greater part of whom were indeed of the same nation [with the citizens of Jerusalem], but not belonging to the city itself. For they were come up from all the country to the feast of unleavened bread; and were on a sudden shut up by an army; which at the very first occasioned so great a straitness among them, that there came **a pestilential destruction** upon them; and soon afterward such **a famine**, as destroyed them more suddenly...

But the entire nation was now shut up by fate, as in prison; and the Roman army encompassed the city when it was crowded with inhabitants. Accordingly the multitude of those that therein perished exceeded all the destructions that either men or God ever brought upon the world."[215]

These images of war horses should not be referred to as the "four horsemen of the Apocalypse." Such labels do more harm than good. What then do we make of these visions? The prophet Zechariah also had the same glimpse into a reality of the spirit realm that helps us contextualize what John saw. John's Jewish audience would have already had this understanding; therefore, it is up to us to become familiar with the Scriptures they already knew:

'I saw in the night, and behold, a man riding on a red horse! He was standing among the myrtle trees in the glen, and behind him were red, sorrel, and white horses. Then I said, 'What are these, my lord?' The angel who talked with me said to me, 'I will show you what they are.' So the man who was standing among the myrtle trees answered, 'These are they whom the Lord has sent to patrol the earth.' And they answered the angel of the Lord who was standing among the myrtle trees, and said, 'We have patrolled the earth, and behold, all the earth remains at rest.'"
Zechariah 1:8–11 (NASB)

'I lifted my eyes and saw, and behold, four chariots came out from between two mountains. And the mountains were mountains of bronze. The first

[215] Josephus, *Wars*, 6:9:2–4 https://penelope.uchicago.edu/josephus/war-6.html

chariot had red horses, the second black horses, the third white horses, and the fourth chariot dappled horses—all of them strong. Then I answered and said to the angel who talked with me, 'What are these, my lord?' And the angel answered and said to me, "These are going out to the four winds of heaven, after presenting themselves before the Lord of all the earth... When the strong horses came out, they were impatient to go and patrol the earth. And he said, 'Go, patrol the earth.' So they patrolled the earth."
Zechariah 6:1–5, 7 (NASB)

Zechariah was privy to a system that is (or was) in place that we will likely not fully comprehend until our Saviour returns. This prophet was gifted with the ability to see what took place in the spirit realm (much like 2 Kings 6:17) after the edict of Cyrus (2 Chronicles 36:22-23), long after the devastating Babylonian invasion that destroyed Jerusalem and the Temple. This event sent great men like Daniel, Jeremiah, and Ezekiel into captivity. Babylon had been given legal right to destroy Jerusalem and exile its inhabitants for 70 years (Jeremiah 25:11; 29:10). God then allowed Persia to overthrow Babylon and used them to liberate the Jews (via Cyrus).

Zechariah and Haggai were commissioned to encourage the people of Israel to rebuild their ruined city and Temple. During this time there was peace again in the Holy Land. The great nations and empires surrounding them were not preparing for war against Israel. Therefore, the horses and chariots of war that Zechariah saw reported peace. Similarly, Daniel caught a glimpse of a spiritual system in place that we may not fully comprehend: High-ranking angels were at war with enemy principalities who had authority over empires (Daniel 10:13, also Colossians 2:15).

Fast forward approximately 600 years. The great empire of the day was not Babylon or Persia, but Rome. God had granted the Roman Empire legal right to invade the Holy Land and destroy Jerusalem and the rebuilt Temple. John, like Jeremiah and Ezekiel, is summoned to warn the people of Judea. And in his visitation with God, he is given spiritual sight (2 Kings 6:17 again) into what is going on around him. This time, John sees the four cavalrymen that Zechariah saw as Rome was *preparing* for war. They represent the assurance that the Word of God will not return void. Rome will overthrow the Holy Land in fulfillment of the Law of Moses.[216]

---

[216] I would venture to suggest that these cavalrymen also went forth before the Assyrian army when they invaded the Ten Northern Tribes of Israel , and before the Babylonians when they invaded Jerusalem. But this is merely conjecture.

"In the interconnected world of heavenly symbols, the seals holding the scroll closed each release an angel of vengeance or catastrophe (reminiscent of those in Ezekiel 9.2), each linked to horses in a way that indicates the inspiration of Zechariah 6…

John introduces horses first, and by color (verses 2, 4, 5b, and 8a). Horses, associated with Greek and Roman armies, signified raw military power (1 Enoch 86.4; 88.3). The four horsemen represent conquest (v 2), internecine violence (v 4), famine and inflation (v 6), and death (v 8)…

With sword, famine, and pestilence,' a traditional prophetic formula for the manifestations of divine vengeance (e.g., Jeremiah 14.12; Ezekiel 5.12,17; 14.21)."[217]

The reader must also keep at the forefront of their minds the fact that hyperbole and dramatic exaggeration was the lingua franca of the Jewish Scriptures. You cannot possibly take every word literally. For instance:

*"I will show wonders in the heavens above
and signs on the earth below,
blood and fire and billows of smoke.
The sun will be turned to darkness
and the moon to blood
before the coming of the great and glorious day of the Lord."
Joel 2:30–31 (NASB)*

The Apostle Peter quotes this prophecy saying that it was currently being fulfilled (almost 2,000 years ago!) in their midst in Acts 2:14–28! Or how about the retelling of the Sinai event where Moses received the Law?

"And when you led his descendants out of Egypt, you brought them to Mount Sinai. You bent down the heavens and shook the earth, and moved the world, and caused the depths to tremble, and troubled the times. Your glory passed through the four gates of fire and earthquake and wind and ice, to give the law to the descendants of Jacob, and your commandment to the posterity of Israel." 2 Esdras 3:17-19 (NRSV)

It behooves the reader, therefore, to be mindful of the continuation of the Jewish writing tradition in John's prophecy. John was raised in this

---

[217] The Jewish Annotated New Testament, Second Edition, ed. Amy-Jill Levine and Marc Zvi Brettler, (New York: Oxford University Press, 2017), p. 550–551.

culture, taught from the Torah, celebrated the Temple feasts from childhood, heard the oral traditions of the Law, and observed the Commandments to the best of his ability (until he met Jesus!). The Jewish style of writing would have been most natural to him.

Additionally, we will see that at times there is a convergence of 'spiritual' and natural. For instance, Josephus and the Roman historian Tacitus, writing of the Jewish-Roman war, recount similar events:

"A few days after that feast [of Pentacost], on the one and twentieth day of the month Artemisius, a certain prodigious and incredible phenomenon appeared: I suppose the account of it would seem to be a fable; were it not related by those that saw it; and were not the events that followed it of so considerable a nature as to deserve such signals. For, before sun setting, **chariots and troops of soldiers in their armour were seen running about among the clouds, and surrounding of cities.**"[218]

"Prodigies had indeed occurred, but to avert them [the Jews] either by victims or by vows is held unlawful by a people which, though prone to superstition, is opposed to all propitiatory rites. **Contending hosts were seen meeting in the skies**, arms flashed, and suddenly the temple was illumined with fire from the clouds."[219]

It may very well have been that not just John, but several others, saw the four cavalrymen released over the Holy Land.

JOSEPHUS AND EARLY ROMAN HISTORIANS

It is worth mentioning that I will continue to quote Josephus and a few other early Roman historians (Tacitus, Cassius Dio, and Suetonius) quite frequently throughout this commentary. Why? Because they provide the historical insight we need in order to understand how the prophecies of John came to pass. Chief among these historical writings are those of Josephus, who was an eye-witness to the Jewish–Roman War.

---

[218] Josephus, *Wars*, 6:5:3. https://penelope.uchicago.edu/josephus/war-6.html
[219] Tacitus, *Histories*, 5:13:1.
https://penelope.uchicago.edu/Thayer/E/Roman/Texts/Tacitus/Histories/5A*.html

When Jerusalem fell the first time, Jeremiah, Ezekiel, and Daniel were eyewitnesses. Not only did these men prophecy concerning destruction of the Holy City (before and after the fall), they were there in the midst of it all. As far as we know, the apostle John was not in Jerusalem when it fell.[220] However, Josephus was. He was a Jewish priest who studied under the Pharisees sect (like the Apostle Paul). He also fought in the Jewish-Roman war as a military leader based in Galilee. His account of the entire ordeal is the only surviving eyewitness record we have. Therefore, Josephus' *Seven Books of the Jewish War* should be considered a supplement to the Book of Revelation, if not the entire New Testament.

> "If any one compares the words of our Saviour with the other accounts of the historian (Josephus) concerning the whole war, how can one fail to wonder, and to admit that the foreknowledge and the prophecy of our Saviour were truly divine and marvellously strange."[221]

As I have mentioned previously, Luke 19-21, Matthew 21-25, Mark 11-13, and John 2:13-22 also spoke of the imminent Roman invasion and destruction of the Holy Land and the Temple. Likewise, what Kings and Chronicles (historical Biblical accounts of the fall of Israel and Judah) are to the prophecies of Isaiah (Israel), Jeremiah and Ezekiel (Judah), Josephus' *Wars* are to Revelation.

THE FIFTH AND SIXTH SEALS

א *(v 9 – 11) "And when he opened the fifth seal, I saw from under the altar the souls of those who were killed because of the word of Elohim and because of the testimony of Yeshua which they had.*

And they cried in a great voice, and they were saying, 'Until when, Yahweh, holy and true, will you not be judging and avenging our blood upon the inhabitants of The Land?'"

And there was given to each of them a white robe, and it was told to them that they rest until the appointed time: a short while for the fulfillment of

---

[220] According to Irenaeus and Polycrates John lived out his final days in Ephesus.
[221] Eusebius, *Church History*, Book 3, Ch. 7.

their companions and brethren also, who were going to be killed, even as they had been."

Verse 9 gives us two groups of people: those who held to the word of God, and those who held the testimony of Jesus. This is in fulfilment of the words of Christ in Matthew 23:

"Woe to you, scribes and Pharisees, hypocrites! For you build the tombs of the prophets and decorate the monuments of the righteous, saying, 'If we had lived in the days of our fathers, we would not have taken part with them in shedding the blood of the prophets.' Thus you witness against yourselves that you are sons of those who murdered the prophets...

Therefore I send you prophets and wise men and scribes, some of whom you will kill and crucify, and some you will flog in your synagogues and persecute from town to town, so that on you may come all the righteous blood shed on earth, from the blood of righteous Abel[22] to the blood of Zechariah the son of Barachiah, whom you murdered between the sanctuary and the altar. Truly, I say to you, all these things will come upon this generation." Matt 23:29–31, 34–36 (NASB)

The prophets of old had the word of God (see also 2 Maccabees 7; 4). And those sent by Jesus held His testimony. In the last months leading up to the destruction of the Temple, Josephus records a most heinous event that perhaps crystalized Jesus' prophecies:

"John [of Giscala, a Jewish rebel leader]… slew moreover many of the priests, as they were about their sacred ministrations… For those darts [arrows] that were thrown by the engines came with that force, that they went over all the buildings, and reached as far as the altar, and the temple itself; and fell upon the priests, and those that were about the sacred offices. Insomuch that many… fell down before their own sacrifices themselves, and sprinkled that altar… with their own blood… and the blood of all sorts of dead carcasses stood in lakes in the holy courts themselves."[223]

---

[222] The theme of avenging righteous blood is also found in 1 Enoch 47; 2 Maccabees 8.3; 4 Ezra 4.35.

[223] Josephus, *Wars*, 5:1:3, https://penelope.uchicago.edu/josephus/war-5.html

א *(v 12) "And I saw when he opened the sixth seal, and there was a great earthquake, and the Sun was like sackcloth of black hair, and the whole moon was if it was like blood.*

John witnesses an illustration of Joel 2:30–32, which I cited earlier in this chapter. Now, Peter has already given us context for this vision in Acts 2:14–28, emphatically stating that in and around 30 AD, the prophecy of Joel was being fulfilled. Placing this scripture *back* into the first century AD allows us to connect a few more dots.

At the end of Matthew 23 (cited above), where Jesus prophesied that the guilt of all the righteous blood shed in Israel would fall on that generation (30 AD to 70 AD is forty years), he concludes with these words:

"Truly, I say to you, all these things will come upon this generation. O Jerusalem, Jerusalem, the city that kills the prophets and stones those who are sent to it! How often would I have gathered your children together as a hen gathers her brood under her wings, and you were not willing! See, your house [the Temple] is left to you desolate. For I tell you, you will not see me again, until you say, 'Blessed is he who comes in the name of the Lord.'" Matthew 23:36–39 (NASB)

His last statement is a quote from Psalm 118. Verses didn't exist in those days - a quote was meant to send the reader to the full picture of what was quoted. Hence, we can assume Jesus is referencing the entire Psalm, which just happens to be God's answer to those who have suffered injustice for His namesake! This is exactly the group of people Matthew 23 and Revelation 6:9–17 address.

But what about Joel 2? Why do Peter in Acts and John in Revelation each quote it? Because Joel 2 was a prophecy concerning Israel of a coming judgement, at that time by the hands of the Romans. The whole chapter speaks specifically of the 30 AD to 70 AD window, when the Holy Spirit was poured out, the new covenant made available, and an open invitation stood for a generation to those under the old covenant to escape the coming judgement for those found guilty under the Law (which was anyone under the Law).

א *(v 13 – 14) "And the stars of the Heavens fell upon The Land, as a fig tree casting its unripe figs when it is shaken by a strong wind.*

And the Heavens were parted like scrolls that are being rolled up, and every mount and every island was shaken from their place.

The mention of the figs here is a direct reference to the prophecy of Jesus in Mark 13:28, which refers to when the disciples asked Jesus when the Temple would be destroyed (see especially Mark 13:24–30, and cross reference with Haggai 2:6–7). Revelation 6:12 to 14 are reference Isaiah 34 (entire chapter). For instance:

> *"And all the heavenly lights will wear away,*
> *And the sky will be rolled up like a scroll;*
> *All its lights will also wither away*
> *As a leaf withers from the vine,*
> *Or as one withers from the fig tree." Isaiah 34:4 (NASB)*

What took place in the days that followed Isaiah's words are used here as a reminder of what would to take place again, this time in the Holy Land. Jewish hyperbole was employed as the prophet Isaiah spoke of the indignation and righteous judgement of God.

א *(v 15 – 17) "And the kings of The Land, and the officials, and captains of thousands,[224] and the wealthy, and the soldiers, and all servant and all sons of the freemen, hid themselves in caves and in the rocks of the mounts,*

And they said to the mounts and rocks, 'Fall on us and hide us from before the face of the Lamb,'

'Because the great day of his indignation has come, and who is able to stand?'"

People did not literally gather together and ask mountains to fall on them! Rather, this is a direct quote from Hosea 10:8, "Then they will say to the mountains, 'Cover us!' And to the hills, 'Fall on us!'" Hosea 10 is also a line by line description of what woes befell Galilee, Samaria, and Judaea. Then who are these people that went into hiding? The "seditious," as Josephus would say—the three factions that took over leadership of the entire region of the Holy Land:

> "And now there were three treacherous factions in the city, the one parted from the other. Eleazar [ben Simon] and his party...
> Those that were with John [of Giscala], plundered the

---

[224] Captain of thousand was a common Roman military rank known as a 'Chiliarch.'

populace, and went out with zeal against Simon [bar Giora]. This Simon had his supply of provisions from the city, in opposition to the seditious…

I shall therefore speak my mind here at once briefly; that neither did any other city ever suffer such miseries; nor did any age ever breed a generation more fruitful in wickedness than this was from the beginning of the world…

I suppose that had the Romans made any longer delay in coming against these villains, that the city would either have been swallowed up by the ground opening upon them, or been overflowed by water; or else been destroyed by such thunder, as the country of Sodom perished by. For it had brought forth a generation of men much more [atheistic] than were those that suffered such punishments. For by their madness it was that all the people came to be destroyed."[225]

These men, along with several false messiahs and false prophets, (more on this in book 3), stirred up the inhabitants of Galilee, Samaria, and Judaea to war against Rome—and then each other. They created their own rule and appointed their own priests. They recruited citizens, rich and poor, to join them. Slaves and the indebted were freed, while the wealthy were stripped of their fortunes and became pawns. Those that didn't join were terrorized and executed. It was a horrendous time. They put up a strong resistance against the Roman war machine, even wounding Titus at one point. But the hammer fall was too strong.

In contrast to those who would hide from the coming indignation of the Lamb, for the righteous who long-suffered during that tribulation, the Lamb was their deliverance: "And then they will see the Son of Man coming in a cloud with power and great glory. But when these things begin to take place, straighten up and lift up your heads, because **your redemption** is drawing near," Luke 21:28 (NASB). This should be read in the context of Luke 21:6–36, where Jesus speaks again of the destruction of the Temple.

We will discover in the next chapter Jesus' providence to deliver those who would dare to believe Him from this calamity. Jesus and his disciples

---

[225] Josephus, *Wars*, 5:1:4, 5:10:5, 5:13:6,
https://penelope.uchicago.edu/josephus/war-5.html

foretold of these events; but at the time it seemed preposterous. And so, like Noah, Jesus' words largely went unheeded.

9 THE FLIGHT TO PELLA: CHAPTER 7

"But whosoever will persevere until the latter end will have life. And
this gospel of the Kingdom will be preached within this entire generation
(age) as the testimony of all the nations, and then comes the
completion... Amen, I say to you, this generation (age) will not pass
away until all these things happen."
— *Matthew 24:13–14, 34, Aramaic Text*

John's dramatic vision continues, with the focus pivoting to those that will
be spared from the Jewish-Roman war. Revelation 8 and 9 then focuses
on the Promised Land and the inhabitants therein who remained for the
catastrophe. The interjection of God's mercy in chapter 7 is a sign of hope
and comfort for His faithful.

In Colossians, Paul remarked that the gospel had been preached "within
this entire generation (age)," (Colossians 1:5–6), and had been proclaimed
"to every creature under heaven," (Colossians 1:23), echoing Matthew 24:14
and Mark 16:15. This notion is reiterated in Romans, where Paul boldly states
that "in all the Land (of Israel) their voice has gone forth, and to the limits
of the Known World their words," (Romans 10:18), and that the Gospel had
"been taught to all Gentiles," (Romans 16:25).

In *Revelation: Dawn of This Age*, I thoroughly discuss the importance of
understanding that Jesus and the Apostles (in the Epistles) were not focused

on the end of the world. "World" is a poor translation of שֵׁרְבְּתָא (γενεά in Greek), meaning generation, family, or age. The age in question in those days was the Mosaic Age, which was coming to a close (Hebrews 8:13). This end would come about with the fulfillment of the Law of Moses (Matthew 5:18), based on the works of those bound under it. Because all had failed to maintain to contractual obligations of the Law (James 2:10, Galatians 5:3), the consequences for breach of covenant would be fulfilled at the end of that age.

Deuteronomy 28, the pivotal chapter that helps us understand why Jerusalem and the Temple were destroyed for a second time, states:

"The Lord will bring a nation against you from far away, from the end of the earth, as the eagle swoops down; a nation whose language you will not understand, a nation with a defiant attitude, who will have no respect for the old, nor show favor to the young." Deuteronomy 28:49–50 (NASB)

The Roman Eagle came from the four winds, Vespasian from the North (via Syria), Titus from the south (via Egypt), with four legions, and descended upon the Holy Land.

א *(v 1 – 4) "And after this, I saw four angels standing over the four corners[226] of the Land, and they were holding the four winds (the four horses)[227], that the winds (horses) would not blow upon the Land, neither upon the Sea[228], neither upon any tree.*

And I saw another angel ascending from the East Sun, and he had the seal of living Elohim, and he cried with a loud voice to the four angels to

---

[226] This is classic Jewish apocalyptic imagery. See 1 Enoch 18 to 36.

[227] We must employ Scriptural self-exegesis like we did in Revelation 6. Upon examination of the four war horses, we discovered that Zechariah had two visions of the same phenomenon. In his second vision, Zechariah is given an interpretation by an angel: "These [horses] are the four spirits of heaven, going out after taking their stand before the Lord of all the earth, with one of which the black horses are going out to the north country; and the white ones are to go out after them, while the spotted ones are to go out to the south country." Zechariah 6:5–6. Here then, angels are holding back these horses of Revelation 6 from riding out against the Holy Land.

[228] This is what I'll call an 'uppercase' Sea יַמָּא which is in reference to the Mediterranean, as opposed to יַמְתָא which would be a 'lowercase' sea, such as the Sea of Galilee or the Dead Sea.

whom it was given to damage[229] the Land and the Sea.

And he said, 'Do not damage the Land, and neither the Sea, and not even the trees, until we seal the royal subjects of Elohim between their eyes.[230]

And I heard the number of those sealed: one hundred and forty four thousand, from each of the tribes of Israel."

The cavalrymen of Revelation 6 are stayed from allowing the Roman invasion to commence until the righteous are marked. This is more likely a vision of comfort and assurance rather than a literal event—a vision that provided a breath of relief to hearers and readers. Jesus would not allow his beloved to suffer under the consequences of the Law.

Returning to Revelation, an angel then rises from the east, a location associated with the Messiah,[231] and is entrusted with the King's signet ring.[232] He is to mark those who would be spared. While this scene echoes the Passover of Exodus (Exodus 12:22–23), it is even more closely a parallel of Ezekiel 9:

"And the Lord said to him, "Go through the midst of the city, through the midst of Jerusalem, and make a mark on the foreheads of the people who groan and sigh over all the abominations which are being committed in its midst," Ezekiel 9:4 (NASB).

Ezekiel 8 and 9 should be read in their entirely in order to see how the former preparations for the destruction of the first Temple mirrored those of the latter.

The Twelve Tribes of Israel were non-existent; at least not in their former state. Recall that the Assyrians displaced the ten northern tribes in 721–722 BC. That is a long time away from 70 AD. Only the southern tribes of Judah and Benjamin remained. The sealing therefore is not a literal representation of those lost tribes; rather, they represent the Diaspora (Jews who had spread abroad; Acts 2:5–13) and the remaining regions of Galilee, Samaria, and

---

[229] The source of calamity shifts from the horses to the angels that now restrain them.
[230] That is to say, their foreheads.
[231] Zechariah 14:4; Joel 3:2, 12; Isaiah 40:3.
[232] For instance, 1 Kings 21:8, Esther 3:12, 8:10.

Judaea. The 144,000 sealed[233] simply represents wholeness and fulfillment, that Jesus has seen all those who are faithfully endured the hardship and injustice (See Hebrews 11:35–38).

א *(v 9 – 10) "Afterward I saw a great multitude who could not be numbered, who were of all people, tribes, nations and languages, standing before the throne and before the Lamb, and they were clothed with white priestly garments[234] and with palms in their hands.[235]*

And they were proclaiming with a great voice and they were saying, 'The redemption of our God—He who sits upon the throne and the Lamb!'"

The scope of the vision then broadens beyond the ancient borders of the Holy Land to the vast expanse of the Roman Empire. In verse 4, the people of Israel were clearly numbered; here, they are without number. Injustice and persecution for the sake of Christ was not an experience unique to the inhabitants of the Land of Israel. All across the known world, Christians were also patiently enduring hardship.

"Neither human help, nor imperial munificence, nor all the modes of placating Heaven, could stifle scandal or dispel the belief that the fire had taken place by order [of Nero]. Therefore, to scotch the rumour, Nero substituted as culprits, and punished with the utmost refinements of cruelty, a class of men, loathed for their vices, whom the crowd styled Christians...

"And derision accompanied their end: they were covered with wild beasts' skins and torn to death by dogs; or they were fastened on crosses, and, when daylight failed were burned to serve as lamps by night. Nero had offered his Gardens for the

---

[233] "the one hundred forty-four thousand are credited with a special degree of purity that involved celibacy, whether out of priestly tradition or reflecting rules for holy war (Exodus 19:15; Leviticus 22:1–9; 1 Samuel 21:4)," The Jewish Annotated New Testament, Second Edition, ed. Amy-Jill Levine and Marc Zvi Brettler, (New York: Oxford University Press, 2017), p. 552.
[234] See my footnote for Revelation 3:5 about priestly garments.
[235] Palm branches are for victory celebrations (1 Maccabees13:51; Matthew 21:18; Mark 11:8).

spectacle, and gave an exhibition in his Circus..."[236]

These are now seen together with the sealed of Israel, who together make up the Bride of the Bridegroom King.

> *"Then one of the elders responded, saying to me, 'These who are clothed in the white robes, who are they, and where have they come from?' I said to him, 'My lord, you know.' And he said to me, 'These are the ones who come out of the great tribulation, and they have washed their robes and made them white in the blood of the Lamb. For this reason they are before the throne of God, and they serve Him day and night in His temple; and He who sits on the throne will spread His tabernacle over them.'"*
> *Revelation 7:13–14 (NASB)*

Lastly, we are introduced to the notion of a heavenly temple: "they serve Him day and night in His temple." Hebrews 8:5 tells us that Moses erected a Tabernacle that was "a copy and shadow of the heavenly things." This distinction between the earthly Temple in Jerusalem and the heavenly one in God's courts will be revisited in Revelation, chapter 11.

ESCAPE TO PELLA IN THE TRANSJORDAN REGION

> *"But when you see Jerusalem surrounded by armies, then recognize that her desolation is near. Then those who are in Judea must flee to the mountains, and those who are inside the city must leave, and those who are in the country must not enter the city; because these are days of punishment, so that all things which have been written will be fulfilled. Woe to those women who are pregnant, and to those who are nursing babies in those days; for there will be great distress upon the land, and wrath to this people; and they will fall by the edge of the sword, and will be led captive into all the nations; and Jerusalem will be trampled underfoot by the Gentiles until the times of the Gentiles are fulfilled."*
> *Luke 21:20–24 (NASB)*

Part of what the "sealing of the 144,000" meant was deliverance from the Roman invasion. We know this to be true because the same thing took place in Ezekiel 9:4, which delivered people from death by the Babylonian sword. The words of Jesus quoted above are a parallel passage of Matthew 24:15–28.

---

[236] Tacitus, *Annals*, 15b:44,
https://penelope.uchicago.edu/Thayer/E/Roman/Texts/Tacitus/Annals/15B*.ht
ml

One fascinating piece of history that has been preserved over time shows us one of the ways the sealing of the 144,000 played out. We are told that **Believers in Jerusalem and surrounding regions were warned prior to the Roman blitzkrieg through an angelic visitation, telling them it was time to leave.** Eusebius (260–340 AD), an early church father and historian, recounts this event as follows:

> "But the people of the church in Jerusalem had been commanded by a revelation, vouchsafed to approved men there before the war, to leave the city and to dwell in a certain town of Perea called Pella... all these things, as well as the many great sieges which were carried on against the cities of Judea, and the excessive sufferings endured by those that fled to Jerusalem itself, as to a city of perfect safety, and finally the general course of the whole war, as well as its particular occurrences in detail, and how at last the abomination of desolation, proclaimed by the prophets, stood in the very temple of God, so celebrated of old, the temple which was now awaiting its total and final destruction by fire, all these things any one that wishes may find accurately described in the history written by Josephus."[237]

Followers of Jesus were given advanced warning prior to the surrounding of Israel and Jerusalem and were therefore able to escape to the nearby town of Pella. But for the hundreds of thousands who did not believe the prophecies of Jesus or the warnings of the followers of Jesus (for example, Acts 6:13-14), they suffered one of the greatest atrocities in Jewish history.

> "It is fitting to add to these accounts the true prediction of our Saviour in which he foretold these very events. His words are as follows: '...pray ye that your flight be not in the winter, neither on the Sabbath day; For there shall be great tribulation, such as was not since the beginning of the world to this time, no, nor ever shall be.' The historian [Josephus], reckoning the whole number of the slain, says that eleven hundred thousand [1.1 million] persons perished by famine and sword, and that the rest of the rioters and robbers, being betrayed by each other after the taking of the city, were slain... These things took place

[237] Eusebius, *Church History*, Book 3, Chapter 5.

in this manner in the second year of the reign of Vespasian, in accordance with the prophecies of our Lord and Saviour Jesus Christ..."[238]

Eusebius continues:

"'And except those days should be shortened, there should no flesh be saved; but for the elect's sake those days shall be shortened' [Matt. 24:22]. By these things He shows them to be deserving of a more grievous punishment than had been mentioned, speaking now of the days of the war and of that siege. But what He saith is like this. If, saith He, the war of the Romans against the city had prevailed further, all the Jews had perished (for by 'no flesh' here, He meaneth no Jewish flesh), both those abroad, and those at home. **For not only against those in Judea did they war, but also those that were dispersed everywhere they outlawed and banished**, because of their hatred against the former.

But whom doth He here mean by the elect? The believers that were shut up in the midst of them. For that Jews may not say that because of the gospel, and the worship of Christ, these ills took place, He showeth, that so far from the believers being the cause, if it had not been for them, all had perished utterly. For if God had permitted the war to be protracted, not so much as a remnant of the Jews had remained, but lest those of them who had become believers should perish together with the unbelieving Jews, He quickly put down the fighting, and gave an end to the war."[239]

Epiphanius of Salamis (310–403 AD), an early church leader, confirms Eusebius' account of the flight to Pella:

"For when the city was about to be taken and destroyed by the Romans, it was revealed in advance to all the disciples by an angel of God that they should remove from the city, as it was going to be completely destroyed. They sojourned as emigrants

---

[238] Eusebius, *Church History*, Book 3, Chapter 7.
[239] John Chrysostom, *Homily of St. Matthew*, Homily 76, Number 2.

in Pella, the city above mentioned, in Transjordania. And this city is said to be of the Decapolis. But after the destruction of Jerusalem, when they had returned to Jerusalem, as I have said, they wrought great signs."[240]

---

[240] Epiphanius of Salamis, *Weights and Measures, The Treatise*, sec 15.

10 THE HOLY LAND IS AFFLICTED: CHAPTER 8

*"Therefore the nostrils of the Lord flared against The Land, bringing
upon it all the curses written in this Scroll, and the Lord uprooted them
from their land with a nostril blast, and in passion, and in great
indignation, and cast them into another land, as is today."*
—— Deuteronomy 29:27–28, Hebrew Translation

In Revelation 8 we are presented with the Promised Land taking centre
stage in a vision reminiscent of Genesis 13:10 and 19:29, where a
beautiful and fertile landscape becomes a vast wasteland. It might seem
redundant to have a prophetic vision concerning the topography, the very
soil of Israel, but we must understand that the ground itself was sacred. It
was part of the promise to Abraham (Genesis 12:7). In fulfillment of
Deuteronomy 28, we see that the Promised Land was to be afflicted:

*"The heaven which is over your head shall be bronze, and the earth which
is under you, iron. The Lord will make the rain of your land powder and
dust; from heaven it shall come down on you until you are destroyed…*

*"You will bring out a great amount of seed to the field, but you will gather
in little, because the locust will devour it. You will plant and cultivate*

vineyards, but you will neither drink of the wine nor bring in the harvest, because the worm will eat it. You will have olive trees throughout your territory but you will not anoint yourself with the oil, because your olives will drop off prematurely. You will father sons and daughters but they will not remain yours, because they will go into captivity. The cricket will take possession of all your trees and the produce of your ground...

[A foreign nation] will besiege you in all your towns until your high and fortified walls in which you trusted come down throughout your land, and it will besiege you in all your towns throughout your land which the Lord your God has given you." Deuteronomy 8:23–24, 38–42, 52 (NASB)

Hence, chapter 8 begins with the devastation that will come upon the Promised Land. Afterward, in Revelation 9, we will see the Roman hoards unleashed to afflict those upon the Promised Land.

THE SEVENTH SEAL

"When the Lamb broke the seventh seal, there was silence in heaven for about half an hour. And I saw the seven angels who stand before God, and seven trumpets were given to them." Revelation 8:1–2 (NASB)

It is incredible to see another instance of the spiritual imagery manifesting in the natural. Such was the case with the 30 minutes of silence in the Temple of Heaven. Consider this historical account Josephus provides of what took place in the earthly Temple:

> "They [the people of Jerusalem] did not attend, **nor give credit to the signs** that were so evident, and did so plainly **foretell their future desolation**. But like men infatuated, without either eyes to see, or minds to consider, did not regard the denunciations that God made to them...

> "[During] the feast of unleavened bread, on the eighth day of the month Xanthicus [Nisan], and at the ninth hour of the night, **so great a light shone round the altar**, and the holy house, that it appeared to be bright day time. Which light lasted for half an hour...

> "Moreover, at that feast which we call Pentecost; as the priests

140

were going by night into the inner [court of the] temple, as their custom was, to perform their sacred ministrations, they said, that in the first place **they felt a quaking, and heard a great noise**: and after that they heard a sound, as of a multitude, saying, "Let us remove hence."[241]

Wow! Could what we just read in Revelation 8:1 have been the cause of what the priests experienced in the Holy Temple? I'm confident enough to say *yes*. Why else would God have manifested such wonders?

One must also take note of the activity that took place within the heavenly temple, which should be contrasted to a similar scene in Revelation 16. Here, incense is burned, representing the prayers of the saints who were martyred. This was heavenly retribution, fulfilling the words of Jesus, in Matthew 23:35, where the guilt of righteous bloodshed in the Holy Land, all the way back to Abel (before the Law), was to be reconciled. Contrast this to Revelation 16, where the full bowls are a fulfillment of what was written in The Law and The Prophets (Moses and Elijah).

THE SUFFERING OF THE PROMISED LAND

The Land of Israel was promised to Abraham as a land flowing with milk and honey. The heartbreaking images that follow in verses 6 through 12 in Revelation 8 depict this lush and fertile region turn from the Garden of Eden to the Dead Sea. The Land, and the creation upon it have become subject to the curse of the Law (Deuteronomy 28:18, 24, 38–40, 42).

The prophetic images in Revelation 8 flow from Ezekiel 5, where the nation of Israel will again suffer destruction in thirds:

"'Therefore as I live,' declares the Lord God, 'Because you have defiled My sanctuary with all your detestable idols and with all your abominations, I definitely will also withdraw and My eye will have no pity, and I also will not spare. A third of you will die by plague or perish by famine among you, a third will fall by the sword around you, and a third I will scatter to every wind, and I will unsheathe a sword behind them." Ezekiel 5:11–12 (NASB)

John's Revelation is very similar to Ezekiel's, therefore it is important to draw on Ezekiel's writings as a guide for interpreting what John's book

[241] Josephus, *Jewish Wars*, Book 6, Chapter 3.

recorded.

Furthermore, another motif that is subtly introduced here is that of the plagues of Egypt. This motif will become overt later on in Revelation, but here the keen student of the Hebrew Scriptures will pick up hints. This too is in fulfilment of the consequence of the Law (Deuteronomy 28:27, 60).

א *(v 6 – 7) "And the seven Angels, who had the seven trumpets, prepared themselves to sound.*

And the first sounded[242], and there was hail and fire mixed with water,[243] and they were cast upon the Land, and the third of the Land was burned, and a third of the trees burned, and all the grass of the Land burned."

Josephus lists many occasions where villages, fields, and crops were set ablaze by the Romans, and at times, even the Jewish factions who vied for power.

> "And truly the very view itself of the country was a melancholy thing. For those places which were before adorned with trees, and pleasant gardens, were now become a desolate country every way; and its trees were all cut down. Nor could any foreigner that had formerly seen Judea, and the most beautiful suburbs of the city, and now saw it, as a desert; but lament and mourn sadly at so great a change. For the war had laid all the signs of beauty quite waste. Nor if any one that had known the place before, had come on a sudden to it now, would he have known it again."[244]

The dramatic image of hail and fire reminds us of the Egyptian plague that struck everything in the open fields (Exodus 9.23–25).

א *(v 8 – 9) "And the second sounded, and there was as a great burning mountain falling into the Sea and a third of the Sea became blood.*

And a third of all creatures that were in the Sea that had breath died,

---

[242] The Aramaic does not have "Angel" in this verse or the ones that follow.
[243] The Aramaic has "water," while the Greek has "blood."
[244] Josephus, *Wars*, 6:6:1, https://penelope.uchicago.edu/josephus/war-6.html

and a third of ships were destroyed."

It is hard to think of Israel and naval battles having any correlation. But the fact is, the Holy Land has along its border the Great Sea (Mediterranean) to the West and the Jordan River to the East, which connects the Sea of Galilee to the North and the Dead Sea to the South. The Jewish-Roman War took place not only in cities and fields, but on open waters as well.

Concerning the Great Sea, Josephus writes:

"[Certain Jews] determined to go off to sea. They also built themselves a great many piratical ships, and turned pirates upon the seas near to Syria, and Phoenicia, and Egypt, and made those seas unnavigable to all men...

"Now as those people of Joppa were floating about in this sea, in the morning there fell a violent wind upon them; it is called by those that sail there "the black north wind," and there dashed their ships one against another, and dashed some of them against the rocks, and carried many of them by force, while they strove against the opposite waves, into the main sea...

"the sea was bloody a long way, and the maritime parts were full of dead bodies; for the Romans came upon those that were carried to the shore, and destroyed them; and the number of the bodies that were thus thrown out of the sea was four thousand and two hundred. The Romans also took the city without opposition, and utterly demolished it."[245]

Concerning the Sea of Galilee (Lake of Gennesareth), Josephus writes:

"Vespasian put upon ship-board as many of his forces as he thought sufficient to be too hard for those that were upon the lake, and set sail after them...

"the Romans ran many of them through with their long poles. Sometimes the Romans leaped into their ships, with swords in their hands, and slew them; but when some of them met the vessels, the Romans caught them by the middle, and destroyed

---

[245] Josephus, *Wars*, 3:9:3, https://penelope.uchicago.edu/josephus/war-3.html

at once their ships and themselves who were taken in them. And for such as were drowning in the sea, if they lifted their heads up above the water, they were either killed by darts, or caught by the vessels; but if, in the desperate case they were in, they attempted to swim to their enemies, the Romans cut off either their heads or their hands...

"one might then see the lake all bloody, and full of dead bodies, for not one of them escaped. And a terrible stink, and a very sad sight there was on the following days over that country; for as for the shores, they were full of shipwrecks, and of dead bodies all swelled."[246]

Concerning the River Jordan and the Dead Sea, Josephus writes:

"[The Roman General Placidus] had driven the whole multitude to the river-side, where they were stopped by the current, [for it had been augmented lately by rains, and was not fordable,] he put his soldiers in array over against them; so the necessity the others were in provoked them to hazard a battle, because there was no place whither they could flee. They then extended themselves a very great way along the banks of the river, and sustained the darts that were thrown at them, as well as the attacks of the horsemen, who beat many of them, and pushed them into the current.

"At which fight, hand to hand, fifteen thousand of them were slain, while the number of those that were unwillingly forced to leap into Jordan was prodigious. There were besides two thousand and two hundred taken prisoners...

"the whole country through which they fled was filled with slaughter, and Jordan could not be passed over, by reason of the dead bodies that were in it, but because the lake Asphaltites [The Dead Sea] was also full of dead bodies, that were carried down into it by the river."[247]

---

[246] Ibid, 3:10:9.
[247] Ibid, 4:7:5–6.

א *(v 10 – 11) "And the third sounded, and a great burning star fell from the sky like a blaze and it fell on a third of the rivers and upon the springs of water,*

And the name of the star is called Absinthe,[248] and a third of the water became like absinthe and a multitude of people died because the waters were made bitter."

The mention of absinthe, or wormwood, takes us to two key Old Testament passages. The first is in Deuteronomy 29:18, where God warns the people of Israel to disallow the root of wormwood to bear forth in their hearts. The second, found in Jeremiah 23:15, warning about the destruction of Jerusalem by the Babylonians, reads, "I will feed them with bitter food and give them wormwood to drink, for from the prophets of Jerusalem ungodliness has gone out into all the land." Further, the bloodied waters also echo another Egyptian plague (Exodus 7.20–21).

א *(v 12) "And the fourth sounded and a third of the Sun was swallowed and a third of the moon and a third of the stars, and a third of them became dark, and a third of the day did not appear, and the night likewise."*

Reminiscent of yet another plague (Exodus 10.21–23), prophetic darkness covered the Holy Land. This ominous image is a classic precursor to the Day of the Lord, which was an appointed time of God's justice manifesting (see Amos 5:18; Joel 3:14). Jesus also prophesied this Day of the Lord in Matthew 24:

"But immediately after the tribulation of those days the sun will be darkened, and the moon will not give its light, and the stars will fall from the sky, and the powers of the heavens will be shaken. And then the sign of the Son of Man will appear in the sky, and then all the tribes of the earth will mourn, and they will see the Son of Man coming on the clouds of the sky with power and great glory. And He will send forth His angels with a great trumpet blast, and they will gather together His elect from the four winds, from one end of the sky to the other."
Matthew 24:29–31 (NASB)

---

[248] Known as *artemisia absinthium*, or *wormwood*, which is a bitter herb, and can be deadly if consumed in large doses.

Just as we read in Revelation 7, Jesus sent angels to seal and gather those who would be spared from the judgment of the Law of Moses. There were signs in the heavens (the chariots of fire mentioned by Josephus), and the balance of spiritual power was shaken (Luke 10:18). There was also another great sign in heaven – perhaps even a "sign of the Son of Man," which Josephus recorded.

> "[The Jews] did not attend nor give credit to the signs that were so evident, and did so plainly foretell their future desolation, but, like men infatuated, without either eyes to see or minds to consider, did not regard the denunciations that God made to them. Thus there was a star resembling a sword, which stood over the city [of Jerusalem], and a comet, that continued a whole year."[249]

א *(v 13) "And I heard one eagle flying in the sky, which said, 'Woe, woe, woe, to the inhabitants of the Land from the sound of the trumpets of the three angels who are going to sound!'"*

The Aramaic reads, "one eagle," representing the Roman empire (4 Ezra 11–12). This vision ironically depicts the agent of their calamity also being their harbinger. The eagle mentioned here is also mentioned by Jesus, who does so in order to harken to the words of God in Deuteronomy 28. Here are three linked passages that all correspond to the same event:

- *"The Lord will bring a nation against you from far away, from the end of the earth, as **the eagle swoops** down; a nation whose language you will not understand, a nation with a defiant attitude, who will have no respect for the old, nor show favor to the young... And it will besiege you in all your towns until your high and fortified walls in which you trusted come down throughout your land, and it will besiege you in all your towns throughout your land which the Lord your God has given you." Deuteronomy 28:49–52 (NASB)*

- *"For just as the lightning comes from the east and flashes as far as the west, so will the coming of the Son of Man be. Wherever the corpse is, there the **eagles** will gather." Matthew 28:27–28 (NASB)*

- *"'I tell you, on that night there will be two in one bed; one will be*

---

[249] Josephus, *Wars*, 6:5:3, https://penelope.uchicago.edu/josephus/war-6.html

taken and the other will be left. There will be two women grinding at
the same place; one will be taken and the other will be left. Two men
will be in the field; one will be taken and the other will be left.' And
responding, they said to Him, 'Where, Lord?' And He said to them,
*"Where the body is, there also the **eagles** will be gathered." Luke*
17:34–37 (NASB)

As for the Woes, they are found throughout the Hebrew Scriptures
(especially Isaiah 5 and Habakkuk 2). When Ezekiel ate a scroll (like John
soon will in Revelation 10), it was said to contain woe (Ezekiel 2:10). He was
then sent by God to proclaim, "Woe, because of all the evil abominations of
the house of Israel, which will fall by the sword, famine, and plague!" (Ezekiel
6:11).

Fast forward to Jesus, who, in the tradition of the prophets of old,
declared woes on two noteworthy occasions. First, in Matthew 11:20–24, He
said, "woe to the cities of Chorazin and Bethsaida." These cities were in Jesus'
homeland of Galilee, and we know historically that Our Saviour's foresight
was razor sharp.

> "[The Jews] provoked the Romans to treat the country
> according to the law of war; nor did the Romans, out of the
> anger they bore at this attempt, leave off, either by night or by
> day, burning the places in the plain, and stealing away the cattle
> that were in the country, and killing whatsoever appeared
> capable of fighting perpetually, and leading the weaker people
> as slaves into captivity; so that Galilee was all over filled with
> fire and blood."[250]

Jesus also spoke woes to the religious leaders in Matthew 23. Speaking
of the same event, Jesus warned them of the coming calamity and
retribution. What Jesus foresaw came about in a most horrific way by
the hands of the Romans.

> "[They slew] many of the priests, as they were about their
> sacred ministrations.... and sprinkled that altar which was
> venerable among all men, both Greeks and Barbarians, with
> their own blood; till the dead bodies of strangers were mingled
> together with those of their own country, and those of profane

---

[250] Ibid, 3:4:1.

persons with those of the priests, and the blood of all sorts of dead carcasses stood in lakes in the holy courts themselves.

…the priests that were pinned with the famine came down, and when they were brought to Titus by the guards, they begged for their lives; but he replied, that the time of pardon was over as to them… So he ordered them to be put to death."[251]

Finally, Josephus tells us of another Jesus, named Jesus, son of Ananus. He was a peasant farmer and a prophet. For seven years he prophesied "woe, woe to Jerusalem," until he was killed by a Roman projectile that hit him atop the walls of Jerusalem. He was constantly mistreated, beaten, and flogged – yet he never spoke a word against his assailants. With respect to this man, Josephus remarks,

"There was one Jesus, the son of Ananus, a plebeian and a husbandman, who, four years before the war began, and at a time when the city was in very great peace and prosperity, came to that feast whereon it is our custom for everyone to make tabernacles to God in the temple, began on a sudden to cry aloud, 'A voice from the east, a voice from the west, a voice from the four winds, a voice against Jerusalem and the holy house, a voice against the bridegrooms and the brides, and a voice against this whole people!'

"[They] brought him to the Roman procurator, where he was whipped till his bones were laid bare; yet he did not make any supplication for himself, nor shed any tears, but turning his voice to the most lamentable tone possible, at every stroke of the whip his answer was, 'Woe, woe to Jerusalem!'

"This cry of his was the loudest at the festivals; and he continued this ditty for seven years and five months, without growing hoarse, or being tired therewith, until the very time that he saw his presage in earnest fulfilled in our siege, when it ceased; for as he was going round upon the wall, he cried out with his utmost force, 'Woe, woe to the city again, and to the people, and to the holy house!' And just as he added at the last, 'Woe, woe to myself also!' there came a stone out of one of the

---

[251] Ibid, 5:1:3, 6:6:1.

engines, and smote him, and killed him immediately; and as he was uttering the very same presages he gave up the ghost.

Now if anyone consider these things, he will find that God takes care of mankind, and by all ways possible foreshows to our race what is for their preservation; but that men perish by those miseries which they madly and voluntarily bring upon themselves."[252]

INTERLUDE: WHERE IS GOD'S LOVE IN ALL THIS?

When you cover this much historical ground, it can be easy to lose sight of the grand love story. Between the time when Israel was first invaded by the Assyrians, to the fall of Jerusalem by the Babylonians, to the Maccabean Revolt against the Greeks, to the advent of Jesus the Messiah, to the fall of Jerusalem under Rome, 800 years of history are covered. In the midst of those years, there are incredible stories of righteous men and women, miracles, angelic visitations, God's favor, and promises fulfilled. That's a lot of ups and downs.

Revelation focuses on a major downer—in fact the most significant in Jewish history. It is the reason Jesus lamented over Jerusalem when He prophesied concerning her destruction (Matthew 23:37). His heart broke because He saw the suffering ahead. But we must remember this is not the end of the story nor the end of the Jewish story. In Romans 9, 10, and 11, Paul writes an incredible discourse on God's grand love story. In those chapters he explains how God is weaving the reconciliation of the Gentile nations to Himself by means of the great calamities that came upon the people of Israel.

"Now if their wrongdoing proves to be riches for the world, and their failure, riches for the Gentiles, how much more will their fulfillment be!"

"... For if their rejection proves to be the reconciliation of the world, what will their acceptance be but life from the dead?

"... For if you [Gentiles] were cut off from what is by nature a wild olive tree, and contrary to nature were grafted into a cultivated olive tree, how much more will these who are the natural branches be grafted into their

---

[252] Ibid, 6:5:3–4.

own olive tree?" Romans 11:12, 15, 24 (NASB)

Did you just catch what Paul wrote? Romans 11 pretty much destroys the Western notion of 'turn or burn'. When he speaks of "life from the dead" in 11:15, he is pulling on Ezekiel 37 and the Jewish dry bones who will come to life again. And in 1 Corinthians 15, when he writes of the Great Resurrection, he is speaking of both Gentiles and Jews:

> *"For since by a man death came, by a man also came the resurrection of the dead. For as in Adam all die, so also in Christ all will be made alive. But each in his own order: Christ the first fruits, after that those who are Christ's at His coming, then comes the end, when He hands over the kingdom to our God and Father, when He has abolished all rule and all authority and power. For He must reign until He has put all His enemies under His feet. The last enemy that will be abolished is death."*
> *1 Corinthians 15:21–26 (NASB)*

To top it all off, Paul concludes his three-chapter exhortation with this mic-drop statement:

> *"For I do not want you, brothers and sisters, to be uninformed of this mystery—so that you will not be wise in your own estimation—that a partial hardening has happened to Israel until the fullness of the Gentiles has come in;* **and so all Israel will be saved.***"*
> *Romans 11:25–26 (NASB)*

We must read through the book of Revelation with these things in mind. What took place in 70 AD was temporal, but God's love story is eternal. As Paul states, let's not be wise in our own estimation. The reason Paul called this a mystery is because it falls beyond our natural comprehension. But if we put on the mind of Christ (1 Corinthians 2:16), then we can immediately step into the flow of his love.

Many people come to the book of Revelation to try to figure out who's in and who's out, who burns and who doesn't. That misses the entire scope of the book. Moreover, there is only one judgement seat, and the name written on it isn't yours or mine. He alone is seeing all ends; we cannot possibly fathom such outcomes. Even with the mind of Christ, some things are for God alone (Matthew 24:36). **But what we can rest assured in is the fact that all of God's judgements are restorative, not retributive.** Case in point: Deuteronomy 30:3–6:

> *"The Lord your God will restore you from captivity, and have compassion*

on you, and will gather you again from all the peoples where the Lord your God has scattered you. If any of your scattered countrymen are at the ends of the earth, from there the Lord your God will gather you, and from there He will bring you back. The Lord your God will bring you into the land which your fathers possessed, and you shall possess it; and He will be good to you and make you more numerous than your fathers.

Moreover, the Lord your God will circumcise your heart and the hearts of your descendants, to love the Lord your God with all your heart and all your soul, so that you may live." (NASB)

This is after all of the curses of Deuteronomy 28 and 29, which is the legal context for all of the calamities in Revelation. Despite all this, God's mercy, not punishment, is the end of the story. Let us therefore look past judgement and keep Revelation within the context of God's grand narrative (chapter 2 of this book).

John's Revelation is a trifecta of hope: First, hope for all the saints in the Matthew 23 and Hebrews 11 hall of faith fame. Second, hope in the end of the Age of Moses and liberation from the curses of the Law, transitioning us into the commensurate launch of *the age of ages*, the Age of Messiah. Finally, John's vision provides all of creation (not just humanity) with the future hope of a restored Eden experience; where heaven and earth become one, where our resurrected mortal and physical bodies do not decay or die, and where we can walk hand in hand with God in the cool of the day upon a renewed planet. Hence the title of this book, *Dawn of All Hope*.

11 ALL THE KINGS HORSES, ALL THE KINGS MEN: CHAPTER 9

"Let not he who is on the housetop go down to get things out of his house. And he who is in the field, let him not turn back to get his cloak... Moreover, pray that your flight will not be in the winter, or on the Sabbath. For then there will be a great calamity, such as has not occurred since the beginning of the age until now, nor will ever be."
— *Matthew 24:17–18, 20–21, Aramaic Text*

Much of Isaiah's ministry was dedicated to prophesying the fall of the Northern Kingdom of Israel. For those who need a refresher, after the death of David's son Solomon, the unified nation split into two kingdoms: The Northern Kingdom of Israel (ten tribes), and the Southern Kingdom of Judah (two tribes, which included Jerusalem and the Temple). God spared the Southern Kingdom of Judah from the Assyrian invasion, which devastated the regions of the Northern Kingdom of Israel. After a short reprieve of about 135 years, the Southern Kingdom of Judah fell to the Babylonians.

This history lesson is vital because the Holy Land fell to the Romans in a similar way. First, Vespasian led a campaign which essentially devastated all of the territories of old Northern Kingdom of Israel, where the ten tribes once inhabited. There was then a short reprieve, and the war ceased as Vespasian headed to Rome for the throne. Titus, son of Vespasian, would then resume the campaign and set his sights squarely on Jerusalem, representing the old Southern Kingdom of Judah.

It is therefore fitting that John's Revelation unfolds in like manner: The Northern Kingdom of Israel falls first, then the Southern Kingdom of Judah, culminating with the fall of Jerusalem and the Temple. Revelation 9 introduces us to the Roman war machine, and takes us through the Roman siege right up to just before Jerusalem falls (Jerusalem is given two entire chapters in Revelation 17 and 18). Hence the sudden shift in Revelation 10, where the vision pauses the unfolding of Israel's future fate (in 70 AD), and turns to the immediate commissioning of John and the measuring of the Temple that was still standing (at the time) in Jerusalem.

א *(v 1) "And the fifth sounded, and I saw a star that had fallen[253] from heaven upon the Land. But there was given to him a key to the well of the deep.[254]"*

Satan is the star. We know this because of the clear allusion to the words of Yeshua in Luke 10:18–19:

"I saw Satan fall from heaven like lightning. Behold, I have given you authority to walk on snakes and scorpions, and authority over all the power of the enemy."

Satan had been dethroned (Luke 4:6, cf. John 12:31, Colossians 2:10–15), and Jesus not only obtained authority over the kingdom of heaven but of the earth as well (Matthew 28:18). This is why it should come as a surprise to the reader to see Satan given a key to the well of the deep. This is where technicalities and legalities within the Mosaic Law came into play.

When the metaphorical gavel fell, and a guilty verdict towards those under the Law was reached, that covenant became of one sin and death (Romans 8:2, 2 Corinthians 3:6). Hebrews 2:14 tells us that Satan works through the power of death. Therefore, with the blood of bulls and goats no longer

---

[253] This verb is in a peal perfect conjugation, meaning the star was already in a fallen state.

[254] This is the same "deep" of Revelation 20:1, which is the Hebrew תְּהוֹם of Genesis 1:2, which the Spirit hovered over.

offering atonement (Hebrews 10:4), Satan is able to accuse those under the Law (much like in Zechariah 3) and afflict them (e.g. Luke 13:16).

Jesus affirms this when He says He came to "destroy the works of the devil," (1 John 3:18). But the unfolding of Jesus' destruction of the devil's works came by means of his New Covenant, and through the demonstration of the power of God's Kingdom. And therein lies the technicality: **for those bound under the Law, there was no longer any covenant protection** (found in Deuteronomy 28:1-14). Rather, there remained for a limited time (a 40-year period that ended with the destruction of the Temple) a legal right for Satan to afflict those under the obsolete covenant.

In this context, consider the words of Paul in Hebrews, writing to those who were once under the Law, at a time when they still had the option to defect back to the old Mosaic system (said option disappeared along with the Temple in 70 AD):

> *"...as you see the day drawing near [and we go] on sinning willfully after receiving the knowledge of the truth, there no longer remains a sacrifice for sins, but a terrifying expectation of judgment and the fury of a fire which will consume the adversaries. Anyone who has ignored the Law of Moses is put to death without mercy on the testimony of two or three witnesses. How much more severe punishment do you think he will deserve who has trampled underfoot the Son of God, and has regarded as unclean the blood of the covenant by which he was sanctified, and has insulted the Spirit of grace?" Hebrews 10:25–29 (NASB)*

Those are harsh words for people under a harsh Law. The testimony of the Two Witnesses (Moses and Elijah; The Law and the Prophets) mentioned in Revelation 11 flow right out of Hebrews 10. What the writer is saying is that as the Day of the Lord was about to descend upon Israel, they were called to be mindful to not reject the New Covenant in favour of the old, because in doing so they would be completely naked and defenseless against the Day of the Lord. And we know that throughout Israel's history, the Day of the Lord was always made manifest though a military attack via a foreign nation.

Returning to the fallen star, Satan is seen being given a key—that is to say, legal right—to the deep, a symbolic holding place for demons (see Luke 8:31; cf. 2 Peter 2:4, Jude 1:6). It was granted to him to summon a demonic hoard that overshadowed both the Roman legions that descended upon the Holy Land from abroad and the factions of Zealots and Jewish rebels who caused

Jerusalem to implode from within (cf. Ephesians 2:2).

This is not the first time we witness celestial beings influencing empires. In Daniel 10, we read of the infamous Prince of Persia who withstood an angel 21 days, hindering him from delivering a message to Daniel. As Robert Altar remarks,

> "The probable reference is not to the Persian emperor but to a celestial *sar* who serves as an angelic patron of Persia. Though there are a couple of episodic hints of such a notion in earlier biblical literature, it basically reflects a new concept of history: celestial agents do battle with one another on behalf of the nations they patronize, and human agency is thus drastically reduced."[255]

Lastly, the roll-call of spiritual antagonists in all of Revelation 9 takes place not in chronological order, but in order of significance. This is important to note. To understand this, let us recall how the siege unfolded:

Vespasian (a Roman general) and his son Titus (a Roman general) came together, each with two legions. Summoned by Nero, Vespasian led the entire campaign. The general decimated Galilee and Samaria to the north, and the southern regions surrounding Jerusalem. Then, to the shock of the empire, Nero committed suicide, and the entire known world held its breath. Three generals succeeded each other in claiming the throne, one killing off the next, in less than a year's time. The legions loyal to Vespasian then proclaimed that he was the new ruler of Rome. Convinced of their sincerity, and recalling the prophetic word he received from Josephus, the general halted the Judean campaign and headed for Rome to claim the throne of Caesar.

Vespasian therefore commissioned his son Titus to finish the job in Judea. Himself a general and skilled in war, the young Titus set his sights squarely on Jerusalem. For five months he besieged the Holy City, cutting off its food supply with an 8 kilometer wall of circumvallation. During that time, Roman scorpions, onagers, and siege towers blasted the city's inhabitants with boulders, stones, and bolts (cross-bow arrows). At the end of the five months, Titus broke through the three walls, slaughtered the priests, razed the Temple, and set the city on fire. He and his legions brought about the end of the Mosaic Age.

---

[255] Alter, Robert. *The Hebrew Bible: Volume 3 – The Writings* (New York: W. W. Norton & Company, 2019), p. 789.

We have then two stages of the three and a half year campaign.[256] First, Vespasian, who marched past the Euphrates and came from the North, destroyed the Holy Land, except Jerusalem. Second, Titus, his son, who marched out of Egypt from the South, destroyed the Holy City and Temple, along with the priests, and fulfilled the requirements of the Law (the curses). Between the two, the most significant achievement was Titus' from a Jewish perspective, since he forever changed their religion and nation.

With these things in mind, we can overlay spiritual aspects as they are revealed in Revelation 9. Verses 1 to 11 display Satan (star) and Vespasian (Abaddon), and with them the Roman legions and Praetorian guards assigned to Titus. We know this because John specifically mentions the five-month campaign (verses 5, 10). Therefore, Revelation 9 introduces the most significant element of the Jewish-Roman war: that spiritual and physical forces coincided to besiege and destroy Jerusalem and the Temple. This stage of the war took place in the third year of the campaign.

In verses 13 to 21, the vision then shifts *back* to the beginning of the war. The Euphrates, much like the Rhine or the Danube rivers in Europe, represent a long-standing territorial and cultural border. It was the checkpoint into the Fertile Crescent from the North. This is where Vespasian broke in, having departed from Greece and riding through Asia Minor (where the seven churches were). The vivid description of the Roman armor and weapons in verses 17 to 19 are unmistakable (more on this below).

Because Revelation 9 reveals those who destroyed Jerusalem first, and those who destroyed the rest of the Holy Land second, we don't need to wonder about the open-ended conclusion to the chapter in verses 20 and 21. Those who didn't repent during Vespasian's campaign would find themselves worse off under Titus. We now have sufficient context to continue on with Revelation 9.

א *(v 2 – 6) "And smoke came up from the well like the smoke of a great furnace which was kindled, and the Sun and the air were darkened by the smoke of the well.*

And from the smoke locusts went out over The Land, and power was

---

[256] The entire Jewish-Roman war lasted 7 years, with an anti-climactic battle in the fortress at Masada, near the Dead Sea. But the last 3 and a half years merely comprised of Rome pursuing the remaining rebel factions.

given to them much like the scorpions of that land have[257].

And it was told them to not do wrong to the grass of The Land, neither any greenery, not even trees. Rather only the people who do not have the seal of Elohim between their eyes.

And it was permitted for them to not (merely) kill them, rather that they be tortured for five months. And their torture was like the torture of a scorpion when it throws itself upon a man.

And in those days people will wish for Death[258] *but it won't happen, and they will envy the dead but Death will flee from them."*

The locust in this instance are not echoing the plagues of the Exodus narrative. We know this because of their description in verse 7, where they were decked with war attire. Instead, the imagery here takes us to the prophet Joel (Joel 1:4–7; 2:1–11), who begins his prophecy with a declaration of the Day of the Lord against Israel.

These specific warriors were given legal right to torture those who were not sealed (which we covered in Revelation 7; see also Ezekiel 9:4–9) during the five-month siege against Jerusalem under Titus. The "torture of a scorpion when it throws itself upon a man" speaks of a slow and agonizing death. Josephus adequately details the protracted sufferings experienced by those who were shut up within the towering walls of Jerusalem, the Great City.

Those who seek death in verse 6 tend to perplex people unnecessarily. It is not literal, in the sense that people are somehow unable to take their own lives. Rather, it is an extension of verse 5, where one would rather die than endure the suffering inflicted by a scorpion sting. Here are but a couple of the several accounts given to us by Josephus.

"[Having heard that a mother ate her child], the whole city was full of this horrid action immediately; and while every body laid this miserable case before their own eyes, they trembled, as if this unheard-of action had been done by themselves. So those

---

[257] "that land have," is the literal Aramaic reading, further solidifying the fact that this is an isolated event, rather than a world-wide occasion.
[258] I have chosen use "death" as a proper noun, picking up on the imagery of Revelation 6:8.

that were thus distressed by the famine, were very desirous to die: and those already dead were esteemed happy; because they had not lived long enough either to hear, or to see such miseries."[259]

"The terror was so very great, that he who survived called them that were first dead happy; as being at rest already: as did those that were under torture in the prisons, declare that upon this comparison those that lay unburied were the happiest."[260]

א *(v 7 – 10) "And the form of the locusts was as the form of horses that are readied for war. And upon their heads were like wreaths whose form was of gold, but their faces were like the faces of men.*

And they had hair like hair of women and their teeth were like those of lions.

And they had breastplates like breastplates of iron and the sound of their dracos[261] were like the sound of the chariots of many horses running to battle. And they had tails like scorpions and a sting in their tails, and their authority is to antagonize people for five months."

The rider and horse were one. Golden wreaths were commonly used in Rome to represent military prowess. Hence, these were top soldiers. The long hair, the "faces of men," and gold wreath are also all telltale standard roman military helmets. If you do an internet search for a Praetorian Guard helmet, a Galea helmet, or a Roman Cavalry helmet, you will have some visual context for what John wrote.[262]

The breastplates are self-explanatory; however, it is worth noting that the mention of their "iron" material would match the construction of Roman

---

[259] Josephus, *Wars*, 6:3:4.

[260] Ibid, 4:6:3.

[261] The Aramaic נבא can can be translated as "wing," but according to Marcus Jastrow's Dictionary (pg. 262), it can also be rendered "a pole with a hook." Within the context of the Roman cavalry described here, a Roman draco (flying dragon), a military standard carried by the draconarius (cavalryman), was the equivalent of the aquila (eagle), carried by the legion's (infantry) standard-bearer, and seemed most fitting to use here.

[262] The Nijmegen Helmet, recently discovered in 1915, would also match the description in the text.

lorica squamata, standard issue body armor for infantry and cavalry. Check the footnote for the roman standards (dracos) below. Now let us move onto the scorpion tails. In addition to their swords, Roman cavalrymen were outfitted with *cheiroballistra* crossbows and *pila* javelins. These weapons were projectiles, hence the imagery of a scorpion's sting.

> "[Titus] gave orders that the commanders should put the army into battle array, in the face of the enemy... So the soldiers, according to custom, opened the cases wherein their arms before lay covered, and marched with their breast plates on, as did the horsemen lead their horses in their fine trappings. Then did the places that were before the city [of Jerusalem] shine very splendidly for a great way. Nor was there any thing so grateful to Titus's own men, or so terrible to the enemy as that sight."[263]

Given the exclusivity of Roman cavalry in these verses, it is fitting that they match the unit that fought alongside Titus. The son of Vespasian gained notoriety when he became the Prefect (chief officer) of the elite soldier group known as the Praetorian Guard, Rome's Navy Seals. Under Titus, they were an equestrian order (eques). These elite soldiers broke through Jerusalem's walls, laid siege to her for 5 months, and destroyed the Holy Temple.

KING ABADDON AND THE SON OF DESTRUCTION

א *(v 11) "And there is over them a king, the angel of the deep, whose name in Hebrew is Abaddon (destruction), and in Aramaic,[264] its name is Shora (principality)."*

I am so excited to discuss the intertextuality between Revelation 9:11, Daniel 10:13, and 2 Thessalonians 2:3. It is amazing!

Abaddon (Strong's H11) means "destruction," or "place of depth/abyss." The Hebrew takes to root "abad" אֲבַד is makes it a near proper name, abaddon אֲבַדּוֹן. Meanwhile, the Aramaic in Revelation takes the same root word found in Daniel 10:13, "sar," שַׂר (Strongs H8269), which means "prince" or

---

[263] Josephus, *Wars*, 5:9:1, https://penelope.uchicago.edu/josephus/war-5.html
[264] Most Bibles today have the Hebrew name and Greek name for the angel. Yet the original text makes no mention of Greek, only the Semitic languages of Jesus' day: Hebrew and Aramaic.

"angelic ruler" (referring to the Prince of Persia). Combining the Hebrew and Aramaic words in Revelation 9:11 we get *Angelic Prince of Destruction*.

What we have here is a synergy of illustrations: the angel of the deep, Abaddon (place of destruction/abyss), and spiritual principality. John saw this angel in his vision and was then given two words that drew from Old Testament imagery[265] to help contextualize it. So much like the Prince of Persia, a Prince of Rome (Prince of Destruction) rose up to threaten the Israelites. The General Vespasian, who would later become Caesar (emperor), was the human expression of Abaddon, much like Darius was the human expression of the Prince of Persia in Daniel. For simplicity sake, Vespasian was Abaddon.

Next, let's look at the connection between Revelation 9:1 and 2 Thessalonians 2. In context, Paul's letter reads as follows:

*"Behold! The Day of the Lord will surely come! Let no one deceive you by any means as if it won't happen. Firstly is the **revolt**, and there be revealed the person of sin, **the son of Abaddon**.[266]*
*He who is an opposer, and he will elevate himself **above all those who call themselves god** and divine; so that even in the Temple of Elohim as a god he will be **installed**, and will demonstrate concerning himself, that he is like a god…*
*So then, that lawless one will reveal himself, whom our Lord Yeshua will cause him to **fulfill his purpose**[267] by the Spirit of His mouth, and will cause him **to desist** through the unveiling of His coming.*
*Indeed, the coming of that one is the effect of Satan, with an **entire army**,[268] and false signs and wonders."*
2 Thessalonians 2:2–4, 8–9, Aramaic Text

This is a much different reading that the Greek-based text in our Bibles. But the language of Jesus provides much more clarity. Paul, perhaps recounting a prophetic dream or open vision, looked roughly 15 to 20 years ahead and saw the rise of Titus. The "revolt" was a clear reference to the

---

[265] Job 26:6, 28:22, 31:12; Proverbs 15:11, 27:20; Joshua 5:14; Daniel 10:13, 12:1.
[266] The same root word found in Revelation 9:11.
[267] The Aramaic root here (suph) is "to come to an end," "to be fulfilled," "to finish." The verb stem, Aphel Imperfect, means Jesus is causing the verb. Given the theological impossibility of Jesus destroying someone, the implication is that Jesus is causing the subject to finish or complete something.
[268] The word חַיִל means "army," "military force," or "heavenly host."

Jewish Revolt of 66 AD, which gave way to the Roman invasion in 67 AD.

If Vespasian was Abaddon, then it would make sense to interpret Titus to be the son of Abaddon. The young general Titus would also make a name for himself by subduing the Jews and razing the Temple to the ground. Upon the Temple mount he would be venerated as a divine emperor by his soldiers.

> "And now the Romans, upon the flight of the seditious into the city, and upon the burning of the holy house itself, and of all the buildings round about it, brought their ensigns to the temple, and set them over-against its eastern gate. And there did they offer sacrifices to them: and there did they make Titus Imperator with the greatest acclamations of joy."[269]

The early church father and apologetic, Tertullian, enlightens the modern reader by explaining how Romans worshipped their ensigns, or standards. These typically had the Roman eagle at the top of a pole, and were incredibly significant to soldiers.

> "But you also worship victories, for in your trophies the cross is the heart of the trophy. The camp religion of the Romans is all through a worship of the standards, a setting the standards above all gods. Well, as those images decking out the standards."[270]

The title of "Imperator" was not just a military one; it had deeper implications. It was a euphemism for emperor. For instance, Julius Caesar attributed the title of Imperator to himself as well. We also know that based on the Imperial Cult of Rome, that to be emperor, or a son of the emperor, was to be divine. And madmen like Caligula and Nero took Julius Caesar's self-deification to a whole new level. This is important because Paul's prophecy that Titus would, "elevate himself above all those who call themselves god and divine," becomes politically charged in this context.

In the years leading up to Titus ascent to the Temple Mount and military victory, Rome was in chaos in 68 and 69 AD following the suicide of Nero. Three other generals vied for the throne, with Vespasian being the fourth.

---

[269] Josephus, *Wars*, 6:6:1, https://penelope.uchicago.edu/josephus/war-6.html
[270] Tertullian, *Apologetics*, chapter 16,
https://www.ccel.org/ccel/schaff/anf03.iv.iii.xvi.html

"The empire, which for a long time had been unsettled and, as it were, drifting, through the usurpation and violent death of three emperors, was at last taken in hand and given stability by the Flavian family."[271]

This was known as *the year of four emperors*. And because it was given that to be emperor was to be divine, three men sought the title of Divius but failed. In this way, Titus fulfilled Paul's prophecy by rising above other who called themselves divine.

And where Paul wrote, "in the Temple of Elohim as a god he will be installed;" the word installed implies "to be situated," or "to be established." The Flavian dynasty (the Roman monarchy under Vespasian), hinged on the military success of the Judean campaign. Therefore, in winning the war, Titus also helped his father (and later himself) secure the throne of Caesar. In this way, Titus' claim to the throne was established.

The Day of the Lord and the coming of Jesus were the same event. Jesus caused Titus to complete his purpose, and also stopped him from doing any more after Titus conquered Judea. Jesus came to end the Mosaic Age. Moreover, Titus' invasion of the Holy Land was, according to Paul, "the effect of Satan, with an entire army," which is exactly what John saw as well in Revelation 9. As for the false signs and wonders, I will cover that at length later on.

Titus was the son of Abaddon (destruction) in 2 Thessalonians 2, and Vespasian was Abaddon in Revelation 9. Both the prophecies of Paul and John spoke of the same event. Looking back to when Jerusalem and the Temple were destroyed the first time, Nebuchadnezzar was the agent of that destruction, and much was prophesied about him prior to those events.[272] It would be bewildering and uncharacteristic of Yahweh God to not have warned the Israelites of second catastrophic event – one that superseded the first one in every way.

An interesting FYI. Vespasian has in his honour a theatre named *Teatro*

---

[271] Suetonius, *Life of Vespasian*,
https://penelope.uchicago.edu/Thayer/E/Roman/Texts/Suetonius/12Caesars/V espasian*.html
[272] Cyrus, the "king of kings," and most powerful ruler of the Known World at that time, crushed Nebuchadnezzar's empire and ultimately freed the Jerusalemites. He is the only non-Jew to be referred to as a "messiah" (anointed one) in the Bible. See Isaiah 45:1.

Flavio Vespasiano, which was built in the 19ᵗʰ century near Rieti, Italy, his homeland. The fresco on the ceiling of the theatre depicts Vespasian and his son Titus in royal procession, following their successful military conquest of Judea (Israel). At about 5 o'clock (bottom right), you can see the golden menorah that was taken from the Holy Temple. **The spoils from the Second Temple were so rich that they funded the construction of the Colosseum in Rome.**

Image Credit: DarioMar19, Teatro Flavio Vespasiano, 2019 (Creative Commons)

א *(v 12) "One woe passes. Behold! There still comes two woes!"*

The woes of Revelation have a mini chiastic structure: In 8:13, an eagle cried out, "Woe! Woe! Woe!" Then Revelation 9 tells us that the first woe is the Roman war machine. In Revelation 11, the second woe is revealed to be the curses of the Law and the Prophets. Lastly, in Revelation 12:12, the third woe is Satan. Revelation 18:10 then closes this structure with those who rule over Judea crying "Woe! Woe! Woe!" over Jerusalem. These three woes are the three catalysts for the great calamity that came upon the Holy Land.

THE ROMAN WAR MACHINE

א *(v 13 – 14) "After this, the sixth Angel sounded, and I heard one voice from the four horns of the altar of gold, which is before Elohim, who said to the sixth angel that had a trumpet: 'Deploy the four angels who had been immobilized[273] at the great river Euphrates.'"*

With the spiritual and physical commanders appointed (Satan and Vespasian), the troops can now be summoned. As mentioned before, the Euphrates would have been a geographical marker to the north in ancient times between Asia Minor and the Fertile Crescent.[274] This scene is also very reminiscent of Ezekiel 9:1–2: "Then He cried out in my presence with a loud voice, saying, 'Come forward, you executioners of the city [of Jerusalem], each with his weapon of destruction in his hand.' And behold, six men came from the direction of the upper gate which faces north."

א *(v 15) "And they were deployed, these four angels who were prepared for an hour and for a day and for a month and for a year; to execute a third of the humans."*

Again, this is in fulfillment of Deuteronomy 28:15–68, in the prophetic tradition of Ezekiel 5:1–5: destruction in thirds. As we look back on these events, we can thank God our Father and our Lord Jesus for the Blood of his New Covenant. "Therefore there is now no condemnation for those who are in Christ Jesus. For the Law of the Spirit of life in Christ Jesus has set you free from the Law of sin and of death," (Romans 8:1–2).

א *(v 16) "And the number of that army of cavalry was two myriad myriads, and I heard their number."*

I'm amazed that so many translations have the number 200,000,000.[275] It might as well say a hundred-billion-trillion! Such an army would be impossible to mobilize, feed, supply, etc. Moreover, how could you possibly transport that many people in a reasonable timeframe?

The Aramaic simply states "two myriad myriads," a singular and a

---

[273] "Deploy… immobilized;" the root words are *to untie* and *to bind,* respectively. But it would be odd for God to bind his own angels. Given the military context, the derivatives I have chosen are more fitting.

[274] Cassius Dio provides a good illustration: "The Jews also were assisted by many of their countrymen from the region round about and by many who professed the same religion, not only from the Roman empire but also from beyond the Euphrates." Roman History, 65:4, https://penelope.uchicago.edu/Thayer/e/roman/texts/cassius_dio/65*.html

[275] I'm not oblivious as to how they arrive at this number: 2 x 10,000 x 10,000 = 200,000,000.

plural.[276] Though this is somewhat enigmatic, we do have a clue from history. Similar to how the word 'dozen' means twelve, a myriad traditionally represented ten thousand in most ancient cultures (though this isn't absolute, since in other instances it just represented a large number). But if we stick with ten thousand, and keep the math simple, we have: ten thousand (10,000) ten thousands (20,000), times 2 (two myriad myriads). **That gives us 60,000.**

If we compare this number to what actually took place when Vespasian and Titus came from the four winds, with four legions, the full might of the Empire, we have an amazing connection to Revelation 9:16:

> "Titus sailed over from Achaia [Greece] to Alexandria [Egypt]… he came suddenly to Ptolemais, and there finding his father, together with the two legions, the fifth and the tenth, which were the most eminent legions of all, he joined them to that fifteenth legion which was with his father: eighteen cohorts followed these legions: there came also five cohorts from Cesarea, with one troop of horsemen, and five other troops of horsemen from Syria.
>
> Now these ten cohorts had severally a thousand footmen, but the other thirteen cohorts had no more than six hundred footmen a piece, with a hundred and twenty horsemen. There were also a considerable number of auxiliaries got together, that came from the Kings Antiochus and Agrippa, and Sohemus, each of them contributing one thousand footmen that were archers, and a thousand horsemen. Malchus also, the king of Arabia, sent a thousand horsemen, besides five thousand footmen, the greatest part of which were archers: so that the whole army, including the auxiliaries sent by the kings, as well

---

[276] The "myriad myriads" formula is also found in Revelation 5:11 and Daniel 7:10, both in Aramaic (though both those passages also add אֶלֶף אֲלְפִים, meaning thousand thousands). However, It is not a stretch to conclude that this is a formula for one plus two equals three, if we compare this to another instance, שְׁמֵי הַשָּׁמָיִם, "heaven heavens" (Deuteronomy 10:14; 1 Kings 8:27), whereby these texts have been used to describe the Third Heaven (cf. 2 Corinthians 12:2–4). Heaven (one) Heavens (two) equals three. See also Talmud, Chagigah 12b. There is also the phrase עָלַם עָלְמַיָּא "age ages" (Daniel 7:18; Ephesians 3:21; Revelation 10:6), which could imply three ages or epoch seasons, as I've discussed at length at the beginning of this book.

horsemen as footmen, **when all were united together, amounted to sixty thousand.**"[277]

While this might seem underwhelming to us today, in the first-century AD this was an obscene number of soldiers. More importantly, this was incredible prophetic accuracy on John's part! Josephus sums up all of those who came against the Holy Land; different nations and kings banded together against the Jews, all under the command of Vespasian and Titus, and this total number of enemies matches the number John heard. Remarkable!

א *(v 17) "Now in this way I saw the horses in a vision, and those sitting upon them had breastplates of fire and chalcedony of brimstone, and the heads of the horses were like the heads of lions, and fire and brimstone and smoke proceeded from their mouths."*

The descriptions of the armies in this Day of the Lord event bears sticking resemblance the visions of the prophet Joel:

"For the day of the Lord is coming;
Indeed, it is near,
A day of darkness and gloom,
A day of clouds and thick darkness.
As dawn is spread over the mountains,
So there is a great and mighty people;
There has never been anything like it,
Nor will there be again after it
To the years of many generations.
A fire consumes before them,
And behind them a flame devours.
The land is like the Garden of Eden before them,
But a desolate wilderness behind them,
And nothing at all escapes them.
Their appearance is like the appearance of horses;
And like war horses, so they run.
With a noise as of chariots
They leap about on the tops of the mountains,
Like the crackling of a flame of fire consuming the stubble…
All faces turn pale…
They storm the city,

---

[277] Josephus, *Wars*, 3:4:2, https://penelope.uchicago.edu/josephus/war-3.html

They run on the wall;
They climb into the houses,
They enter through the windows like a thief.
Before them the earth quakes,
The heavens tremble,
The sun and the moon become dark,
And the stars lose their brightness." Joel 2:1–7, 9–10 (NASB)

Where Revelation 9:17 and Joel 2:3 both speak of fire, both prophecies make a clear reference to Genesis 13:10 and 19:29: The region of Sodom (east of Jerusalem) was like the Garden of Eden before that region was destroyed by the rain of fire and brimstone.

א *(v 18 – 19) "And by these three blows a third of the humans were executed; by the fire, by the brimstone and by the smoke that proceeded from their mouths,*

Because the power of the horses was in their mouths, and also in their tails."[278]

The allusions to Joel 2 continue with a mix of vivid word-pictures depicting the horses to be dragon-like creatures (fire breathing). The description concludes by referencing the scorpion tail again (Revelation 9:10), which was a dream-like vision of the Roman cavalry's artillery. The vision of this ferocious demonic army, led by Satan, was meant to inspire fear and repentance. Those who would hear these words of John read aloud in the days leading up to the Revolt should have trembled and, hopefully, warned anyone and everyone they knew in the Holy Land.

But the shocking reality was that there were those who did not turn from their wayward path, as we will read in the closing verses.

א *(v 20 – 21) "And those humans that remained, those not executed by the blows, these did not turn from the work of their hands: to not worship devils, and idols of gold and of silver and of brass and of wood and of stone, which do not see and do not hear, nor able to walk.*

And they did not turn from their murders, or from their incantations, or

---

[278] The Aramaic does not have the Greek embellishment, "for their tails were like unto serpents, and had heads, and with them they do hurt."

from their fornication."

This pattern of forewarning and ignorance is found throughout the Hebrew Scriptures. But since these verses stem from Deuteronomy 28, then Revelation 9:20–21 serves to fulfill Deuteronomy 29:14–20:

"Now it is not with you alone that I am making this covenant and this oath, but both with those who stand here with us today in the presence of the Lord our God… you have seen [the Egyptian's] abominations and their idols made of wood and stone, silver and gold, which they had with them; so that there will not be among you a man or woman, or family or tribe, whose heart turns away today from the Lord our God, to go to serve the gods of those nations; that there will not be among you a root bearing poisonous fruit and wormwood.

And it shall be when he hears the words of this curse, that he will consider himself fortunate in his heart, saying, 'I will do well though I walk in the stubbornness of my heart in order to destroy the watered land along with the dry.' The Lord will not be willing to forgive him, but rather the anger of the Lord and His wrath will burn against that person, and every curse that is written in this book will lie upon him…"

Moses then continues,

"Now the future generation, your sons who rise up after you and the foreigner who comes from a distant land, when they see the plagues of that land and the diseases with which the Lord has afflicted it, will say, 'All its land is brimstone and salt, burned debris, unsown and unproductive, and no grass grows on it, like the overthrow of Sodom and Gomorrah… which the Lord overthrew in His anger and in His wrath.' All the nations will say, 'Why has the Lord done all this to this land? Why this great outburst of anger?' Then people will say, 'It is because they abandoned the covenant of the Lord, the God of their fathers… Therefore, the anger of the Lord burned against that land, to bring upon it every curse which is written in this book…"
Deuteronomy 29:22–25, 27 (NASB)

Then in chapter 31, God spoke to Moses as he was about to die, saying,

"The Lord said to Moses, 'Behold, you are about to lie down with your fathers; and this people will arise and play the prostitute with the foreign gods of the land into the midst of which they are going, and they will abandon Me and break My covenant which I have made with them.'"
Deuteronomy 31:16 (NASB)

I know that was a lot of reading from Deuteronomy, but without this baseline knowledge that first-century Jews would have had, it is not possible to interpret Revelation from their perspective.

In closing, I will leave you with the reflections of Flavius Josephus, who lamented over the destruction of his own country and kin. The "seditious" he speaks of are the same ones Revelation 9:20–21 alluded to. These were the Zealots and rebel factions that became a fatal disease within the Holy Land.

> "[I] must be allowed to indulge some lamentations upon the miseries undergone by my own country. For that it was a seditious temper of our own that destroyed it, and that they were the **tyrants** among the Jews who brought the Roman power upon us, who unwillingly attacked us, and occasioned the burning of our holy temple. Titus Caesar, who destroyed it, is himself a witness, who, during the entire war, pitied the people who were kept under by **the seditious**, and did often voluntarily delay the taking of the city, and allowed time to the siege, in order to let the authors have opportunity for **repentance**."[279]

> "And now, as the city [of Jerusalem] was engaged in a war on all sides, from these treacherous crowds of **wicked men**, the people of the city, between them, were like a great body torn in pieces...

> "they fought against each other, while they trod upon the dead bodies as they lay heaped one upon another, and taking up a mad rage from those dead bodies that were under their feet,

---

[279] Josephus, *Wars*, Preface, 4. https://penelope.uchicago.edu/josephus/war-pref.html

became the fiercer thereupon."[280]

"But [Jerusalem] was most of all unhappy before it was overthrown, while those [Romans] that took it did it a greater kindness for I venture to affirm that the **sedition** destroyed the city, and the Romans destroyed the sedition, which it was a much harder thing to do than to destroy the walls; so that we may justly ascribe our misfortunes to our own people, and the just vengeance taken on them to the Romans."[281]

"[But] the seditious… **did not repent,** but suffered the same distress to come upon themselves; for they were blinded by that fate which was already coming upon the city, and upon themselves also."[282]

---

[280] Ibid, 5:1:5.
[281] Ibid, 5:6:1.
[282] Ibid, 5:13:7.

12 THE PROPHET IS SUMMONED: CHAPTER 10

*"I will send them prophets and apostles, and some of them they will kill,
and some they will persecute, so that the blood of all the prophets,
shed since the foundation of the world, may be charged against this
generation."*
— Luke 11:49–50 (NASB)

John was both an apostle and a prophet. But as I suggested at the beginning
of this book, his prophetic office was given a specific assignment in the
final years leading up to the fall of Jerusalem. Like the prophet Ezekiel,
John is given an official commissioning, which I have also mentioned several
times. Moreover, John's mission must be understood both in light of the
prophetic tradition of his predecessors, and, in light of the prophetic words
of Jesus concerning Israel.

*"Woe to you! For you build the tombs of the prophets, and it was your
fathers who killed them…For this reason also, the wisdom of God said,
'I will send them prophets and apostles, and some of them they will kill,
and some they will persecute, so that the blood of all the prophets, shed
since the foundation of the world, may be charged against this generation,
from the blood of Abel to the blood of Zechariah, who was killed between*

the altar and the house of God; yes, I tell you, it shall be charged against this generation.' Luke 11:47, 49–51 (NASB)

The prophecies of Jesus and the prophecies of old are brought together in a final crescendo in Revelation. Additionally, John is given something of great significance: a scroll. This was the same scroll given to Ezekiel, as we shall see.

א *(v 1 – 2a) "And I saw another angel[283] who descended from Heaven and he wore a cloud and a rainbow of heaven on his head. And his appearance was like the Sun, and his legs like pillars of fire.*

And there was in his hand a small scroll opened..."

John's prophetic encounter here almost mirrors that of his predecessor:

"[And] on that which resembled a throne, high up, was a figure with the appearance of a man. Then I noticed from the appearance of His waist and upward something like gleaming metal that looked like fire all around within it, and from the appearance of His waist and downward I saw something like fire; and there was a radiance around Him. Like the appearance of the rainbow in the clouds on a rainy day, so was the appearance of the surrounding radiance...
Then I looked, and behold, a hand was extended to me; and behold, a scroll was in it." Ezekiel 1:26–28, 2:9 (NASB)

Given the undeniably similar experiences here between Ezekiel and John, we can benefit from the fact that Ezekiel's account provides us with context and interpretation. First, we must understand the audience. Ezekiel was sent to the house of Israel in the days of the Babylonian siege under Nebuchadnezzar, who destroyed Solomon's Temple and razed Jerusalem. In Ezekiel's commissioning, he is told:

"Son of man, I am sending you to the sons of Israel, to a rebellious people who have rebelled against Me; they and their fathers have revolted against Me to this very day. So I am sending you to those who are impudent and obstinate children, and you shall say to them, 'This is what the Lord God says:' As for them, whether they listen or not—for they are a rebellious house—they will know that a prophet has been among them.

---

[283] The Aramaic lacks "mighty," found in Greek texts.

'Open your mouth wide and eat what I am giving you.' Then I looked, and behold, a hand was extended to me; and behold, a scroll was in it. When He spread it out before me, it was written on the front and back, and written on it were songs of mourning, sighing, and woe…

So I opened my mouth, and He fed me this scroll. And He said to me, 'Son of man, feed your stomach and fill your body with this scroll which I am giving you.' Then I ate it, and it was as sweet as honey in my mouth."
Ezekiel 2:3–5, 8–10, 3:2–3 (NASB)

Ezekiel's audience was the house of Israel. And as we have discovered over and over, John's prophetic audience was also the house of Israel. You can pretty much take Ezekiel 2 and apply it to the audience of John's day. With that established, we must now turn our attention to a crucial part of the John and Ezekiel experience: the contents of the scroll. To do this, I'll need to go through Revelation 10 in a non-linear fashion; but I believe it will be worthwhile.

UNRAVELLING THE SMALL SCROLL

א *(v 8 – 10) "And I heard a voice from Heaven again speaking with me and saying, 'Go! Receive the small scroll that is in the hand of the angel who stands on The Land and upon the Sea.'*

And I went to the angel and I told him to give me the little scroll and he said to me, 'Take and eat it, and your belly will be bitter to you, but it will be like honey in your mouth.'

And I received the small scroll from the hand of the angel, and I ate it, and it was like sweet honey in my mouth and when I had eaten it, my belly was bitter."

John's experience again parallels that of Ezekiel's. The two are given a small scroll to place in their mouths as part of a commissioning ceremony, whereby they are then sent to prophesy to their countrymen. Because of this, we can turn to the major prophet's account once again, as it provides us with commentary regarding the nature of this scroll.

A literal Hebrew translation of Ezekiel 2:10 reads,

"and there were written upon it dirges, and a sound of moaning, and a lamenting song."

Each of the three words used denote a type of song or sound that is melancholy and grievous, which tells us that the scroll Ezekiel was given was a song. This is our first clue. Ezekiel is then told to eat this song scroll. In one of Israel's most defining moments, when they were with Moses in the wilderness, they were all given a similar command:

"The Lord said to Moses, "Behold, you are about to lie down with your fathers; and this people will arise and play the prostitute with the foreign gods of the land into the midst of which they are going, and they will abandon Me and break My covenant...

"Now then, write this song for yourselves, and teach it to the sons of Israel; put it on their lips, so that this song may be a witness for Me against the sons of Israel. For when I bring them into the land flowing with milk and honey, which I swore to their fathers, and they eat and are satisfied and become prosperous, then they will turn to other gods and serve them, and spurn Me and break My covenant. Then it will come about, when many evils and troubles find them, that this song will testify before them as a witness -for it shall not be forgotten from the mouth of their descendants... So Moses wrote down this song on the same day, and taught it to the sons of Israel." Deuteronomy 31:16, 19–22 (NASB)

Robert Alter provides wonderful insight into what is call the Song of Moses:

"traditionally called in Hebrew Shirat Ha'azinu, after the first word of the poem... Moses is enjoined to "put it their mouths," that is, to make them learn it by heart. A similar idiom for memorization is attested in other ancient Semitic languages, and in postbiblical Hebrew, the idiom for 'by heart' is be'aal peh, literally, 'in/on the mouth.' ...The textual permanence of the poem thus makes it an eternal 'witness' that will confront every generation of the people of Israel."[284]

The Song of Moses (found in Deuteronomy 32) was so significant to the people of Israel that Yahweh told them to place it alongside the Ark of the Covenant (Deuteronomy 31:26). Not only do we have the Song of Moses recording in the Book of Deuteronomy, but it was also written as a standalone work (a small scroll) and placed beside the Ark. The words of this small scroll were to "put in the mouths" of Moses and the Israelites. This is our second clue.

---

[284] Alter, Robert. *The Hebrew Bible: Volume 1 – The Five Books of Moses* (New York: W. W. Norton & Company, 2019), p. 1035.

The Song itself is a heavy one, and effectively summarizes Israel's story. Through much calamity and suffering, the people of Israel will have a change of heart. To some degree, Romans 9 to 11 encapsulates the essence of the Song, connecting it to Yahweh's broader narrative of restoration. Because the means by which Israel experiences better days comes through all of the terrible events written in the song, it is fitting to call it a song of lament.

Thus, for Ezekiel to have been given a small scroll of "dirges, and a sound of moaning, and a lamenting song," in the context of his prophetic commissioning, which he is to prophecy the doom of Jerusalem in accordance with the word of Moses in Deuteronomy, **then it is likely that the scroll Ezekiel ate was the Song of Moses**. And given the connection between John and Ezekiel's mission, **then it is also likely that John ate the same scroll: the Song of Moses**. In light of this, the fact that the Song of Moses takes center stage in Revelation 15:3, "and they sang the song of Moses," makes sense, as it is the prelude to the fall of Jerusalem in chapters 16 to 19.

One very notable difference between John's and Ezekiel's experiences is the aftertaste. Both prophets recount that the song scroll tasted like honey. But John then adds that when it hit his stomach, it became bitter (מָרַר, which can also mean "grieved"). Why? I believe it is because of what took place after the prophetic ministries of Ezekiel and John ended.

Jeremiah and Daniel prophesied that after 70 years in captivity, things would turn around for Israel. [285] And they did. King Cyrus, in his famous edict, allowed the Jews to return to their homeland and rebuild their Temple. Remarkably, the antithesis of this occurred 70 years after the Jewish Revolt. In 66 AD, the Jews kicked the hornet's nest and the wrath of Rome fell upon them. 70 years later, in 136 AD, the revolt of Simon bar Kokhba (he was a big deal) was crushed and almost 600,000 of the remnant of Jews were killed.[286] Further, Roman emperor Hadrian (son of Vespasian) renamed Jerusalem to Aelia Capitolina, and built a temple dedicated to Jupiter on the Temple Mount.

The bitterness or grief that John experienced when eating the song scroll makes sense given the outcome of these events. Ezekiel experienced no such

---

[285] Jeremiah 25:1–11; 29:1–10; Daniel 9:1–2.
[286] Cassius Dio, *Roman History*, 69:14:1,
https://penelope.uchicago.edu/Thayer/e/roman/texts/cassius_dio/69.html

bitterness, because after the prophet's death his people would experience a remarkable change of circumstances. However, after John fell asleep, his kin and country would experience a change in circumstances that went from bad to worse. 136 AD brought an age of dirges, moaning, and lamenting for the Israelites.

א *(v 2b) "and he placed his right foot upon the Sea, but the left upon The Land."*

For Jerusalemites, the North has traditionally been where evil and devastation had descended from (Assyria, Babylon, Greece, Rome). With this in mind, consider the placement of the angel's feet: the right foot on the Sea (יַמָּא, in which case it would be the Mediterranean), and left foot on the land of Israel. This likely positions the angel to the North of Jerusalem, facing South and overlooking the Holy Land.

א *(v 3 – 7) "And he cried out with a voice as loud as a roaring lion, and once he cried out, seven thunders spoke with their voices.*

And when the seven thunders spoke I was getting ready to write, but I heard a voice from the Seventh Heaven,[287] saying, 'Close up that which was spoken by the seven thunders and do not write it.'

Now the angel who I saw standing on the Sea and upon the dry land, was raising his hand to Heaven,

and he swore by Him who lives to the age of ages, Him who created Heaven and that which is in it, and The Land and that which is in it: 'Never again will this season happen.[288]

Rather, in the days of the seventh angel, when he prepares to sound, the

---

[287] Unique to the Aramaic, "seven heavens" is an ancient Semitic concept, going as far back as Mesopotamian society. In the Talmud, the seventh heaven is the Araboth (ערבות), where Ezekiel's throne vision originated (Chagigah 12b). In 2 Cor. 12:2–4, Paul visits the third heaven, what the Talmud calls Shehaqim (שחקים); cf. Deuteronomy 10:14 and 1 Kings 8:27, וּשְׁמֵי הַשָּׁמָיִם, heaven of heavens. The Greek likely dropped this because the lack of Jewish context would have confused the Hellenic reader.

[288] A short but dense oath, דְּתְוּב זַבְנָא לֹא נֶהֱוֵא, it speaks of an era or specific time period that has a start date and an end date, and the events therein, never taking place again.

mystery of God is shall complete itself,[289] *which he declared to his servants the Prophets.'"*

The forty-year transition period of epoch seasons, a seismic shift from the Age of Moses to the Age of Messiah, shall never take place again. Never again will the Law be able to demand blood. Never again can anyone come under the curses of the Tablets of Stone, the Law of Moses. To take an oath and swear it by Yahweh God Himself is not a light thing (Matthew 5:33–36). This was a deeply profound theological statement, in which the angel declared that season and all that participated in it: the curses, the calamities, the guilt of all the righteous blood ever shed; NEVER AGAIN. [290]

When the seventh angel sounds (verse 7), the transition of epoch seasons will be complete. This seventh angel with be seen again twice in John's vision (11:15 & 16:17), but the anticipated sounding of the trumpet takes place in the following chapter. Therefore, 10:7 and 11:15 are connected, and speak of the same event.

> *"Never again will this season happen. Rather, in the days of the seventh angel, when he prepares to sound, the mystery of God is shall complete itself… And the seventh angel sounded, and there was a great voice in the Heavens, saying, 'It is now the Age of the Kingdom of Elohim and His Messiah, and He will dominate for the age of ages."*
> *Revelation 10:6–7, 11:15, (Aramaic Text)*

This is such a powerful combination! Of course, much had to happen in between, which I will cover in the next chapter. But it is important to not lose sight of these connected events and what they meant. The Mosaic Age and all that it required was completed:

The Kingdom Age,
     the Age of Messiah,
          the Thousand Years,
               the Age of Ages;

All these descriptions refer to the same period of time in history—a time that was now fully manifested. No longer would it be eclipsed by the Age of Moses. "But now once at **the consummation of the ages** He has been

---

[289] The Ithpaal Perfect is an intensive force in a reflexive voice.
[290] Even in the Talmud, it states that the reason the second temple was destroyed was because of the bloodshed of the righteous prophets of Yahweh God. See Shabbat 33a.

revealed to put away sin by the sacrifice of Himself," (Hebrews 9:26). Following the activities of this seventh angel, we see it make an appearance again in 16:17, this time with the final bowl poured out over Jerusalem. The events of Revelation 11—the preparation of Jerusalem and the Temple's destruction—are completed in Revelation 16 to 19. With the Temple and sacrificial system destroyed, the Mosaic Age ended.

THE MYSTERIES OF GOD

"Now to Him who is able to establish you according to my gospel and the preaching of Jesus Christ, according to the revelation of the mystery which has been kept secret for long ages past, but now has been disclosed, and through the Scriptures of the prophets, in accordance with the commandment of the eternal God, has been made known to all the nations, leading to obedience of faith; to the only wise God, through Jesus Christ, be the glory forever. Amen." Romans 16:25–27 (NASB)

One final item we must cover is the "the mystery of God," mentioned in verse 7. This is a massive topic, one far too grand for the scope of this book. But I will hit some of the main points that relate to Revelation. On the one side of verse 7, it mentions the prophets of old speaking of the mystery of God's plan for Israel. Many of these prophecies we have already covered, so I will add a bit of social-proof in order to help you understand that even a first-century Jews like Josephus was aware of the fulfillment of prophecies during the last days of his nation:

"These [wicked] men therefore trampled upon all the laws of men; and laughed at the laws of God: and for the oracles of the prophets they ridiculed them, as the tricks of jugglers. Yet did these prophets foretell many things concerning [the rewards of] virtue, and [punishments of] vice, which when these zealots violated, they occasioned the fulfilling of those very prophecies belonging to their own country. For there was a certain ancient oracle of those men, that 'The city should then be taken, and the sanctuary burnt, by right of war, when a sedition should invade the Jews: and their own hands should pollute the temple of God.' Now while these zealots did not [quite] disbelieve these predictions, they made themselves the instruments of their accomplishment."[291]

"And who is there that does not know what the writings of the ancient prophets contain in them? And particularly that oracle which is just now going to be fulfilled upon this miserable city. For they foretold, that this city should be then taken, when some body shall begin the slaughter of his own countrymen. And are not both the city, and the entire temple now full of the dead bodies of your countrymen? It is God therefore, it is God himself who is bringing on this fire to purge that city and temple by means of the Romans; and is going to pluck up this city [Jerusalem], which is full of your pollutions."[292]

Moving on to the other side of the mystery that the angel refers to in Revelation 10:7, we find the mystery Paul mentions in Romans 11:25. The mystery is that Israel would suffer great calamity and be exiled into the nations of the earth in order to allow Gentiles to be brought into unity with the Father—only for Israel to then also have a prodigal son experience as well in the latter days.

> *"See then the kindness and severity of God: to those [Jews] who fell, severity, but to you [Gentile], God's kindness, if you continue in His kindness; for otherwise you too will be cut off. And they also, if they do not continue in their unbelief, will be grafted in; for God is able to graft them in again...*
> *For I do not want you, brothers and sisters, to be uninformed of this mystery—so that you will not be wise in your own estimation—that a partial hardening has happened to Israel until the fullness of the Gentiles has come in; and so all Israel will be saved."*
> *Romans 11:22–23, 25–26 (NASB)*

Paul shares along similar lines in Ephesians 3:

> *"...when you read you can understand my insight into the mystery of Christ, which in other generations was not made known to mankind, as it has now been revealed to His holy apostles and prophets in the Spirit; to be specific, that the Gentiles are fellow heirs and fellow members of the body, and fellow partakers of the promise in Christ Jesus through the*

---

[291] Josephus, *Wars*, 4:6:3, https://penelope.uchicago.edu/josephus/war-4.html
[292] Ibid, 6:2:1.

gospel…

and to enlighten all people as to what the plan of the mystery is which for ages has been hidden in God, who created all things; so that the multifaceted wisdom of God might now be made known through the church to the rulers and the authorities in the heavenly places. This was in accordance with the eternal purpose which He carried out in Christ Jesus our Lord." Ephesians 3:4–6, 9–11 (NASB)

There is then the mystery of the coming of God in flesh, that he would become the New Adam, and suffer death, only to be raised to life, raising us with Him (see Romans 5)!

"…we speak God's wisdom in a mystery, the hidden wisdom which God predestined before the ages to our glory; the wisdom which none of the rulers of this age has understood; for if they had understood it, they would not have crucified the Lord of glory." 1 Corinthians 2:7–9 (NASB)

"For since by a man death came, by a man also came the resurrection of the dead. For as in Adam all die, so also in Christ all will be made alive… then comes the end, when He hands over the kingdom to our God and Father, when He has abolished all rule and all authority and power. For He must reign until He has put all His enemies under His feet. The last enemy that will be abolished is death." 1 Corinthians 15:21–22, 24–25 (NASB)

And Luke shares these words of Jesus:

"Now He said to them, 'These are My words which I spoke to you while I was still with you, that all the things that are written about Me in the Law of Moses and the Prophets and the Psalms must be fulfilled.' Then He opened their minds to understand the Scriptures, and He said to them, 'So it is written, that the Christ would suffer and rise from the dead on the third day, and that repentance for forgiveness of sins would be proclaimed in His name to all the nations, beginning from Jerusalem…'" Luke 24:44–47 (NASB)

God also established this age of Christ; the Kingdom Age. In this 'upside down' kingdom we conquer through love, laying down our lives, and co-labour with Him to disciple the nations into sonship and unity with our Father. In this way, he began a work of restoration of all creation.

Paul writes,

"But the things which God previously announced by the mouths of all the prophets, that His Christ would suffer, He has fulfilled in this way. Therefore repent and return, so that your sins may be wiped away, in order that times of refreshing may come from the presence of the Lord; and that He may send Jesus, the Christ appointed for you, whom heaven must receive until the period of restoration of all things, about which God spoke by the mouths of His holy prophets from ancient times." Acts 3:18–21 (NASB)

"He made known to us the mystery of His will, according to His good pleasure which He set forth in Him, regarding His plan of the fullness of the times, to bring all things together in Christ, things in the heavens and things on the earth. In Him we also have obtained an inheritance, having been predestined according to the purpose of Him who works all things in accordance with the plan of His will." Ephesians 1:9–11 (NASB)

"Behold, I am telling you a mystery; we will not all sleep, but we will all be changed, in a moment, in the twinkling of an eye, at the last trumpet; for the trumpet will sound, and the dead will be raised imperishable, and we will be changed... then will come about the saying that is written: 'Death has been swallowed up in victory.'" 1 Corinthians 15:51–52, 54 (NASB)

Lastly, I want to mention the greatest and perhaps most significant mystery of all: that God Almighty chose to dwell in us!

"I was made a minister of this church according to the commission from God granted to me for your benefit, so that I might fully carry out the preaching of the word of God, that is, the mystery which had been hidden from the past ages and generations, but now has been revealed to His saints, to whom God willed to make known what the wealth of the glory of this mystery among the Gentiles is, the mystery that is Christ in you, the hope of glory." Colossians 1:25–27 (NASB)

13 THE LAW & THE PROPHETS: CHAPTER 11, PART 1

"And after sixty and two weeks The Messiah will be killed, and it is not for himself; and the City of Holiness shall be destroyed with the King who comes, and its end is in an overwhelming flood, and it is until the end of the war of the judgments of destruction. And he shall strengthen the covenant with many, one week and half of a week, and he shall cancel sacrifice and offering, and upon the wings of abomination destruction shall rest upon the desolation until the end of the judgments."
— *Daniel 9:26–27, Aramaic (Peshitta Bible)*[293]

Chapter 11 of Revelation ends with a natural break in the narrative flow of events thus far, since chapter 12 of the Apocalypse takes a dramatic departure from the build-up that began in chapter 6. This chapter is massive in terms of significance and the themes it covers; therefore, I chose to end my book at Revelation 11, having broken up its commentary into two parts. The sequence of visions that follow in chapter 12 charge ahead on a new prophetic path all the way to the 20th chapter. My next book will cover the remainder of John's Vision.

---

[293] Bauscher, David. *The Holy Peshitta Bible Translated*, Lulu.com, p. 1690.

LEO DE SIQUEIRA

It was not coincidence that the Holy Temple was placed at the center of this Vision; it was Divine design. The Temple was at the center of the Jewish religious and cultural universe. Their civic laws, civic Holidays, and of course their connection point with Yahweh God, all stemmed from their Temple. Hence, the collapse of not just the physical building, but the cessation of the priesthood and sacrificial system, along with the displacement of the holy contents within the temple;[294] had a devastating impact on the Jews.

The realization of this dramatic and history-altering effect was even felt by Jesus Himself. No one believed him at the time, when the Temple glistened in all her glory. The Jews had built upon the humble structure that Nehemiah and company erected after their return from Babylon through King Herod substantial financial investments, increasing the Temple's adornments and overall footprint.

But Jesus looked ahead and saw what was coming. In perhaps His most profound and empathetic statement concerning the fate of the Temple, Jesus was quoted as follows:

"When He approached Jerusalem, He saw the city and wept over it, saying, "If you had known on this day, even you, the conditions for peace! But now they have been hidden from your eyes. For the days will come upon you when your enemies will put up a barricade against you, and surround you and hem you in on every side, and they will level you to the ground, and throw down your children within you, and they will not leave in you one stone upon another, because you did not recognize the time of your visitation." Luke 19:41–44 (NASB)

These are sobering words. This was real, not prophetic, hyperbole. The Hebrew story that began in the slave pits of Egypt and embarked across the wilderness with signs and wonders; the story which testified of great men like David and Daniel; the story that saw Judeans returning from Babylonian exile and rebuilding their city; this story would take an unfathomable turn for the worse in the days leading to the end of the Mosaic Age.

Jesus and even his followers warned the people. But not only were the warnings rejected, they were considered treasonous, and were twisted in order to be used against them:

---

[294] Josephus notes the Golden Table, the Menorah, great sums of gold objects, coins, and most significantly, the Book of the Law and the holy veils; these were all taken to the royal palace in Rome (*Wars*, 7:5:5–7).

- *"We heard Him say, 'I will destroy this temple that was made by hands, and in three days I will build another, made without hands.'"*
  Mark 14:58 (NASB)

- *"Those passing by were hurling abuse at Him, shaking their heads and saying, "Ha! You who are going to destroy the temple and rebuild it in three days, save Yourself by coming down from the cross!"*
  Mark 15:29–30 (NASB)

- *"This man [Stephen] does not stop speaking against this holy place and the Law; for we have heard him say that this Nazarene, Jesus, will destroy this place and change the customs which Moses handed down to us."*
  Acts 6:13–14 (NASB)

The author of Hebrews goes to great lengths to prepare the people of Israel to embrace the fact that the Temple system would come to an end:

"[For] if perfection was through the Levitical priesthood (for on the basis of it the people received the Law), what further need was there for another priest to arise according to the order of Melchizedek, and not be designated according to the order of Aaron?
...For, on the one hand, there is the nullification of a former commandment because of its weakness and uselessness (for the Law made nothing perfect); on the other hand, there is the introduction of a better hope, through which we come near to God...
For if that first covenant had been free of fault, no circumstances would have been sought for a second...
When He said, 'A new covenant,' He has made the first obsolete. But whatever is becoming obsolete and growing old is about to disappear...
He takes away the first in order to establish the second."
Hebrews 7:11, 18–19, 8:7, 13, 10:9 (NASB)

Peter also wrote of this transition of covenant seasons in 2 Peter 3. This passage is quite difficult to translate from the Aramaic, quite possibly because Peter wasn't eloquent in his writing (Acts 4:3). In the original language, this letter is dramatically different from the Greek version. But it is much more in line with the Jesus we hear in the Gospels, and fits within the narrative of

God's overarching love story.

2 Peter 3:10–13 reads:

"Yahweh is not delaying Himself[95] in his promises as men would consider delay, but he is longsuffering for your spirit, because he is not willing that a single person should perish, but rather that everyone come to repentance.

However the Day of Yahweh comes as a thief; in which Heaven shall suddenly cross beyond[296] the obsolete principles,[297] where by means of being set ablaze these (principles) will be disannulled,[298] and The Land and the deeds therein will be exposed.

Therefore, until all of these (principles) are disannulled, it is right for you to be in your way of life as those who are holy and in the worship of God, while you expect and eagerly desire the coming of the Day of Yahweh, in which Heaven proves itself to be true[299] through fire, and the obsolete principles will be disannulled, by means of being set ablaze they will be brought low.[300]

---

[295] Ishtaphel participle is a self-causing verb conjugation.

[296] This is the same עָבַר from the Book of Joshua, "to pass over." The word carries with it a profound image of Yehoshua (Joshua) leaving Moses in the wilderness and crossing over into the Promised Land. Yeshua (Jesus) in the same way caused us to cross over from the Covenant of Moses into the Covenant of Jesus.

[297] אֶסְטוֹכְּסָא is an incredibly difficult word to translate, partially due to its limited use. The word seems to derive from an ancient *classical elements* worldview. But the two other instances in the New Testament of this word being used are by Paul, and both times in the same context. In Galatians 4:3 and 9 and Colossians 2:8 and 20, he uses the same word in reference to **not coming under the legal requirements of Law of Moses**, almost in a derogatory sense. Therefore, "obsolete principles" is a euphemism for the Law of Moses, or at the very least, the contractual obligations of the Law. See J. P. Margoliouth's Supplement to the Thesaurus Syriacus, p. 26, and Jennings' Lexicon to the Syriac, p. 26.

[298] The Ithpeel Imperfect 3rd plural can mean, "was let go," "dismissed," "loosed," or even "disannulled," or "divorced" (See William Jennings' Lexicon to the Syriac, pg. 230). All of this speaks of being set free from the requirements of the Law of Moses (perhaps an allusion to Hebrews 8:13).

[299] Ithpeel participle, reflexive verb of מֶתְבַּחְרִין, "to prove," "to examine," "to test."

[300] The root of נְשַׁחֵן is "to spring up," or "flourish," like a beautiful flower. The conjugation of the verb here is an antithesis, and therefore means "to be brought low," "to bend," "to be held in small esteem," or "to sink down" (See Payne's p. 596, Jennings' p. 230, and Jastrow's p. 1627).

Then Heaven is renewed and Earth is renewed, according to His promise.
Be anticipating this; those in whom righteousness dwells."
2 Peter 3:10–13, Aramaic Translation

Peter never had in mind that God would destroy the earth but that Heaven would initiate the transition of epoch seasons. The Day of the Lord so often mentioned in the New Testament always spoke of the same day: the *day* in which judgement would come one last time against those who had breached the Law of Moses. Paul, also writing of the Judeans who ignorantly (Romans 10) thought no harm could ever come upon them, said:

"But concerning the times and the seasons, brethren, you have no need that
I should write to you. For you yourselves know perfectly that the day of the
Lord so comes as a thief in the night. For when they say, "Peace and
safety!" then sudden destruction comes upon them, as labor pains upon a
pregnant woman. And they shall not escape. But you, brethren, are not in
darkness, so that this Day should overtake you as a thief."
1 Thessalonians 5:1–4 (NASB)

Both 2 Peter 3:10–13 and 1 Thessalonians 5:1-4 encompass so much of what we have already read and expound John's Revelation. Keywords, such as "Day of the Lord" and "as a thief," are recurring motifs and refer to the same event. All passages quoted in this chapter thus far have helped lay a necessary foundation from which we can build our understanding of the 19 verses in Revelation 11.

THE TEMPLE VISION

א *(v 1) "And there was given to me a reed like a rod, and the angel was*
standing and saying, 'Rise! And measure the Temple of God, and the
altar, and those who worship in it…"

The measuring of the Temple here is the antithesis of the Ezekiel event (Ezekiel 40–47). This is a very important distinction that must be made. Revelation 11 opposes Ezekiel 40 to 47. Only Revelation 21-22 compliments the Old Testament vision, and the second Johannine experience aligns with Ezekiel's narrative:

"In the visions of God He brought me into the land of Israel and set me
on a very high mountain, and on it to the south there was something like
a structure of a city. So He brought me there; and behold, there was a man
whose appearance was like the appearance of bronze, with a thread of flax
and a measuring rod in his hand; and he was standing in the gateway."

Ezekiel 40:2–3 (NASB)

Revelation 21 to 22 and Ezekiel 40 to 47 tell of angels measuring, while in Revelation 11, John measures. Also consider that John measures not only the Temple, but the people in it. The meaning of this is that human hands bring destruction, but heavenly hands bring hope and new life.[301] As we will explore further soon, the second measuring experience in Revelation shares a vision of a future hope and new creation with Ezekiel's. Lastly, both Ezekiel 40 to 47 and Revelation 21 to 22 take place after the destructions of the first Temple (Solomon's), and the rebuilt (second) Temple (a.k.a. Nehemiah's Temple or Herod's Temple). Meanwhile, Revelation 11 takes place *before* the destruction of the second Temple.

Ezekiel's measuring experience was very long—seven chapters worth. But sandwiched between the angelic visitation and the vision of a New Eden, Yahweh gave Ezekiel a message for the people of Israel. God's words to the prophet in chapters 43 and 44 provide us with context for Revelation 11:

"Son of man, this [Temple mount] is the place of My throne and the place of the soles of My feet, where I will dwell among the sons of Israel forever. And the house of Israel will not again defile My holy name...

'Son of man, inform the house of Israel of the temple, so that they will be ashamed of their wrongdoings; and have them measure the plan. And if they are ashamed of everything that they have done, make known to them the plan of the house, its layout, its exits, its entrances, all its plans, all its statutes, and all its laws...

'You shall say to the rebellious ones, to the house of Israel, 'This is what the Lord God says: 'Enough of all your abominations, house of Israel, when you brought in foreigners, uncircumcised in heart and uncircumcised in flesh, to be in My sanctuary to profane it, My house, when you offered My food, the fat, and the blood and they broke My covenant—this in addition to all your abominations. And you have not taken responsibility for My holy things yourselves, but you have appointed foreigners to take responsibility for My sanctuary.'''
Ezekiel 43:7, 10–11, 44:6–8 (NASB)

---

[301] This by no means implies that John was responsible for the deaths of those slain within the Temple compounds. Rather, that he was taking inventory of all things that would suffer judgement and redemption under the Law.

John's measuring of the Temple was a symbolic reminder (remember he was on Patmos, not in Jerusalem) of Yahweh's words to the people of Israel via the prophet Ezekiel. John's prophecy was not to blanket those who earnestly sought to uphold the sacredness of the Temple (i.e. the Maccabean Revolt and the miracle that became Hanukkah). It was for a seditious people, a last generation that would perpetuate the great calamities that came upon the Temple Mount.

> "…when [John of Giscala] could no longer plunder the people, he betook himself to sacrilege, and melted down many of the sacred utensils, which had been given to the temple; as also many of those vessels which were necessary for such as ministered about holy things: the caldrons, the dishes, and the tables…
>
> Whereas this man, who was a Jew, seized upon what were the donations of foreigners: and said to those that were with him, that it was proper for them to use divine things… I suppose that had the Romans made any longer delay in coming against these villains, that the city would either have been swallowed up by the ground opening upon them, or been overflowed by water; or else been destroyed by such thunder, as the country of Sodom perished by. For it had brought forth a generation of men much more atheistically than were those that suffered such punishments. For by their madness it was that all the people came to be destroyed." [302]

Jesus, who looked ahead and saw these perilous times, spoke of the same men, saying:

> *"And at that time many will fall away, and they will betray one another and hate one another. And many false prophets will rise up and mislead many people. And because lawlessness is increased, most people's love will become cold." Matthew 24:10–12 (NASB)*

Now if the mention of "false prophets" completely distracted you from everything else in that passage, allow me to satisfy your curiosity:

> "A false prophet was the occasion of these people's

---

[302] Josephus, *Wars*, 5:13:6, https://penelope.uchicago.edu/josephus/war-5.html

destruction, who had made a public proclamation in the city that very day, that God commanded them to get upon the temple, and that there they should receive miraculous signs of their deliverance. Now there was then a great number of false prophets suborned by the tyrants to impose on the people, who denounced this to them, that they should wait for deliverance from God; and this was in order to keep them from deserting, and that they might be buoyed up above fear and care by such hopes… Thus were the miserable people persuaded by these deceivers…"[303]

Josephus makes several mentions of false messiahs and false prophets, and those other mentions will be discussed in the next book where I unpack Revelation 13 and 16. But in this case, Josephus wrote concerning the destruction of the temple. Jesus too, in Matthew 24, spoke of the same event. Therefore, we have congruency between the prophetic word and historical accounts.

The Apostle John was summoned to eat the song scroll of Moses, which foretold the great calamity that would come upon the Holy Land. He then performed a symbolic act to remind the inhabitants of Judea of the prophecies of Ezekiel in order to further contextualize the destruction of the Holy Temple. And as we have learned from Josephus, the wickedness of a few erased the good deeds of many who went before them in times past.

THE HOLY OF HOLIES

א *(v 2) "But the **inner court**[304] for the Temple expel for the outsider,[305]*

---

[303] Ibid, 6:5:2, 3.

[304] This is a significant distinction from the Greek, which has "outer court." The Aramaic continues to support an early dating of when Revelation was written, since the inner court only existed until 70 AD. This verse also provides a clearer understanding of chapter 11 in relation to the destruction of the Temple. For the "outer court" to be given to the Gentiles makes no sense, since the outer court was always the "court of the Gentiles" anyway.

[305] This enigmatic sequence of words is reminiscent of Hebrew word plays found in the Old Testament: וַלְדָּרְתָא דָּלְגֵו מֶן הֵיכְלָא אַפֵּק מֶן לְבַר with the preposition מֶן ("for" in this case instead of "from") being used twice to juxtapose the use of the inner court. I could have translated this as follows: "But the inner court of the Temple cast out," but we would have totally missed the literary brilliance: The inner court, sacred and holy, would become the outer court, which was the court of the

192

and do not measure it, because it has been given to the Gentiles, and upon the Holy City they will trample forty two months."

Revelation 11:2 contains within it the entire Flavian campaign. Forty-two months, or three-and-a-half years, was the duration of the Roman siege against the Jews. The next verse reiterates this timeframe with "1,260 days," which are again 3.5 years. Numerology and sequencing of events was a big deal in Jewish history; and we see that even Josephus illustrates this too:

"One cannot but wonder at the accuracy of this period thereto relating. For the same month and day were now observed [9th of Av], as I said before, wherein the holy house was burnt formerly by the Babylonians. Now the number of years that passed from its first foundation, which was laid by King Solomon, till this its destruction, which happened in the second year of the reign of Vespasian, are collected to be one thousand, one hundred, and thirty: besides seven months, and fifteen days. And from the second building of it, which was done by Haggai, in the second year of Cyrus the King, till its destruction under Vespasian, there were six hundred, thirty nine years, and forty five days."[306]

"And thus was Jerusalem taken, in the second year of the reign of Vespasian, on the eighth day of the month Gorpeius [Elul, A.D. 70]. It had been taken five times before: though this was the second time of its desolation. For Shishak, the King of Egypt; and after him Antiochus, and after him Pompey, and after them Sosius and Herod, took the city; but still preserved it. But before all these, the King of Babylon conquered it, and made it desolate: one thousand, four hundred, sixty eight years, and six months, after it was built...

It was demolished entirely by the Babylonians, four hundred, seventy seven years, and six months after him. And from King David, who was the first of the Jews who reigned therein, to this destruction under Titus, were one thousand, one hundred, and seventy nine years. But from its first building, till this last

---

Gentiles. This leads us right into the next part of the verse, where the inner court is given to the Gentiles!

[306] Josephus, *Wars*, 6:4:8, https://penelope.uchicago.edu/josephus/war-6.html

destruction, were two thousand, one hundred, seventy seven years… And thus ended the siege of Jerusalem."[307]

It is also fascinating to read that the inner court is mentioned here. As we discovered when we studied Revelation 9, Titus stormed the inner court of the Temple and stood upon the Temple Mount (Mount Moriah) while his soldiers worshipped their gods, and declared Titus to be "Imperator." Revelation 11:2 is a crystal-clear connection and fulfillment of the prophecies of Jesus in Luke 19, 21, and Matthew 24.

> *"For the days will come upon you when your enemies will put up a barricade against you, and surround you and hem you in on every side, and they will level you to the ground, and throw down your children within you, and they will not leave in you one stone upon another, because you did not recognize the time of your visitation.*
>
> *But when you see Jerusalem surrounded by armies, then recognize that her desolation is near. Then those who are in Judea must flee to the mountains, and those who are inside the city must leave, and those who are in the country must not enter the city; because these are days of punishment [or, "vengeance"], so that all things which have been written will be fulfilled…*
>
> *for there will be great distress upon the land, and wrath to this people; and they will fall by the edge of the sword, and will be led captive into all the nations; and Jerusalem will be trampled underfoot by the Gentiles until the times of the Gentiles are fulfilled."*
> *Luke 19:44–44; 21:20–24 (NASB)*

Matthew's account of the same discourse is perhaps more enigmatic, but this is only because he chose to tie in Old Testament prophecies as well:

> *"Therefore when you see the abomination of desolation which was spoken of through Daniel the prophet, standing in the holy place —let the reader understand— then those who are in Judea must flee to the mountains."*
> *Matthew 24:15–16 (NASB)*

This "abomination" was first demonstrated by Antiochus IV Epiphanes when he defiled the Temple in 168 BC and sacrificed a pig upon the alter. It was a precursor of what would happen again. Antiochus did not destroy the Temple (desolation); rather, the Greeks were driven out in the Maccabean

---

[307] Ibid, 6:10:1.

Revolt. The abomination that came through desolation was fulfilled by Titus; whose soldiers both destroyed the holy Temple and sacrificed its worshippers.

The "times of the Gentiles" in Luke 21:24 was, like many of Jesus' sayings, near-term and long-term. These "times" for sure account for the forty-two month (3.5 years) Roman campaign against the Holy Land. This was near-term. But the "times" (notice the plural) is eschatological as well, weaving in God's design of reconciling all tribes, peoples, and nations to Himself: "a partial hardening has happened to Israel until the fullness of the Gentiles has come in; and so all Israel will be saved." (Romans 11:25-26). It would therefore seem that Luke 21:24, Revelation 11:2, and Romans 11:11-33 all share a thematic connection.

These "times" become far-reaching, and hope-filled, in accordance with God's grand love story:

> *"Therefore repent and return, so that your sins may be wiped away, in order that times of refreshing may come from the presence of the Lord; and that He may send Jesus, the Christ appointed for you, whom heaven must receive until the period of restoration of all things, about which God spoke by the mouths of His holy prophets from ancient times."*
> *Acts 3:19–21 (NASB)*

> *"In all wisdom and insight He made known to us the mystery of His will, according to His good pleasure which He set forth in Him, regarding His plan of the fullness of the times, to bring all things together in Christ, things in the heavens and things on the earth."*
> *Ephesians 1:8–10 (NASB)*

A FUTURE HOPE AFTER MEASURING THE TEMPLE

Before concluding this section pertaining to the destruction of the second Temple, we must revisit the connection between John's two measuring accounts and Ezekiel's. Revelation 11 is only part of the story. Chapters 21 and 22, in conjunction with Ezekiel 40–47, give us the long-term vision of what Yahweh has in store.

> *"Our fathers worshiped on this mountain [Mount Gerizim], and you Jews say that in Jerusalem [Mount Moriah, the Temple Mount] is the place*

where one ought to worship."

Jesus said to her, "Woman, believe Me, the hour is coming when you will neither on this mountain, nor in Jerusalem, worship the Father... But the hour is coming, and now is, when the true worshipers will worship the Father in spirit and truth; for the Father is seeking such to worship Him. John 4:20-23 (NASB)

That God would decide to abide in us (John 15, 17) and make us His Holy Temple (1 Corinthians 3:17, 6:19; 2 Corinthians 6:16; Ephesians 2:21, 22) is already mind-blowing. Just pause for a moment and think about this – in you is the Holy of Holies, where once only a High Priest could enter.

The Epistle of Barnabas, written sometime between 70 and 130 AD, is an early church document often attributed to the same Barnabas who ministered with the Apostle Paul. In said document, speaking of the destruction of the Second Temple, the author remarks,

> "For a holy temple unto the Lord, my brethren, is the abode of our heart...
>
> Moreover I will tell you likewise concerning the temple, how these wretched men being led astray set their hope on the building, and not on their God that made them, as being a house of God...
>
> But what saith the Lord abolishing the temple? '...Behold they that pulled down this temple themselves shall build it.'
>
> So it cometh to pass; for because they went to war it was pulled down by their enemies...
>
> Again, it was revealed how the city and the temple and the people of Israel should be betrayed. For the scripture saith; 'And it shall be in the last days, that the Lord shall deliver up the sheep of the pasture and the fold and the tower thereof to destruction.' And it came to pass as the Lord spake...
>
> Before we believed on God, the abode of our heart was corrupt and weak, a temple truly built by hands; for it was full of idolatry and was a house of demons, because we did whatsoever was contrary to God.

But it shall be built in the name of the Lord. Give heed then that the temple of the Lord may be built gloriously.

How? Understand ye. By receiving the remission of our sins and hoping on the Name we became new, created afresh from the beginning. Wherefore God dwelleth truly in our habitation within us."[308]

Consider this: when Jesus said, "You are the light of the world. A city on a hill can't be hidden" (Matthew 5:14), he wasn't making up a new word-picture. He was taking an existing understanding that *the Temple was the light of the world*, which was at the center of a city build on a hill (Jerusalem).

"Had I [King Herod] known that the Rabbis were so circumspect, I should not have killed them. Now tell me what amends I can make. Rabbi ben Buta replied: '...go now and attend to the light of the world – which is the Temple, of which – it is written, And all the nations become enlightened by it.'"[309]

Now, *you and I* are the light of the world— the Temple! And because the ultimate High Priest entered into the Heavenly Temple once and for all (Hebrews 9:12), that High Priest, Jesus, dwells in us (2 Corinthians 13:5; Romans 8:10).

When Jesus said in John 14:2, "Many are the abodes in my Father's house," he was not speaking of mansions in heaven. The Aramaic word "abode" stems from the root word "unity," which fits perfectly within the context of John 15 and 17, where Jesus speaks of *abiding* in Him. The Bible doesn't really provide us with any concrete reference to God specifically having a house in heaven. But there are over 40 Biblical references to the House of God being the Temple.

Jesus confirmed this when He, quoting Isaiah 56:7 said, "my house will be called a house of prayer" (Matthew 21:13), and in John 2:16 when He was driving money changers out and exclaimed, "stop making My Father's house a place of business!" In this context, the House of God with many abodes was the Temple. And Jesus went to prepare permanent access to the House of God, so that they (and we) may abide there. The great mystery here is that

---

[308] Epistle of Barnabas, 6:15; 16:1–9,
http://www.earlychristianwritings.com/text/barnabas-lightfoot.html
[309] Babylonian Talmud: Tractate Baba Bathra, 4a.,
https://halakhah.com/bababathra/bababathra_4.html

we became this temple, and the Shekinah Glory of God is no longer found in the Holy of Holies; it is found in you and I! Consider yourself the Third (and final) Temple. We do indeed live in the age of ages!

But as is always the case with our Heavenly Father, there is yet more. When John experienced a measuring event for the second time, he explicitly writes that there is no temple, for God's dwelling place is among mankind once more (Revelation 21:3, 22). It is the new polis, the city-state of God's people, that is symbolically measured. While not wanting to take too much away from the next book, which covers Revelation 21 and 22, I do want to emphasise one major point:

> *"And he showed me a river of the water of life, clear as crystal, coming from the throne of God and of the Lamb, in the middle of its street. On either side of the river was the tree of life, bearing twelve kinds of fruit, yielding its fruit every month; and the leaves of the tree were for the healing of the nations." Revelation 22:1–2 (NASB)*

John didn't see something unique; he saw something that built upon the prophetic experience of his predecessor Ezekiel. The former prophet, after his temple measuring experience, witnesses progressively deeper water flowing out of the temple, to the point that he can't stand in it any longer.

> *"Then he brought me back to the door of the house; and behold, water was flowing from under the threshold of the house toward the east, for the house faced east. And the water was flowing down from under, from the right side of the house, from south of the altar... Again he measured a thousand; and it was a river that I could not wade across, because the water had risen, enough water to swim in, a river that could not be crossed by wading.*

> *"And he said to me, 'Son of man, have you seen this?' Then he brought me back to the bank of the river... Then he said to me, 'These waters go out toward the eastern region and go down into the Arabah; then they go toward the [Dead] sea, being made to flow into the sea, and the waters of the sea become fresh. And it will come about that every living creature which swarms in every place where the river goes, will live... And by the river on its bank, on one side and on the other, will grow all kinds of trees for food. Their leaves will not wither and their fruit will not fail. They will bear fruit every month because their water flows from the sanctuary, and their fruit will be for food and their leaves for healing.'" Ezekiel 47:1, 5, 6, 8, 9, 12 (NASB)*

This vision has a profound theological impact on Western eschatology.

God's spirit, illustrated as water (John 4:14; 7:37–39), flows out of the Temple, first south of the alter, which is the Hinnom Valley (Gehenna), then heads East across the Arabah wilderness, falls off the Jordan Rift Valley, and in to the Dead Sea. And He brings the Dead Sea to life.

Now, do you know what was traditionally believed to be at the bottom of the Dead Sea? The Pentapolis (five cities) of the Valley of Siddim (Genesis 13:10, 14:1–3), **where Sodom and Gomorrah were**. That region was described as being like the Garden of Eden before it was destroyed. But then Ezekiel sees Spirit-life flowing into the Valley of Siddim and healing the waters that buried Sodom and Gomorrah. How can this be?

> *"Nevertheless, I will restore their fortunes, the fortunes of Sodom and her daughters, the fortunes of Samaria and her daughters, and along with them your own fortunes, so that you will bear your disgrace and feel ashamed for all that you have done when you become a consolation to them. Your sisters, Sodom with her daughters and Samaria with her daughters, will return to their former state, and you with your daughters will also return to your former state." Ezekiel 16:53–55 (NASB)*

You see, the whole of Ezekiel 16 must be understood in context: Jerusalem becomes a great harlot (like Revelation 17-19), and her guilt is worse than that of Sodom and Gomorrah (like Matthew 10:15), and therefore she suffers great calamity. But when God brings about the restoration of Jerusalem, He restores Sodom and Gomorrah as well (much like Romans 11:11–26)!

Therefore, although in Revelation 11 John measures Jerusalem and the Temple for destruction, we know from Romans 9 through 11 that this is the trigger event for a massive restoration campaign initiated by God Himself. "God was in Christ reconciling the world to Himself, not counting their wrongdoings against them, and He has committed to us the word of reconciliation," (2 Corinthians 5:19). And at the end of it all, even Sodom and Gomorrah, along with Jerusalem, are restored.[310] Because of these things, though we mourn the tragedy and suffering experienced by those who suffered through the years leading up to the fall of Jerusalem and her Temple in 70 AD, we may also rejoice as we look ahead to the grand restoration of Jews, Gentiles, and all of creation itself (Romans 8:20–23; 11:25–26)!

---

[310] Now how does this tie in to the last judgement, the sea of fire and brimstone, and the Book of Life? In the next book I take a much deeper dive into all these matters.

199

"For it was the Father's good pleasure for all the fullness to dwell in Him [Jesus], and through Him [Jesus] to reconcile all things to Himself, whether things on earth or things in heaven, having made peace through the blood of His cross." Colossians 1:19–20 (NASB)

14 THE LAW & THE PROPHETS: CHAPTER 11, PART 2

> *"Do not think that I will accuse you before the Father; the one who accuses you is Moses, in whom you have put your hope.."*
> — John 5:45 (NASB)

The short but dramatic temple scene quickly shifts its focus from the Temple itself to the symbolic contents within it. John does not leave the temple mount. He is still standing (figuratively) in the same place he was when he was measuring the vicinity.

As we discovered from the Aramaic text, Revelation 11:2 tells us that the inner court was to be trampled on by the Gentiles, which suggests that John was overlooking the inner court. Therefore, with our focus still upon the inner court, Revelation 11:3 takes us inside the Temple itself. Here once lied one of the most symbolic and defining articles of Jewish Identity: The Ark of the Covenant.[311]

---

[311] I say once because when the Temple was first destroyed under Nebuchadnezzar in 587 BC, the Ark of the Covenant was lost during the war and never recovered.

The Ark represented the Law of Moses, since it contained the tablets of stone written by the hand of God on Mount Sinai (Exodus 34:1). But the Law itself did not make up the whole of the Jewish Scriptures; there were also the Prophets,[312] which together became known as the Law and the Prophets (the Hebrew Bible). Though the Ark was gone, there were copies of the Sacred Scriptures within the Temple compounds since the priests ministered there daily.

So what does the Law and the Prophets have to do with the two witnesses? As we will discover below, they are one and the same; which is why the focus of Revelation 11 takes us from the inner court to the inner Temple.

Granted, much speculation has come and gone over who these mysterious figures could have been. Unfortunately, a literal reading of their description and actions has gained much consensus and garnered much fervor. This has created an anticipation of a cinematic experience to unfold, much like in the days of the Exodus. Others have taken to a literal historical approach, linking them to the apostles Paul and Peter, since both were martyred in Rome around the same time. However, there is another way to interpret these verses, one that I believe is more harmonious with the unfolding these visions that revealed the consummation of the Mosaic Age and its final judgement.

א *(v 3 – 4) "And I will grant my two witnesses to prophesy one thousand two hundred and sixty days while wearing sackcloth.*

These ones are two olive trees and the two menorahs, who in the presence of Yahweh of His whole Land are standing."

For those familiar with the Old Testament prophets, you'll notice that we have a parallel image to the two witnesses in Zechariah 4. There, Zerubbabel and Joshua are interpreted to be those who were standing before the Lord at

---

Although the Book of Maccabees says the ark was hidden in a cave on Mount Nebo by Jeremiah, saying that its location "shall remain unknown until God gathers his people together again and shows his mercy" (2 Maccabees 2:7). The Temple also contained at one point the Book of the Covenant (the Five Books of Moses (i.e. Genesis to Deuteronomy). Also see 2 Kings 23:2.

[312] The "Prophets" where the "Law and Prophets" are mentioned assumes the Ketuvim (Writings) as well, which makes up the Law, Prophets and Writings (Torah, Nevi'im, Ketuvim, which become acronyms for the word Tanakh, the Hebrew Bible). See Luke 24:27, 44, Matthew 5:15, and Acts 13:15 for examples.

that time. They were there as Messianic representatives (king and priest) to oversee the rebuilding of Jerusalem and the Temple. The Messianic hope in Zechariah peaks throughout chapters 9 to 14 as pictures of Jesus and His eternal kingdom are depicted.

In contrast, however, the witnesses John sees here in chapter 11 make it clear that these are not the same ones in see in Zechariah. The only common theme between the figures in Zechariah versus the ones in Revelation have to do with the Temple. In Zechariah, they are summoned for rebuilding it, while in Revelation, they are summoned for its destruction (notice also the plumb line to *measure* the Temple in Zechariah), hence the sackcloth.

It is worth noting the similarities between the prophetic encounters of Zechariah and John. Like he does with Ezekiel, John also parallels Zechariah to some degree. Here are the most notable occasions:

Zechariah	Revelation
A vision of Joshua as High Priest	A vision of Jesus as High Priest
	A scroll of curses
Four coloured horses and chariots	Four coloured horses
A vision of Jerusalem	A vision of Jerusalem
A plumb line for the Temple	A measuring stick for the Temple
Two Witnesses	Two Witnesses
A scroll of curses	
Cup of wrath for Jerusalem	Cup of wrath to Babylon (Jerusalem)
A battle in Megiddo	A battle in Megiddo (Harmagedon)
	Nations gather against Jerusalem
	God's fire consumes Magog
Cleansing the Land by Fire	Cleansing the earth by Sea of Fire
Nations gather against Jerusalem	
God destroys those enemies	
A new Jerusalem rises	A new Jerusalem descends
The nations will walk in God's light	The nations will worship God
A river of life flows east and west	A river of life flows from the throne

Returning to the matter of the Two Witnesses, one major clue to the identity of these two prophetic figures of Revelation 11 can be found in Luke 16. This is Jesus' parable about the rich man and the poor man, Lazarus. It powerfully alludes to the notion that the Law and Prophets bore witness to the people of Israel:

"And [the rich man] said, 'Then I request of you, father, that you send

203

him [Lazarus] to my father's house——for I have five brothers——in order that he may warn them, so that they will not come to this place of torment as well.' But Abraham said, 'They have Moses and the Prophets; let them hear them.' But he said, 'No, father Abraham, but if someone goes to them from the dead, they will repent!' But he said to him, 'If they do not listen to Moses and the Prophets, they will not be persuaded even if someone rises from the dead.'" Luke 16:27-31 (NASB)

This parable is dense, and to fully unpack it is beyond the scope of this book. Though within our context of Revelation, I offer these thoughts. First, two times Abraham personifies the Torah by calling it "Moses and the Prophets." Second, the number of the rich man's brothers are five, a number rich in Exodus imagery: The Five Books of Moses, the grouping of fives in the structure of the Tabernacle (the 5 offerings, 5 curtains, 5 pillars, 5 bars, 5 ingredients for holy oil, 5 ingredients for incense). Third, his dialogue is with father Abraham, meaning he was a descendant of Abraham (John 8:39). Fourth, the one who "rises from the dead" is Jesus, meaning they won't believe his testimony. **The rich man therefore is a personification of Israel**.

Next, in the same way that Moses represented the first five books of the Bible, there was also a sole figure that represented the books of the prophets: Elijah. This is why Moses and Elijah appearing before Jesus in the pivotal transfiguration event.

"And while He was praying, the appearance of His face became different, and His clothing became white and gleaming. And behold, two men were talking with Him; and they were Moses and Elijah, who, appearing in glory, were speaking of His departure, which He was about to accomplish at Jerusalem." Luke 9:29-31 (NASB)

Moses and Elijah were speaking of His "departure," which in Aramaic is מפקנ, meaning exodus! This was a commissioning event, where the Law and Prophets (Moses and Elijah) representing the first covenant were acknowledging the new Exodus event where Jesus was instituting a new Covenant. Moses and Elijah had looked ahead to this day with great anticipation, and it was finally at hand!

Indeed, even on the way to Emmaus Jesus said to his followers,

"You foolish men and slow of heart to believe in all that the prophets have spoken! Was it not necessary for the Christ to suffer these things and to come into His glory?" Then beginning with Moses and with all the

Prophets, He explained to them the things written about Himself in all the Scriptures." Luke 24:25-27 (NASB).

To recap so far, John's vision in chapter 11 took him to the inner court, then to the inside of the Temple itself. We know this because while John was still standing in the inner court, God began to speak of His two witnesses who continually stand in His presence. The only two witnesses in the Temple would have been the Law and the Prophets, or, Moses and Elijah.

"Take this Book of the Law and place it beside the ark of the covenant of the Lord your God, so that it may remain there as a witness against you." Deuteronomy 31:26 (NASB)

The Law and the Prophets, Moses and Elijah, were witnesses against those bound by that covenant. Corresponding with Abraham's closing remarks to the rich man, take note of Jesus' words to the religious leaders in John 5:

"Do not think that I will accuse you before the Father; the one who accuses you is Moses, in whom you have put your hope. For if you believed Moses, you would believe Me; for he wrote about Me. But if you do not believe his writings, how will you believe My words?" John 5:45–47 (NASB)

Abraham said to the rich man, "If they do not listen to Moses and the Prophets, they will not be persuaded even if someone rises from the dead."

KEY DESCRIPTIONS OF MOSES AND ELIJAH

Revelation 11:3 tells us that the Law and the Prophets would prophesy for three and a half years—the exact duration of the Roman siege, which lead to the fall of the Temple in 70 AD. And what was it that they prophesied? Think back to all the Old Testament prophecies we have explored so far in this book! From Deuteronomy to Ezekiel, time and time again God spoke of the great Day of the Lord that would bring about the end of the Mosaic Age and the Temple system.

Revelation 11:10 gives us another important piece of information because it refers to the two witnesses as the **"two prophets."** It is a given that Elijah was a prophet, but we must also remember that Moses was considered a prophet as well (Deuteronomy 34:10).

In 11:4 they are described as olive trees and menorahs, which stand in the presence of God and the whole Land of Israel. The oil is the source of fuel for the menorah in the Temple, an allusion to the Exodus event when the Tabernacle of Moses was first built and the oil and the menorah were placed inside of it. They are in His presence (in the Holy Place), and He is described as the God of the whole Land. In John's day the Holy Land was fractured; North and South had long divided, and Samaritans were considered half-breeds; yet Yahweh was still the God of the entire Promised Land, which He swore to Abraham and His descendants.

א   *(v 5 – 6) "And whoever seeks to dispute[313] them, fire goes forth from their mouths and consumes their legal adversaries;[314] yet for those who choose to dispute them, afterwards it will be granted that they be executed.*

Now to these authority is upon them to close up the skies so that rain would not descend in the days of their prophecy, and there is to these authority to turn water to blood and to strike the Land with all plagues, as much as they choose."[315]

Verse 5 is charged with legalistic language, not militaristic. The Law and the Prophets had long prophesied these "days of vengeance" (Luke 21:22). The great calamities that befell the inhabitants of the Holy Land came about as a result of a judicial verdict. It was no different than capital punishment for someone who commits a first-degree murder.

They broke the Law, and now they would suffer the consequence of the Law (Romans 2:12, Galatians 5:3; James 2:10). To reject this verdict is to "dispute" it. As I footnoted below, the ones who dispute the prophecies of Moses and Elijah are considered legal adversaries; in other words, they are trying to appeal the verdict in court. However, the sentence had already been pronounced. Because of this, it was "granted that they be executed," which is to say, capital punishment.

---

[313] The root word here is "to dispute," "to do wrong," "to trouble," or "to litigate." So while the implication is to do someone harm, it is not a physical harm, it is a battle of words and legalities. See also my footnote on Revelation 2:11 in this book.

[314] Closely linked to the word Beelzebub. Compare בעלדבבא "accuser, legal adversary" (that is, the devil), and בעלזבוב "Beelzebub "lord of the high house," which implies lord of the underworld. See William Jennings' Lexicon to the Syriac New Testament, p 39, and J. Payne Smith's Syriac Dictionary, p 51.

[315] In typical Old Testament Hebrew style, we have two word-plays at hand: first, it is *granted* (legal right is given) to the witnesses to judge, just as it is *granted* (legal right is given) that those who objected these judgements be executed (capital punishment). Second, just as these adversaries may *choose* to dispute the witnesses, the witnesses may also *choose* to inflict plagues.

The authority to close the skies (Elijah) and strike the Land of Israel with plagues (Moses) was a sobering reminder of God's justice against those who lead His Covenant people astray (Ahab and Jezebel) and those who bring them into spiritual slavery (Pharaoh). As I have quoted numerous times, Josephus tells how seditious men tormented and subdued their own kinsmen, while false prophets and false messiahs led many others astray in those days. The historian also spared no detail in recounting how these ones suffered the Roman hammer fall as a result of their treachery.

THE TEMPLE SYSTEM DESTROYED

א *(v 7) "And when their covenantal obligation[316] is fulfilled, the Beast that ascends from the Sea[317] will make war with them, and will overcome them, and will execute them."*

When I first saw this verse in the Aramaic text my jaw hit the floor and I was filled with excitement! My interpretation isn't even a paraphrase; it is a literal word-for-word translation. The "covenantal obligation" is directly related to the legal requirements of the Law and the Prophets, as footnoted. The curses of the Law and the prophecies of the Prophets are then fulfilled at the end of the destruction of Jerusalem and the Temple.

As Jesus said,

"For truly I say to you, until heaven and earth pass away, not the smallest letter or stroke of a letter shall pass from the Law, until all is accomplished!" Matthew 5:18 (NASB)

Then the Beast of the Sea, which was the Roman Empire, laid siege against Jerusalem, and destroyed the Temple. The Law and the Prophets – specifically the sacrificial system – was overcome and "executed." This too is congruent with Scripture.

"When He said, "A new covenant," He has made the first obsolete. But

---

[316] The word סהדותא here can mean "testimony" in a legal sense, as one who is providing evidence. But equally, it can mean "covenantal obligation," and the lexicon specifically connects this word to the Tablets of Stone and the Ark of the Covenant! See The Comprehensive Aramaic Lexicon, http://cal.huc.edu/getlex.php?coord=620411459&word=5

[317] The Aramaic has "Sea" here and not "Abyss." This is the first mention of the Beast of the Sea, who appears again in greater detail in Revelation 13. As we will discover in my next book, The Beast of the Sea (ימא, meaning a large Sea – hence the uppercase "S", meaning the Mediterranean) is the Roman Empire.

whatever is becoming obsolete and growing old is about to disappear."
Hebrews 8:13 (NASB)

That last line in Hebrew 8:13, "about to disappear," in the original language literally means "to be ruined" or "to be damaged." This word stems from the root word "to destroy." The writer of Hebrews spoke of the first covenant not only becoming obsolete but also coming to ruin!

Finally, in Matthew 5:18 just quoted above, Jesus spoke of heaven and earth passing away. In book 1 of this series, I explained at length how that expression was a euphemism for the Temple. What He was saying was that only after the temple "passed away" (literal meaning, "to cross over," like the Israelites did when they left the wilderness) would the Law be fulfilled of its contractual obligations. In Luke 21, Jesus makes this connection for us:

"But when you see Jerusalem surrounded by armies, then recognize that her desolation is near...
because these are days of punishment, so that all things which have been written will be fulfilled...
and Jerusalem will be trampled underfoot by the Gentiles until the times of the Gentiles are fulfilled...
Truly I say to you, this generation will not pass away until all things take place. Heaven and earth will pass away, but My words will not pass away." Luke 21:20, 22, 24, 32, 33 (NASB)

Additionally, as previously mentioned, Zerubbabel (King) and Joshua (Priest) stood as witnesses to the rebuilding of the Temple in Zechariah. They represented God's original intent: before the covenant of the Law was cut between God and the Hebrews, Yahweh invited them to "be to Me a kingdom of priests and a holy nation" (Exodus 19:6). This notion is also expressed by Peter (1 Peter 2:9), and alluded to indirectly in Hebrews by the mention of Melchizedek, king of Salem, priest of the Most High God (Hebrews 7:1).

However, the Hebrews rejected God's invitation. "Now all the people witnessed the thunderings, the lightning flashes, the sound of the trumpet, and the mountain smoking; and when the people saw it, they trembled and stood afar off. Then they said to Moses, "You speak with us, and we will hear; but let not God speak with us, lest we die." (Exodus 20:18-19). Therefore they received the covenant of the Law through Moses.

So in juxtaposition to Zerubbabel and Joshua, Moses and Elijah stood as witnesses to the destruction of the Temple in 70 AD instead of its rebuilding.

For the Tanakh (Law, Prophets, Writings) was the "law of sin and death" (Romans 8:2), and "the power of sin" (1 Corinthians 15:56). Paul would even go so far as to say that the "Law brings wrath" (Romans 4:15), and that the "letter [of the Law] kills" (2 Corinthians 3:4-6). The refusal of apostate Israel and its religious leaders to embrace the covenant offered by God through His Son meant that they chose to remain bound by the terms and conditions set by the Law of Moses (John 5:45).

A secondary implication of the presence these witnesses is that they testified regarding the adultery apostate Israel had committed, thereby nullifying their marriage contract with God. Repeatedly throughout Ezekiel and Revelation apostate Israel is referred to as a harlot, having been unfaithful to God time and time again.

Although Jesus was willing to forgive the woman caught in adultery (John 8:11), the Law of Moses could not. "In the Law Moses commanded us to stone such a woman," the Pharisees declared when then caught a woman in the act of adultery (John 8:5). In contrast, the harlot Jerusalem was stoned to death by Roman stones.[318]

While the Temple was still erected, during the 40-year transition from the Age of Moses to the Age of Messiah, Paul wrote to his Jewish listeners that they could divorce themselves from the covenant under Moses by means of death and thus not be found guilty of adultery. This death was figurative in the sense that to be born anew in Christ, one first died in the waters of baptism (Romans 7:1-6).

> "When an obligation has ceased, the instrument creating it is canceled by the court by being torn or cut crosswise through the date, through the names of the witnesses, or through other important parts of the document. Hence any document which bears such cuts or scissions is invalid, the presumption being that its validity has ceased by a judicial act."[319]

Upon the destruction of Jerusalem and the Temple, the Romans symbolically destroyed copies of the original ketubah (marriage covenant) between Yahweh and Israel, which were the Scrolls of the Torah.

---

[318] These stones were projectiles launched from ballistas, carroballists, cheiroballistas and scorpios, all various forms of catapults designed to hurls large and small stones.

[319] Shulhan Aruk, Hoshen Mishpat, 52, 1; B. B. 168b.

א *(v 8) "And their corpses were upon the public square of that Great City, which spiritually is called Sodom and Egypt, where their Yahweh[320] was crucified."*

Remembering that John never dropped his measuring stick as he stood in the inner court of the Temple, from whence Moses and Elijah emerged, he then witnessed the Roman Beast attack them. Now they lay in the "public square," which could likely be taken to mean the outer courts of the Temple Mount. Further confirmation of this location is now provided: Jesus was crucified just beyond the boundaries of the Temple, in the city of Jerusalem.

Jerusalem is now identified as both Sodom[321] and Egypt, a theme that will continue throughout Revelation. Both of these lands suffered supernatural calamities. The very example of what not to be would end up defining them. "Truly I say to you, it will be more tolerable for the land of Sodom and Gomorrah on the day of judgment, than for that city," (Matthew 10:15).

Incredibly, Jesus is not mentioned by his earthly name. Instead, he is identified in the fullest measure of who He is: Yahweh God. While the Greek reads, "where our Lord was crucified," the original language provides much more depth. For Yahweh was and is the God of Israel. Jesus was Yahweh God incarnate (Emmanuel). Therefore, Jerusalem was the place where the God of Israel, Yahweh, was crucified. How sobering is this verse?

א *(v 9 – 12) "And their corpses were seen by their people and kinsmen, and by foreigners and Gentiles for three and a half days, but their corpses would not be abandoned so as to be placed in tombs.*

Now the sojourners[322] of the Land were rejoicing over them and made

---

[320] While difficult to read, not just theologically but grammatically, I chose to keep the translation as literal as possible. John often uses מריא in reference to Jesus, which (as mention earlier in this book) in Syriac means Yahweh (ie. the Tetragrammaton, YHWH).

[321] Not the first time. See Ezekiel 16:46–56, Isaiah 1:9–10 and Jeremiah 23:14.

[322] This verse is enigmatic because of the grammatical nuance found in the noun "inhabitant/dweller," found twice in the verse. The first instance is only found once in the New Testament. עמורא in Ashuri square script, or ܥܡܘܪܐ in Aramaic (dukhrana.com ID 2:15942, sedra.bethmardutho.org #15719), differs subtly from ܥܡܘܪܐ (dukhrana.com ID 2:15943, sedra.bethmardutho.org #15720), which is found three times in the New Testament, but only in the book of Revelation (3:10, 8:13, 11:10b). Those three times the noun means "dweller" or "inhabitant." But the nuanced version found in 11:10a can mean "alien/foreigner," or "immigrant."

themselves glad, and were sending gifts to one another, on account of[323] the Two Prophets who tormented the inhabitants[324] of the Land.

And thence, after three days and a half, the Living Spirit from Elohim entered into them and they stood on their feet, and the Spirit of Life fell upon them,[325] and great reverence[326] came over those who saw them.

And they heard a great voice from Heaven that said to them, 'Ascend to here.' And they ascended to Heaven in a cloud and their legal adversaries were forced to look upon them."[327]

This section of Scripture continues from the aftermath of the fall of the Temple and destruction of Jerusalem. The "people and kinsmen" are the Israelites on the one hand, and the "foreigners (literal meaning is 'foreign languages'), and Gentiles are the Roman soldiers on the other. The three and a half days represent both a contraction of the three and a half years in which the Flavian campaign lasted until the Great City was destroyed, and the duration in which Titus and his men stood upon the Temple Mount.

> "Titus ordered those, whose business it was, to read the list of
> all that had performed great exploits in this war... and rejoiced
> in them in the same manner as a man would have rejoiced in
> his own exploits. He also put on their heads crowns of gold,
> and golden ornaments about their necks, and gave them long
> spears of gold, and ensigns that were made of silver, and... he
> plentifully distributed among them, out of the spoils, and the

---

These of course were the Roman soldiers who has been in their midst for over three years.

[323] The word מֶטֵל in this context here means "concerning," "about," "because of," "by means of," or "on behalf of." See, The Comprehensive Aramaic Lexicon http://cal.huc.edu/getlex.php?coord=620400936&word=

[324] As mentioned above, עמורא in Ashuri square script, or ܥܡܘܪ̈ܐ in Aramaic (dukhrana.com ID 2:15943, sedra.bethmardutho.org #15720), is found three times in the book of Revelation (3:10, 8:13, 11:10b). Those three times the noun means "dweller" or "inhabitant." But the nuanced version found earlier in 11:10a can mean "alien/foreigner," or "immigrant."

[325] "and the Spirit of Life fell upon them" is not found in the Greek texts.

[326] דחלתא is a word that related to deities, and means "reverential awe," "religion," or "fear" in the sense of being afraid of a god. It does not imply terror.

[327] "forced to look upon them," is due to the Aphel inflection on the verb, which, like the Hebrew Hiphil, is a forced or causative action.

other prey they had taken, silver, and gold, and garments.

So when they had all these honours bestowed on them, according to his own appointment made to every one, and he had wished all sorts of happiness to the whole army, he came down, among the great acclamations which were made to him: and then betook himself to offer thank-offerings [to the gods], and at once sacrificed a vast number of oxen…

And when he had stayed three days among the principal commanders, and so long feasted with them, he sent away the rest of his army to the several places where they would be every one best situate: but permitted the tenth legion to stay, as a guard, at Jerusalem: and did not send them away beyond Euphrates, where they had been before."[328]

From Josephus we learn that after three days, they began to leave (the half day). We also learn that Titus distributed gifts, and he and all his men were filled with merriment and gladness. This connects nicely to verse 10. The Romans were the "sojourners" who were rejoicing over the destruction of the Temple and the conquest of Jerusalem. And it was "on account of the Two Prophets," which is to say, the Two Prophets were the cause or means by which all these events took place. These Witnesses "tormented" the Judeans and other inhabitants of the Holy Land by way of the contractual obligations of the Law and the oracles of destruction in the Prophets.

Then comes the mysterious resurrection. In verse 9 we read that "their corpses would not be abandoned so as to be placed in tombs," that is to say, their end isn't death. The Spirit of God then comes upon them and lifts them up, and they ascend. In 2 Kings 2:11 we know that Elijah ascended to Heaven in a chariot. But what many don't know is that Jewish tradition holds to the belief that Moses too ascended into heaven.[329] It is fitting then that the two great prophets are vindicated and affirmed by Yahweh God, since ascension into Heaven is a symbol of great honour.

As for the words, "their legal adversaries were forced to look upon them," I imagine one of two scenarios. First, it is a picture of the sobering realization that came upon those who had survived long enough to see that day of destruction. Perhaps they remembered in their hearts the Song of Moses, which was written specifically to serve as a reminder *after* calamity had come

[328] Josephus, *Wars*, 7:1:3, https://penelope.uchicago.edu/josephus/war-7.html
[329] See, Ginzberg, Louis, *The Legends of the Jews*, Volume 3.

upon them (Deuteronomy 31:21). Or, it could have been that the legal adversaries were the demonic hordes, led by Beelzebub (recall that "legal adversaries" is almost identical to the proper noun Beelzebub), who were made to look upon the vindication of Moses and Elijah. And they were forced to see (to perceive) that the destruction of the Temple was not a triumph for Satan, but actually worked against him, factoring into His gradual and overall defeat.

א *(v 13 – 14) "And in that hour there was a great terror[330] and one tenth of the City fell, and the names of men who were killed in the shaking[331] were seven thousand, but the remnant were in reverential awe and gave glory to Elohim who is in Heaven.*

Behold! Two woes have past. But behold! A third woe comes immediately!"

The vision concludes its description of the destruction of the Temple by telling us that the Temple Mount complex fell to the Romans. Jerusalem, in terms of size, took up an area of approximately 0.5 square miles, while the Temple had a footprint of approximately 0.05 square miles,[332] which is 1/10th of the city.[333] Moreover, many modern scholars and archeologists have determined the population of Jerusalem in the first century CE was around

---

[330] "Earthquake" is an unlikely translation. The Aramaic noun זוּעָא matches the spelling in Marcus Jastrow's Lexicon (p. 389), where the word is defined as "trembling, fear." This stems from the root word verb "to shake, stir, trouble." Hence, earthquake can be implied (such as Matthew 27:54 or Acts 16:26), but the same word is used in 8:24 and John 5:4 in relation to water. Here, because the noun is preceded with adjective "great," it makes sense to heighten the intensity of the word from "trembling" to "terror." This same root word is used in Hebrews 12:27: "Yet once more I will shake not only the earth, but also the heaven."

[331] See footnote above. Because the adjective "great" is not present, I deescalated the word back to "shaken," and thus maintain its symbolic meaning (in connection to Hebrews 12:27).

[332] Gibbon, Edward. *The Decline and Fall of the Roman Empire*, Vol. 2, (E. P. Dutton & Company, 1914), p 381; and, Hollis, F.J. *The Archaeology of Herod's Temple: With a Commentary on the Tractate Middoth*, (London, 1934), cited in Lundquist, John M. *The Temple of Jerusalem: Past, Present, and Future*, (Greenwood Publishing Group, 2008), p 103.

[333] I have to give credit to Daniel Morais for working out the math on this on his commentary on Revelation 11:13: "27 stadia X 607ft/1stadia=16.389 ft or 3.104 miles. Since the outer walls of the city of Jerusalem roughly approximated the rectangular proportions of the Temple, a circumference of 3.104 miles would give an average length of .6208 miles and an average width of .9312 miles. .6208 X .9312 = .5781 square miles." https://www.revelationrevolution.org

70,000 people.[334] Therefore, the 7,000 who fell were also a tenth of the population of the city—at least from a prophetic perspective.

This calamity was not caused by an earthquake, but a great shaking or terror. This prophetic keyword reminds us not only of what the Romans did, but perhaps more importantly, why they did it.

> *"For then there will be a great tribulation, such as has not occurred since the beginning of the world until now, nor ever will again. And if those days had not been cut short, no life would have been saved; but for the sake of the elect those days will be cut short." Matthew 24:21–22 (NASB)*

> *"[There will be] people fainting from fear and the expectation of the things that are coming upon the world; for the powers of the heavens will be shaken." Luke 21:26 (NASB)*

> *"And His voice shook the earth then, but now He has promised, saying, 'Yet once more I will shake not only the earth, but also the heaven.' This expression, 'Yet once more,' denotes the removing of those things which can be shaken, as of created things, so that those things which cannot be shaken may remain." Hebrews 12:26–27 (NASB)*

This great calamity was in fulfillment of the Scriptures and prophecies of Jesus. The suffering that those within the walls of the Great City underwent was horrendous, as we have already discussed. Citizens were terrorized by both Roman soldiers and three different internal rebel factions. It was a great tribulation indeed.

"But as for the legions that came running thither, neither any persuasions, nor any threatenings could restrain their violence... [The Jews] were every where slain, and every where beaten. And as for a great part of the people, they were weak, and without arms, and had their throats cut wherever they were caught. Now round about the altar lay dead bodies, heaped one upon another; as at the steps going up to it, ran a great quantity of their blood: whither also the dead bodies that were slain

---

[334] Wilkinson, John, *Ancient Jerusalem, Its Water Supply and Population, PEFQS 106*, p. 33–51 (1974), and, Rocca, Samuel, *Herod's Judaea: A Mediterranean State in the Classical World*, p. 333 (2008), and, Stephen S. Smalley, *The Revelation to John: A Commentary on the Greek Text of the Apocalypse*, (Downers Grove, IL: IVP Academic, 2005), p 286.

above on the altar fell down."[335]

In stark contrast to those suffering within the walls of Jerusalem, the remnant —the 144,000 who were given a mark and led out of the Holy Land prior to the invasion—these ones were in awe and worshiped Yahweh God. And with that, the second woe is concluded. The third woe won't be experienced until Revelation chapter 12, where John's vision takes a dramatic shift in its focus and message.

Josephus' words summarize Revelation 11:1-13 quite brilliantly from a historical perspective:

> "So Titus retired into the tower of Antonia, and resolved to storm the temple the next day, early in the morning, with his whole army, and to encamp round about the holy house. But as for that house, God had, for certain, long ago doomed it to the fire; and now that fatal day was come, according to the revolution of ages; it was the tenth day of the month Lous, Av, upon which it was formerly burnt by the king of Babylon; although these flames took their rise from the Jews themselves, and were occasioned by them; for upon Titus's retiring, the seditious lay still for a little while, and then attacked the Romans again, when those that guarded the holy house fought with those that quenched the fire that was burning the inner court of the temple."[336]

I love that he wrote, "according to the revolution of ages," because that fits so well with the framework of the ending of the Mosaic Age. This theme will be revisited again in the following verse (15). The forty-year transition period had come to a close, and the Messianic Age remained.

Revelation 11 presents us with a climactic end to the Temple sacrificial system and all of the requirements of the Law of Moses having been met. The consequences for breach of covenant were carried out, and the covenant has ceased. But we must guard our hearts to not be dismissive, for God honoured Moses and Elijah (The Law and the Prophets) and they were seen ascending to God. As Paul wrote,

"But if the ministry of death, engraved in letters on stones, came with glory

---

[335] Josephus, *Wars*, 6:4:6, https://penelope.uchicago.edu/josephus/war-6.html
[336] Ibid, 6:4:5.

so that the sons of Israel could not look intently at the face of Moses because of the glory of his face, fading as it was, how will the ministry of the Spirit fail to be even more with glory? For if the ministry of condemnation has glory, much more does the ministry of righteousness excel in glory. For indeed what had glory in this case has no glory, because of the glory that surpasses it. For if that which fades away was with glory, much more that which remains is in glory." 2 Corinthians 3:7–11 (NASB)

THE AGE OF MESSIAH IN FULL SPLENDOR

א *(v 15 – 17) "And the seventh angel sounded, and there were great voices in Heaven, who were saying, 'It has become the Kingdom Age[337] of our Elohim and His Messiah, and He has dominion[338] unto the age of ages.'[339]*

And the twenty four Elders who are in the presence of Elohim seated upon their thrones, fell on their faces and worshiped Elohim,

And they were saying, 'We give thanks to You, Yahweh Elohim Almighty, who is and has been, for you have conquered[340] in your great warrior might[341] and you have dominated.'"[342]

The main thrust of Revelation 11 has to do with the Law of Moses, the sacrificial system and the Mosaic Age. The Temple, representing both the Torah and Age of Moses, was measured for destruction. You may consider this as a sort of planned decommissioning. The Law and the Prophets (Moses and Elijah) had one last legal obligation to perform before the requirements of that contract could be fulfilled.

---

[337] הות מלכותה דעלמא, "to be" in the peal perfect (like the Hebrew Qal); "kingdom" is a *singular* noun; "age, epoch season," the Hebrew עוֹלָם 'olam.'

[338] This verb "to reign/to be made king" is in the Aphel (a causative force) Perfect, meaning a completed and intense action. It does not say, "He *will* reign," rather, a literal meaning could be, "He has dominated."

[339] לעלם עלמין.

[340] This verb, "to take away," or, "to command," has several idioms, including, "to conquer." Context determines the best use. The word that follows, "army/force," made this an easy choice.

[341] חילא means "army/force," a "military unit," or can imply supernatural strength. I have attempted to maintain the militaristic essence while combining it with strength; hence, "warrior might."

[342] See footnote on "dominion" above.

The Age of Messiah began when Jesus ascended from death in resurrection power. But even after the disciples witness heaven receiving Him, for the next 40 years (a generation) sacrifices continued to be offered daily in the Temple. This period of time, one of a kind in history, saw two overlapping covenants with Yahweh God in force. As I wrote at length in my first book, *Dawn of This Age*, this reality caused some Jews who came to Christ to struggle with the temptation to return back to the Law. Hence the countless exhortations in letters like Galatians, Romans, and especially Hebrews, admonishing those wavering to not place themselves under bondage to the Law once again.

In light of all this it should come as no surprise that *after* the Temple is destroyed (the Law and the system), the angels *then* proclaim, "It is become the Kingdom Age of our Elohim and His Messiah." This is proclamation that the transition period of epoch seasons had come to an end. The consistent mistranslation of the word "olam/alam" (age) in most translations as "world" causes much confusion here. Adding to the issue is the fact that the Greek is κόσμος (cosmos), which rightly should be translated as "world" or even "creation." So it could be that the root cause here goes a long way back, right to the early transcribers who made copies of the Aramaic into Greek.

"[God] caused Him to rise from the house of the dead and established Him at His right hand in the Heavens, far above all principalities, authorities, military powers, and magistrates, and far above every name that is named, not only in this age, but also in the one being readied."
Ephesians 1:20–21, Aramaic Translation

Sticking with the original language, within the context of Revelation 11, it makes sense to read that the Age of Messiah now stood alone, no longer overlapping with the Age of Moses.

"Once the Holy One of holies had come, both vision and prophecy were sealed. And the kingdom of Jerusalem ceased at the same time, because kings were to be anointed among them only until the Holy of holies had been anointed. Moses also prophesies that the kingdom of the Jews shall stand until His time, saying, 'A ruler shall not fail from Judah nor a prince from his loins, until the things laid up for him shall come and the Expectation of the nations Himself.' And that is why the Savior Himself was always proclaiming 'The law and the prophets prophesied until John.'"[343]

As a result, Jesus would reign unto the age of ages; which is to say, right through to the end of this age. Incidentally, the Greek flips from cosmos to aion here, τοὺς αἰῶνας τῶν αἰώνων (the age of ages is the age you and I are currently living in: the final epoch season before heaven and earth become one). This heavenly statement fits the existing framework of Scripture we have relating to the period of time that Jesus reigns:

"And Jesus came up and spoke to them, saying, 'All authority in heaven and on earth has been given to Me. Go, therefore, and make disciples of all the nations… I am with you always, to the end of the age.'" Matthew 28:18–20 (NASB)

*"For as in Adam all die, so also in Christ all will be made alive. But each in his own order: Christ the first fruits, after that those who are Christ's at His coming, then comes the end, when He hands over the kingdom to our God and Father, when He has abolished all rule and all authority and power. For He must reign until He has put all His enemies under His feet. The last enemy that will be abolished is death."
1 Corinthians 15:22–26 (NASB)*

This is in no way to imply that Jesus in the future will somehow lose his place as king, or stop sitting at the right hand of the Father, or anything along those lines! Away with the thought. Instead, what we have here are harmonious passages in Scripture that support one another. But these passages are not the whole picture, nor do they tell the whole story.

א *(v 18 – 19) "'And the Gentiles were incited, and your indignation came, and the time of the dead to be judged,[344] but you will give reward to your royal subjects the prophets, and to the holy ones, and to those who revere your Name, to the small with the great, but you shall ruin those who have ruined[345] the Land.'*
Now the Temple in Heaven was opened, and the Ark of the Covenant belonging to Him appeared in the Temple, and there were lightnings and

---

[343] Athanasius (345 AD), *Incarnation*, Chapter 6.
[344] Readers must maintain John's first death/second death paradigm in mind. See Matthew 8:22 to understand which "dead" are being referenced here. Those under the Law were being judged.
[345] A Hebrew-styled word-play: Yahweh will "ruin" ("to damage," "to disfigure," "to destroy") those who have done the same to the Holy Land. This is a very typical Old Covenant 'eye for an eye' method of vindication.

thunders and noises and tremors and large hail."

Verse 7 reveals that the Beast of the Sea, the Roman Empire, rose up to destroy the Temple. Then verse 7 provides us with a picture of who was at the scene of the crime: "their corpses were seen by their people and kinsmen, and by foreigners and Gentiles." The Jews on one side and the Romans on the other.

With these details in mind, verse 18 tells us what we already know from history; that the Romans were incited (literally: provoked to anger). The added layer that is significant theologically is that the Romans were the medium for God's indignation (righteous judgement), by way of contractual obligation through the Law. This was an isolated incident, pertaining only to those who "ruined" the Land of Israel.

The reward He will give (conjugated in future tense) is to His holy ones. But the "time of the dead to be judged," a statement preceded by two past tense verbs, "incited" and "came," implies that this *has* taken place.

In *Dawn of This Age*, I explained how the first death/second death, and first resurrection/second resurrection paradigm that John uses, works. In short, those who exist outside of Yeshua are already dead, while those who are born anew are resurrected. Meanwhile, the second death is the Sea of Fire and Brimstone, and the second resurrection is the Great Resurrection of 1 Corinthians 15 and Revelation 19. That said, the "dead" who were judged mentioned here in 11:18 are those who are already dead: those not born anew in the Messiah.

"And He said to another, 'Follow Me.' But he said, 'Lord, permit me first to go and bury my father.' But He said to him, 'Allow the dead to bury their own dead; but as for you, go and proclaim everywhere the kingdom of God.'" Luke 9:59–60 (NASB)

"And the son said to him, 'Father, I have sinned against heaven and in your sight; I am no longer worthy to be called your son.' But the father said to his slaves, 'Quickly bring out the best robe and put it on him, and put a ring on his finger and sandals on his feet; and bring the fattened calf, slaughter it, and let's eat and celebrate; for this son of mine was dead and has come to life again; he was lost and has been found.' And they began to celebrate." Luke 15:21–24 (NASB)

"And when you were dead in your wrongdoings and the uncircumcision of

219

your flesh, He made you alive together with Him, having forgiven us all our wrongdoings." Colossians 2:13 (NASB)

Jesus, in His parable, put it so beautifully: for this son of mine was dead and has come to life again; he was lost and has been found. We are dead when we wander as orphans, but when we encounter the Father, we are not only found, but we come into resurrection life! Therefore, the "dead" in verse 18 are the same ones who have been on the receiving end of all of the woes from Revelation chapter 6 onward.

"Wait, but what about the goodness of God?" you might be wondering. As I have said earlier, all of God's judgements a restorative, not retributive. While I will dive much deeper into this in the next book, let us ponder the words of the Apostle Peter in one of his letters:

"For Christ also suffered for sins once for all time, the just for the unjust, so that He might bring us to God, having been put to death in the flesh, but made alive in the spirit; in which He also went and made proclamation to the spirits in prison [literally: Sheol], who once were disobedient when the patience of God kept waiting in the days of Noah, during the construction of the ark, in which a few, that is, eight persons, were brought safely through the water. Corresponding to that, baptism now saves you— not the removal of dirt from the flesh, but an appeal to God for a good conscience—through the resurrection of Jesus Christ...

For the gospel has for this purpose been preached even to those who are dead, that though they are judged in the flesh as people, they may live in the spirit according to the will of God." 1 Peter 3:18–21, 4:6 (NASB)

How's that for a theological bombshell? Perhaps Peter's description of the Harrowing of Sheol is the answer to the cliff-hanger in Luke 16, where we are unclear concerning the future fate of the rich man in Sheol. In what was either a parable, or a generalization of the fate of those under the Law, the rich man, now repentant, was separated from Abraham by a great chasm. We know from other passages that Abraham—and by deductive reasoning, Lazarus—were in God's kingdom.[346] Surely then when Jesus descended into

---

[346] Luke 13:28, "when you see Abraham… in the kingdom of God." Though it should be noted that Luke 13:22–30 as a whole can be understood as a sort of prologue to the story of Luke 16:19–3, since in both instance Jesus is addressing Jews who chose to not repent (which in their context meant to stay under the Law and die in breach of covenant). The key verse being, "The last will be first, and the first will be last."

Sheol, as Peter revealed, he would have been among those gathered to hear the gospel preached to them. But this is a topic for book 3. Suffice to say that Revelation 11:19 is not the end of the story for the Jews who were slain in the 'days of vengeance' when the Temple was destroyed (Romans 11:26).

Lastly, verse 19 concludes chapter 11 the same way it began: with the Ark of the Covenant! The contrast is that first we have John standing in the inner court of the Temple as the Ark of the Covenant is indirectly mentioned via the Two Witnesses: Moses and Elijah. But the Temple is then destroyed, and symbolically the Law and the Prophets are destroyed with it. Nevertheless, the heavenly Temple stands, and in it, Yahweh has in safe keeping His copy of the original contract signed on Mt Sinai.

> *"We have such a high priest, who has taken His seat at the right hand of the throne of the Majesty in the heavens, a minister in the sanctuary and in the true tabernacle, which the Lord set up, not man... Now if He were on earth, He would not be a priest at all, since there are those who offer the gifts according to the Law; who serve a copy and shadow of the heavenly things, just as Moses was warned by God when he was about to erect the tabernacle; for, 'See,' He says, 'that you make all things by the pattern which was shown to you on the mountain.'" Hebrews 8:1–2, 4–5 (NASB)*

What Revelation 11:19 explains then is that like any other ancient near eastern covenant,[347] two parties (God and Israel) kept a copy of a covenantal agreement (a contract). The Israelites kept theirs in an Ark, and Yahweh kept His in an Ark. Thus, even though it is believed by most scholars today that the Ark of the Covenant that was carried from the wilderness into the Promised Land was lost after the Babylonian invasion, Yahweh had His copy on hand, meaning the contract was still ratified and binding unto death.

---

[347] Genesis 21:22-34 and 31:43-53; 1 Samuel 18:3 and 23:18.

15 CONCLUDING THOUGHTS

*"'Son of man, can these bones live?' And I answered, 'Lord God, You
Yourself know...'*
*Then He said to me, "Son of man, these bones are the entire house of
Israel; behold, they say, 'Our bones are dried up and our hope has
perished. We are completely cut off.' Therefore prophesy and say to them,
'This is what the Lord God says: "Behold, I am going to open your
graves and cause you to come up out of your graves, My people; and I
will bring you into the land of Israel. Then you will know that I am the
Lord... And I will put My Spirit within you and you will come to life,
and I will place you on your own land."'*
— *Ezekiel 37:3, 11–14 NASB*

If Yahweh God were austere and solely focused on a contractual
relationship with mankind, then Revelation could have very well ended
at chapter 11. The Israelites failed to keep their end of the agreement;
just ask Moses, who prophesied all the way back at the beginning. The
consequences for non-compliance that were written in the agreement were
executed, and the terms were satisfied. End of story.

But that was far from the end. What follows in chapters 12 to 19 is God's
romance with His first love. Ezekiel 16 as a whole serves as a backdrop for

what those chapters in Revelation are all about. Here are a few highlights from the prophet's book, though I highly recommend you read the entire chapter yourself.

"Thus says the Lord God to Jerusalem (all of Israel), 'Your [spiritual] origin and your birth are from the land of the Canaanite; your [spiritual] father was an Amorite and your [spiritual] mother a Hittite. And as for your birth, on the day you were born your navel cord was not cut, nor were you washed with water for cleansing, nor were you rubbed with salt or even wrapped in cloths. No eye looked with pity on you to do any of these things for you, to have compassion on you; but you were thrown out in the open field, for you were loathed on the day that you were born.

"When I passed by you and saw you squirming in your [newborn] blood, I said to you while you were there in your blood, 'Live!' Yes, I said to you while you were there in your blood, 'Live!' I made you (Israel) multiply like plants [which grow] in the field, and you grew up and became tall and you reached the age for [wearing] fine jewelry; your breasts were formed and your hair had grown, yet you were naked and bare.

Then I passed by you [again] and looked on you; behold, you were maturing and at the time for love, and I spread My skirt over you and covered your nakedness. Yes, I swore [an oath] to you and entered into a covenant with you,' says the Lord God, 'and you became Mine. Then I washed you with water; yes, I [thoroughly] washed away from you the [clinging] blood and anointed you with oil. I also clothed you with embroidered cloth and put sandals of porpoise skin on your feet; and I wrapped you with fine linen and covered you with silk. I adorned you with ornaments and I put bracelets on your wrists and a necklace around your neck. I also put a ring in your nostril and earrings in your ears and a beautiful crown on your head. Thus you were adorned with gold and silver, and your dress was [made] of fine linen and silk and embroidered cloth. You ate fine flour and honey and oil; so you were extremely beautiful and you advanced and prospered into royalty. Then your fame went out among the nations on account of your beauty, for it was perfect because of My majesty and splendor which I bestowed on you,' says the Lord God.

"But you trusted in and relied on your beauty and prostituted yourself [in idolatry and its debauched rituals] because of your fame, and you poured out your immoralities on every [willing] passer-by and your beauty was his

[as you worshiped the idols of the Gentile nations]. 1*You took some of your clothes and made for yourself [decorated] high places and shrines of various colors and prostituted yourself on them——things which should never have come about and taken place…*

Moreover, you took your sons and your daughters whom you had borne to Me, and you destroyed them as sacrifices [to your man-made gods]. Were your gross immoralities so small a matter? You slaughtered My children and offered them up to [worthless] idols, forcing them to pass through the [hideousness of the] fire. And in all your repulsive acts and prostitutions (idolatrous immoralities) you did not [pause to] remember the days of your youth, when you were naked and bare, squirming in your [newborn] blood.

Then it came about after all your wickedness ('Woe, woe to you!' says the Lord God)… you offered your body to every passer-by and multiplied your obscene immorality… and yet even with this you were not satisfied…

You adulterous wife, who welcomes and receives strangers instead of her husband! Men give gifts to all prostitutes, but you give your gifts to all your lovers, bribing the pagan nations to come to you [as allies] from every direction for your obscene immoralities… therefore, listen, I will gather all your lovers (pagan allies) with whom you took pleasure, and all those whom you loved with all those whom you hated; I will even gather them against you from every direction and will expose your nakedness to them that they may see all your nakedness [making you, Israel, an object of loathing and of mockery, a spectacle among the nations].

Nevertheless, I will remember [with compassion] My covenant with you in the days of your youth, and I will establish an everlasting covenant with you… And I will establish My covenant with you, and you will know [without any doubt] that I am the Lord, so that you may remember [in detail] and be ashamed and never open your mouth again because of your humiliation, when I have forgiven you for all that you have done," says the Lord God." Ezekiel 16, Abridged (AMP)[348]

Yahweh God shifts from matters of covenant to matters of identity and the heart. Ultimately, he restores his unfaithful wife.[349] Much of Revelation details the calamities, but in the end there is hope. And this theme of valleys and mountain tops is found throughout the Scriptures. I say all this to remind you that as heavy as some of these chapters of Revelation can be, they aren't the end of the story. And if there is one thing that has surprised me the most on my personal journey of discovery throughout the Scriptures, it is how often I find mercy triumphing over judgement (James 2:13).

What would happen if those who identify themselves today as Jews by either ethnicity, or religion, or both, were to discover that they do not need to rely solely on the promises of God in the Hebrew Scriptures to find hope for tomorrow? What if they were to discover that John's prophetic visions were also a beacon of hope, where the burden of performance is lifted knowing the Mosaic Age and the temple system no longer holds them accountable to the Law? That they can find an open invitation to a covenant not requiring "the blood of goats and calves, but through His [Jesus] own blood, He entered the holy place once for all time, having obtained eternal redemption" (Hebrews 9:12). We could very well see the words of Paul in Romans 9, 10 and 11 come to pass.

As for us who are those that Paul would call Gentiles, my hope is that by digging deep into the Language of Jesus, we may see the Book of Revelation in a new light. More importantly, that we may be able to reconcile the person of Jesus—the one who stooped down to raise the woman caught in adultery and washed the feet of Judas knowing he was about to betray Him—that this Jesus may be found in Revelation. Lastly, my hope is that this commentary allows the reader to encounter the Father heart of God, who stood outside his house waiting for his wayward son to come home, may be encountered in the Apocalypse of John. May we forever do away with the paradigm of the angry Dad who beat His oldest son because He was mad at the other children.

"[God] made known to us the mystery of His will according to that which seemed good to Him, which good thing He purposed in himself, with respect to an administration of the completion of the epochs of time to bring back again to their original state all things in the Christ, the things in the heavens and the things on the earth..." Ephesians 1:9–10 (WET)[350]

---

[349] Much like Hosea when he married Gomer.
[350] Wuest, Kenneth. *The New Testament: An Expanded Translation* (Eerdmans Publishing, Grand Rapids: 1961)

CLOSING REMARKS

What a journey this book has been. I myself am deeply impacted by all that I have discovered. As much as I would have liked to continue with the entire commentary in this volume, I find that very few people are willing to pick up a 600 page book these days (900 if you include the prelude, *Dawn of This Age*). Moreover, working in installments affords me time to work though manageable chunks without feeling too overwhelmed by the full scope of the project.

With all sincerity and humility, I wish to thank you for taking the time to read this book. I trust in the goodness of our Heavenly Father, Yahweh God, by His Holy Spirit, to lead you and guide you in all truth. Jesus is the Good Shepherd, and His sheep hear his voice. May His voice be crystal clear in your hearts and minds and all other voices made silent.

I also ask in the Spirit of God's love and grace that you do not let points of disagreement and nuances in belief cause us to break the unity of the Spirit (Ephesians 4:3). In these times, the Accuser is looking for every opportunity to bring division and strife within the Body of Christ. Let us therefore set our hearts and minds on the things above and focus our efforts on maintaining connection and honour (Romans 12:10).

Please pray for me, for my wife, and for my children. Pray that we would continue to walk in His grace, and that we would encounter greater measures of His love and His goodness (Ephesians 1:18). I ask that you bless and not curse or judge (Matthew 7:1). Thank you for your love and for your prayers.

Finally, let us not forget that the world will know us by our love (John 17). May we focus on the united banner of Jesus the Messiah, and may we rally around what we all know to be foundational and true: Yeshua! It is all about Him: Jesus is risen, Jesus is Lord, Jesus is the Saviour of all creation!

CHRISTUS VINCIT,

CHRISTUS REGNAT,

CHRISTUS IMPERAT!

"He has rescued us completely from the tyrannical rule of darkness and has translated us into the kingdom realm of his beloved Son. For in the Son all our sins are canceled and we have the release of redemption through his very blood.

"He is the divine portrait, the true likeness of the invisible God, and the first-born heir of all creation. For through the Son everything was created, both in the heavenly realm and on the earth, all that is seen and all that is unseen. Every seat of power, realm of government, principality, and authority—it was all created through him and for his purpose! He existed before anything was made, and now everything finds completion in him.

"He is the Head of his body, which is the church. And since he is the beginning and the firstborn heir in resurrection, he is the most exalted One, holding first place in everything. For God is satisfied to have all his fullness dwelling in Christ. And by the blood of his cross, everything in heaven and earth is brought back to himself—back to its original intent, restored to innocence again!

"Even though you were once distant from him, living in the shadows of your evil thoughts and actions, he reconnected you back to himself. He released his supernatural peace to you through the sacrifice of his own body as the sin-payment on your behalf so that you would dwell in his presence. And now there is nothing between you and Father God, for he sees you as holy, flawless, and restored, if indeed you continue to advance in faith, assured of a firm foundation to grow upon." Colossians 1:13-23 (TPT)[351]

Amen! Amen!

ABOUT THE AUTHOR

Leo De Siqueira has a passion to dig deeper into the Scriptures in order to better understand the heart of God towards mankind. While attending Tyndale University College in Toronto, Leo focused his studies on translating Biblical Hebrew and early church history. He and his wife Melanie have three beautiful children and serve their local church in Calgary, Canada.

If this book blessed you in any way, please consider leaving an encouraging review. It may just be what someone needs to help them decide if this book is for them. And please consider lending your copy to a friend. Let's encourage as many as we can with this good news! Thank you.

Made in United States
Troutdale, OR
08/23/2023

12329439R00142